The Khat Controversy

Stimulating the Debate on Drugs

**David Anderson, Susan Beckerleg,
Degol Hailu and Axel Klein**

Oxford • New York

English edition
First published in 2007 by
Berg
Editorial offices:
1st Floor, Angel Court, 81 St Clements Street, Oxford OX4 1AW, UK
175 Fifth Avenue, New York, NY 10010, USA

Berg is the imprint of Oxford International Publishers Ltd.

This book has been produced with the support of the Economic and Social Research
Council and the Arts and Humanities Research Council

Library of Congress Cataloguing-in-Publication Data

The khat controversy : stimulating the debate on drugs / David Anderson
... [et al.].
        p. cm. — (Cultures of consumption series ; ISSN 1744-5876)
Includes bibliographical references and index.
ISBN-13: 978-1-84520-250-7 (cloth)
ISBN-10: 1-84520-250-3 (cloth)
ISBN-13: 978-1-84520-251-4 (pbk.)
ISBN-10: 1-84520-251-1 (pbk.)
 1. Qat. 2. Drug traffic. 3. Drug control. I. Anderson, David,
1957–

HV5822.Q3K53 2007
362.29′9—dc22

                                                        2007008137

British Library Cataloguing-in-Publication Data

A catalogue record for this book is available from the British Library.

ISBN   978 1 84520 250 7 (Cloth)
        978 1 84520 251 4 (Paper)

Typeset by JS Typesetting, Porthcawl, Mid Glamorgan
Printed in the United Kingdom by Biddles Ltd, King's Lynn

www.bergpublishers.com

Contents

List of Tables and Figures

Tables

Figures

Acknowledgements

This book has benefited from insights, comments, and assistance provided by a number of people. Degol Hailu says thank you to the following people. In Ethiopia Samuel Assefa's support has been instrumental in facilitating access to the various institutions visited during the fieldwork. Amin Abdella gave his time unreservedly and made invaluable contributions to data collection and analysis. Thank you goes to Demeska Tamiru who from the outset showed his eagerness to identify data and literature. Mesfin Hailu's patience and support during the arduous travels across Ethiopia were unparalleled. In Djibouti, without the insights and hard work by Ahmed Araita, our research there would not have been possible. Hassan Chehem supplied interesting stories and anecdotes. Neil Carrier's careful reading of the literature in French was great help. Most of all, the book greatly benefited from various individuals, government officials, farmers, traders, retailers, exporters and community leaders who gave their time to answer questions and satisfy the authors' curiosity.

Susan Beckerleg would like to thank all the people, named and unnamed, interviewed during fieldwork in Kenya, Uganda and Rwanda. In particular, Mahmoud Abdulkadr, Salim Brek, Umaru Sendi, Mahmoud Abdi Jamaa and Salima Said are thanked for their generous time and trouble. A number of local researchers assisted in data collection and deserve thanks and acknowledgement. In Kenya Ali Swaleh assisted throughout the fieldwork period and the first Uganda visit. In Uganda Abu Famau, Musa Almasi and Mzee Hasan were of great assistance. Nuur Sheekh in Kenya and Saidi Famau in Uganda carried out interviews and wrote reports, the findings of which are incorporated into this book. Data from the Uganda consumers' survey was entered onto a database by Jason Dowling. Colette Jones is thanked for helping with the technical analysis of our survey data. Swaleh Jumbe, who drove the team in North East Uganda, is thanked for his exemplary work. Finally, Abdul Rahman of Mandera is thanked for allowing us to travel in his convoy from Wajir, for entertaining us to lunch and dinner and for helping us to gain access to the Mandera airstrip.

The final section of the book could not have been written without the support of friends and colleagues from the UK Somali community. Axel Klein would like to thank Muna Deria, Warsan Fowzi, Ahmed Sheik, Saeed Abdi, Sado Omar, Nasir Warfa, Mohamud Ege, Abdul Araru, Hassan Isse, Mahdi Ali and Yakoub Aden Abdi. Further thanks to Akalu and Ralph Beckford for their openness; to Janice Zima and Nadia Lovell for their hospitality; and to the Streatham neighbourhood office for their dedication.

–1–

Introduction: Going Global
The Khat Controversy

Khat is the most recent plant-based psychoactive substance to spread across global markets. It has traditionally been consumed in East Africa and the Middle East, where it is also known as the 'flower of paradise', *qat* (transliterated from Arabic), *miraa* (its Kenyan name), *chat* (Ethiopian) and numerous other names which locals use to differentiate various varieties.[1] The actual plant is an evergreen shrub of the *Celastraceae,* which grows best at an altitude of 5,000–8,000 feet (approx. 1,500–2,500 metres). Wild khat trees can grow as high as 80 feet in an equatorial climate, but the farmed variety is kept at around 20 feet with constant pruning (Kennedy 1987; Goldsmith 1994; Lemessa 2001).

Wild plants have been found from Afghanistan to South Africa, but the cultivation of khat has for centuries been confined to a narrow geographical belt ranging from Yemen in the Arabian peninsula to the Meru highlands of Kenya. Over the last twenty years khat has become a global commodity, openly on sale in London and Amsterdam, and covertly in Toronto, Chicago and Sydney. Though global availability of this delicate product would be unthinkable without dramatic advances in transport technology, the key behind this commercial development has been the growth of sizeable markets in Djibouti, Somalia and major urban centres in Ethiopia, as well as across Europe and North America. It is safe to say that the unfolding problematic surrounding the use of khat in Western countries has corresponded to the arrival of large numbers of Somali and Ethiopian refugees from the web of conflict that has been haunting the Horn of Africa for the past thirty years.

Host countries in the West have responded in different fashions to this new phenomenon, with tolerance in the UK and the Netherlands but prohibition in Scandinavia and North America. Across these borders a consensus has formed over the likelihood of transmission. Khat, it is generally assumed, will not catch on among mainstream consumers. Not only are these already generously supplied with a range of mind-altering substances, but also Western consumers are unlikely to take to the involved and unfashionable mode of administration – the khat chew. Yet, this European indifference should not lead us to ignore the sharp rise in incidence of khat use in other parts of the world. The data from eastern Africa show how the border of khat use is shifting in all directions. It seems to fit ideally into the consumption trends and patterns of sociability of African towns, and provides a cost-effective

1

alternative to alcohol. The spread of khat production and use has therefore become an issue of global concern.

Tales of Origin

The first origins are shrouded in pastoral myth which, as we find later in the book, repeats itself as a motif in the propagation of use along the 'khat frontier'. Accordingly a shepherd, observing how happy and energetic his goats get every time they chew from this plant, experiments with chewing it himself and finds the effect pleasing (Getahun and Krikorian 1973; Trimingham 1952; Weir 1985). There is an ongoing discussion of whether cultivation originated in Yemen (Burton 1930) or Ethiopia (Weir 1985; Kennedy 1987), with no conclusive evidence on either side of the argument. This is not the only dispute along the Red Sea littoral, where claims to the first domestication of coffee and the residence of the Queen of Sheba remain to be settled.

Once its stimulant properties are recognized, khat becomes invested with spiritual significance and takes on cosmological value. This finds expression in one popular Ethiopian story relating that when God came to earth all plants bowed before him – showing their ultimate reverence. The exception was khat: a plant which stood straight with a posture of disrespect. Then God cursed – *forever you be chewed by humans*.[2] For causing such divine displeasure khat has traditionally been prohibited by the Ethiopian Orthodox Church. Islamic clergy, by contrast, welcomed khat's stimulating effects as a divine gift to assist in their studies (Hill 1965). Over the centuries khat has gained an important place in Muslim observance and rituals of piety in Eastern Ethiopia, particularly the Harerge region. For centuries, religious scholars have been chewing khat while spending long hours of the day and night reciting passages from the Holy Qur'an and praying to Allah (Gebissa 2004). This practice is continued to this day in this ancient seat of Islamic learning. Here khat is referred to as the 'flower of paradise', and prayers are offered before the beginning of the chew. Scholars maintain that, in contrast to alcohol consumption, the use of khat is not banned by the Qur'an (Almedom and Abraham 1994: 249–50).

In Ethiopia, then, khat has long played a symbolic function to distinguish Christianity from Islamic powers. Khat is first officially recorded in 1330 when the Muslim leader Sebra'din of Ifat threatens to sow khat in the backyard of emperor Amde Syon (Gebissa 2004). Conversely, khat chewing was forbidden to Orthodox Ethiopian Christians, and has only in recent years been used widely across the country. Earlier generations proved far less tolerant. The young emperor Lij Iyasu (1911–1916), the grandson of emperor Minelik, was excommunicated and lost his throne after being accused of chewing khat with Muslims in Harar.

In spite of the strong association between Muslims and khat use, the status of the substance within Islam is not uncontested. Yemen probably has the longest tradition of use, and the theological debate dates back to the fifteenth and sixteenth centuries, when arguments centred on the degree to which the plant can be considered an intoxicant (Varisco 2004: 111–12). To some extent the religious debate on khat persists, but the liberal interpretation that permits khat chewing among Muslims has gained the upper hand. Hence, Kennedy found in his Yemeni study that about 60 per cent of both men and women reported that chewing 'draws one close to Allah' (Kennedy 1987: 128). According to Kennedy:

> Since its introduction hundreds of years ago, Islamic scholars and judges have been divided on the question of whether or not qat should be placed in the category of *haram* (forbidden) substances, along with alcohol, hashish, etc. As we noted earlier, some have argued that analogous to wine it has consciousness-altering properties, and since it is on the basis of such properties that alcohol was forbidden by the prophet, qat too should be forbidden. However, the prevailing legal ruling in Yemen has usually been the more strict interpretation; that since it was not explicitly mentioned in the Qur'an it should not be forbidden. (ibid.: 108)

The debate over the religious status of khat continues among East African and Yemeni Muslims. In Europe the discussion of khat has been from the start decidedly scientific. It entered the world of botanical knowledge after the return of the Danish expedition to Yemen in 1761. It was Carsten Niebuhr who conducted the first recorded self-experiments on khat, and Peter Forsskål to whom we owe the first botanical description and classification of *Catha edulis* (Forssk.). These early reports were followed in the course of the nineteenth and twentieth centuries by sophisticated pharmacological analyses of the psychoactive mechanisms, and more exhaustive accounts of the incidence and context of use.

Richard Burton, that most intrepid of Victorian gentleman travellers, visited Harar, the heartland of khat production in Ethiopia, in 1856 and was struck by the regularity of use. One of the first European experimenters, he was quick to note the pattern of administration and the combination with other substances, and offered a ready assessment of its psychoactive potency: 'The people of Harar eat it every day from 9 a.m. till noon, when they dine and afterwards indulge in something stronger – millet beer and mead' (Burton 1966: 196–7).

Burton's report is not only one of the earliest, but also one of the most positive by a European. The spectacle of large numbers of Yemeni or Ethiopian men sitting together with wads of vegetable matter in their cheeks, flaccid gums, discoloured teeth and glassy eyes, did nothing to recommend either khat or its users to colonial administrators. When early medical examinations were interpreted within a socio-economic context, such as the strain on household income and the drag on labour productivity, khat began increasingly to be considered as a menace to the development of the region. Once again, this is a discussion that is continuing today.

Chewing Khat and its Effects

At harvest, khat is picked as a leaf, packed into bundles and wrapped in banana leaves to keep fresh. The consumer opens this bundle, often known as *marduuf* in Somalia (Elmi 1983a), *robta* in Yemen (Kennedy 1987) and *zurba* in Ethiopia, and delicately picks out leaves and stems. The leaves and/or the tender stems are worked into a wad in the cheek of the consumer. These are masticated over the course of the session, lasting anything between two and eight hours depending on context and occasion. The taste of the fresh leaves being slightly bitter, many users accompany their bundle with water and sweet drinks. Tea has traditionally been served, but fizzy, sugary drinks are increasingly popular. In most settings khat chewing has become associated with intense nicotine consumption, hubbly bubblies or *ma'daa* in Yemen, cigarettes in Ethiopia, Somalia and Kenya.

Chewers report an immediate emotional effect of euphoria, which increases the sense of well-being and can facilitate social interaction. Indeed, khat seems to greatly exacerbate the chewers' urge to express themselves, albeit at the expense of their listening skills. The initial stage of a typical khat-chewing session is therefore characterized by a din of voices, with all attendant speaking excitedly and at the same time. Zaghloul describes the chewing experience as follows:

> The chewer feels elation and well-being together with increased levels of energy and alertness; his self-esteem is enhanced. He becomes communicative and enjoys social interaction while having a sensation of heightened perceptive and imaginative ability as well as a … greater … capacity to associate ideas. For the observer, khat is seen to induce a state of mild euphoria and excitement accompanied by loquacity and, sometimes, hyperactivity and hypo-manic behaviour. (Zaghloul et al. 2003: 80)

This initial euphoria is followed by a quieter and more inward-looking mood. This is the phase celebrated in Arabic poetry as the time when musicians receive their inspiration. And then, in turn, comes a long and melancholic period. Some chronic users have been found to carry on chewing in order to postpone the comedown (Griffiths 1998; Hassan et al. 2002). In Ethiopia khat chewers may also come down to a 'soft landing' by drinking alcohol.

Studies on the use of illicit drugs suggest that the effect of any substance is largely conditioned by the context, the company and the expectations of the user, known among drug researchers as the set and setting (Zinberg 1984). With reference to khat, we therefore find different traditions of use. Among Ethiopian farmers, for instance, khat is popular as a performance enhancer taken early in the morning to ease the hardships of agricultural labour. In Addis Ababa, by contrast, university students, lorry drivers and night watchmen chew khat to stay awake and alert. In Yemen and Somalia there are ancient traditions of khat use in religious and scholastic settings, with many Qur'anic schools supplying khat for their students when reciting the *suras* of the Qur'an late into the night. Khat, like all stimulants, is therefore used in both social and formal settings.

The energizing effect does not preclude its use in strictly controlled ritual conditions, as is the case with hallucinogens or narcotics (Rudgley 1993). Hence the main function of khat is a communal one, stimulating sociability. Secluded, individual use remains rare and meets with disapproval among urban Ethiopians and Somalis. Like all stimulants, khat upsets established sleep patterns and proves exhausting after repeat administration. The disruption of natural bodily as well as social rhythms can cause disturbances in the mental well-being and social adjustment of some users. For most occasional users, however, the recovery phase is fairly benign, particularly when compared to that of other drugs.

Pharmacology of Khat

Attempts at isolating the psychoactive agents in khat date back to the nineteenth century, when Fluckiger and Gerock identified the first alkaloid in khat and called it katin (Halbach 1972). It was close to a hundred years later when research at the United Nations Narcotics Laboratory specified three main alkaloids, as cathinone, norpseudoephedrine (cathine) and norephedrine. For decades the efforts of chemists and pharmacologists had been frustrated by the acute instability of this alkaloid, which is only prevalent in the fresh vegetable matter. In the fresh leafs cathinone combines with cathine, norpseudoephedrine, and several other alkaloids, tannins and other ingredients not all of which have as yet been identified (Al-Hebshi and Skaug, 2005).

When the khat leaves are chewed, the cathine and cathinone are effectively extracted, isolated by enzymes active in the saliva and then directly resorbed through the oral mucosa. The effectiveness of the method has been demonstrated in controlled experiments where volunteers managed to extract around 90 per cent of both cathinone and cathine by chewing for over an hour (Toennes et al. 2003). Once absorbed the terminal elimination half life of cathinone was 1.4 hours, and for cathine 5 hours. The maximal plasma concentration for cathine occurred at 2.3 hours for cathinone and at 2.6 hours for cathine (ibid.; Widler et al. 1994).

The Advisory Council on the Misuse of Drugs comments that:

> drugs with a fast onset of action have a high addictive potential. Although chewing khat is an efficient way to extract the active ingredients, it takes a long time to reach maximal plasma levels, and hence khat has less reinforcing properties than other stimulants such as amphetamine and cocaine. (ACMD 2006: 16)

Neuro-physiological Consequences of Khat Use

It is now well established that the chemical structure of cathinone resembles that of amphetamine. It also affects the central and peripheral nervous systems in a similar manner (Kalix 1999; Woolverton and Johanson 1984; Zelger et al. 1980). Animal experiments testing for discrimination and preference (Johanson and Schuster 1981; Woolverton and Johanson 1984) have found cathine to be rewarding in a manner similar to that of amphetamine or cocaine.

The effective mechanism of all three substances – khat, cocaine and amphetamines – is believed to work through increasing the concentrations of dopamine, a neurotransmitter, in specific regions of the brain. The sudden release of dopamine at presynaptic storage sites inhibits its re-uptake, and can eventually produce depletion of central dopamine (Schechter 1990a, 1990b) possibly leading to depression and aggressive behaviour. Cathinone also impacts on serotonin and the noradrenaline transporters (Glennon and Liebowitz 1982; Nielsen 1985; Rothman et al. 2003).

Moreover, cathinone seems to affect the 'mesocorticolimbic reward system', which is the neural base of all addictions (Deslandes et al. 2002; Spanagel and Weiss, 1999). Drugs act by stimulating this system, which is usually activated by natural rewards, such as food or sex. Where drugs succeed in circumventing the negative feedback system of this system, they may be responsible for the phenomenon of craving and explain the addictive potential of substances (ACMD 2006).

Peripherally, cathinone and cathine both have sympathicomimetic effects, through the release of noradrenaline at the presynaptic storage sites. The short-term physiological effects of khat are therefore a reflection of the sympathicomimetic and central dopaminergic activity, with increases in heart rate, diastolic and systolic blood pressure, arterial constriction, increased lipolysis, metabolic rate and oxygen consumption (Brenneisen et al. 1990; Hassam et al. 2000; Kalix 1991; Toennes *et al.* 2003; Widler et al. 1994).

Khat and Mental Health

International research on the implications of khat use for mental health is ongoing. Studies abound linking khat use with a range of adverse conditions, yet none has been based on sufficiently large sample populations or has been able to discount confounding factors to allow for firm conclusions to be drawn either way. Many of the psychiatrists and mental-health practitioners working in the field are agreed, however, that khat is a powerful trigger of a range of conditions. What remains to be determined are dosage, usage patterns, contributing factors and individual predisposition.

The bulky nature of khat, where large quantities of vegetable matter need to be consumed for extreme effects to occur, is a natural protective factor in the current pattern of use. Nevertheless, over long periods of time chronic use can lead to heavy levels of intoxication, which may trigger disorders. These include observed loss of appetite, mood swings, feelings of anxiety, problems with sleeping, irritability and depression. In most chewers these conditions disappear 24 hours after the end of their chewing session. There are, however, links between khat use and paranoid psychosis: hypomanic illness with grandiose delusions have been reported from case studies in the UK as well as in Somaliland (Odenwald et al. 2005). Moreover, in the Horn of Africa patients with khat-induced psychosis present in psychiatric hospitals (Dhadphale et al. 1981; UNDCP 1999).

Much concern has therefore centred on two questions – the addictive potential of khat and the related one regarding patterns of consumption. The International Classification of Diseases, ICD-10, provides a manual for the classification of mental disorders (see Table 1.1). A case can be diagnosed as dependent if three of these symptoms occur, though it is important to recognize that while some criteria are biologically measurable others are not. It must also be noted that long-term use which does not result in harm and where the user is controlled would not be considered dependent use.

Addictive drugs work by stimulating the body's innate reward system, triggering a sense of pleasure and well-being by activating these neurological processes. As discussed above, some of the psychoactive ingredients of khat – particularly cathinone – fulfil this function, and hence khat has got dependence potential. Animal experiments, for what they are worth, support this contention. Rats held in laboratory conditions, for instance, will self-administer oral khat extract and cathinone in a

Table 1.1 Criteria for Substance Dependence in ICD-10

Three or more of the following must have been experienced or exhibited together at some time during the previous year:

1. a strong desire or sense of compulsion to take the substance
2. difficulties in controlling substance-taking behaviour in terms of its onset, termination, or levels of use
3. a physiological withdrawal state when substance use has ceased or been reduced, as evidenced by the characteristic withdrawal syndrome for the substance; or use of the same (or closely related) substance with the intention of relieving or avoiding withdrawal symptoms
4. evidence of tolerance, such that increased doses of the psychoactive substance are required to achieve effects originally produced by lower doses
5. progressive neglect of alternative pleasures or interests because of psychoactive substance use, increased amounts of time necessary to obtain or take the substance or to recover from its effects
6. persisting with substance use despite clear evidence of overtly harmful consequences, such as harm to the liver through excessive drinking, depressive mood states consequent to heavy substance use, or drug-related impairment of cognitive functioning. Efforts should be made to determine that the user was actually, or could be expected to be, aware of the nature and extent of harm

Source: WHO 1992.

dependent fashion, with evidence of development of tolerance. This leads to a higher rate of consumption to achieve the same effect, while the natural dopamine levels are falling steadily (ACMD 2006).

There is no research, however, to show similar patterns of dependency in humans. Indeed, khat seems a relatively benign substance, as even chronic users can come off the substance and find relief from unpleasant side effects after short periods of abstinence. In Yemen, Ethiopia and parts of Kenya, traditional cultures of consumption have set parameters for safe and moderate use.

Along the frontier of khat use, be this in Africa or in the diaspora, such rituals and customs have yet to be elaborated and established. It is possible that, without such culturally embedded controls on consumption, excessive use can trigger a range of psychiatric conditions. And even in the heartland of khat, as we demonstrate below, the patterns of consumption are changing. The concern is often not about the medical consequences of use, but over the social and economic implications.

An informed assessment is provided by Kennedy, who reviews the medical evidence as well as studying the health effects of khat chewing among a sample of Yemeni men and women chewers. Twenty years ago he concluded that 'it must be evident that while the medical case against qat is weaker than the literature would lead us to believe, the drug clearly cannot be discounted as a health threat' (Kennedy 1987: 232). He goes on to identify the most harmful effects of qat chewing as being on the family – poor people who cannot afford to buy the substance as well as care properly for their families (ibid.). This argument of khat being detrimental to family life and finances is strongly made by Somali groups in the Diaspora.

Locating the Material in the Global Debate on Khat

British and French colonial authorities did try at different times to put an end to the khat trade in Djibouti (1956/57), Somaliland (1921–1957), Aden (1957/58) and Kenya (1945–1956). These official restrictions, as with subsequent attempts in independent Somalia and Yemen, proved impossible to enforce and short-lived. Only in Saudi Arabia has khat cultivation been largely eradicated and availability reduced.

Today, with the distribution of khat across global markets, and emerging cultures of consumption from Lamu (Kenya) to Lambeth (London), the discussion over the legal status of khat is once again an urgent topic. Governments in Europe and North America with neither tradition nor knowledge of khat use are now considering legislation to safeguard the well-being of their immigrant communities. Moreover, the control of mind-altering substances is the preserve of a number of international organizations working under the aegis of the United Nations. The World Health Organization and the International Narcotics Control Board have long-standing interests in generating information and leading a discussion on the control of khat.

It is customary, in such deliberation, to invite an interdisciplinary panel of experts to inform lawmakers on the pharmacology of the substance, the mental and physical health implications, and the impact on crime. What is rarely heard in any such forums are the perspectives of the users and producers. In dealing with most other plant-based psychoactive substances with a global reach, such an endeavour would be impossible because of the legal status. For the present, khat – a licit substance in a majority of countries, an illegal drug in some, a major cash crop in a few – provides a unique research opportunity which allows testing the efficacy and impact of distinct control regimes, with parallels valuable for discussion of other substances.

The objective of this book, therefore, is to document some of the processes of production, distribution and cultural transmission within Africa and among the Somali and East African diaspora in Europe and North America. By looking at cultures of consumption, the discussion veers into directions that are conventionally ignored or at best marginalized in drug-policy discussions. Most importantly, perhaps, are the economic implications of khat production for rural producers and traders across eastern Africa. By providing a detailed analysis of the economic costs and benefits of the khat industry, this book voices the concerns and interests of stakeholders who rarely earn consideration in policy debates.

For instance, according to World Bank figures, sub-Saharan Africa is now the only region where per capita income fell from 1985 onward. While the development agenda focuses on trade, aid and debt-relief, little is said about the entrepreneurship that can flourish in the least developing countries if the market is less dependent on international demand. One commodity chain that proves this argument is the production, marketing and consumption of khat. The khat industry mainly relies on domestic demand and on market opportunities from neighbouring countries (a classic example of regional trade). The khat export to Europe, North America and Australia is also destined to the diaspora where – unlike with coffee, tea and cocoa – multinational companies do not possess monopolies over its importation and processing. Tariffs are not imposed on khat imports and, since it is not cultivated in developed countries, agricultural subsidies in the developed world are inapplicable.

The khat industry, therefore, has grown significantly despite the controversy surrounding the plant and the policy ambivalence toward its cultivation. For instance, farmers in Ethiopia do not receive direct support from government institutions nor do producers and exporters receive special treatment such as subsidies and tax incentives. Even under this policy negligence, the khat industry has become the second largest foreign-exchange earner nationally, and the first in eastern Ethiopia. Nationwide, the contribution of khat to development finance and employment opportunities cannot be overemphasized. Farmers responded to declines in cereal and coffee prices as well as deterioration in agricultural value added.[3] The interesting question is how khat has become such an important cash crop. The first three chapters will attempt to answer this question by tracing the khat commodity chain.

The third section of the book, Chapters 8–10, picks up the discussion over the status of khat ongoing in the UK since the early 1990s. There is considerable pressure to follow the United States, Canada and Scandinavia and bring the substance under control. Somali community groups, often led by women, have been vociferous in their campaign against the evils of khat. They cite a range of adverse conditions from cultural isolation to domestic violence, family break-up, and the drain on financial resources to substantiate their arguments. Yet, the data from Canada and Scandinavia suggest that prohibiting the importation of khat does little to promote the integration of the Somali migrants. In the UK, the khat trade has provided fledgling Somali entrepreneurs with a business opportunity where they can operate with advantage and accumulate capital. There is no reported diversification into other drugs, and the police emphatically dissociate khat use and distribution from organized crime.

What the situation from Sweden and Canada suggests is telling for the formation of drug markets in general. When supply is cut while demand remains high the market will reconfigure underground. Business transactions will assume all the features of a criminal drug economy, and the supply will be taken over by criminals who will eventually consolidate into networks. For the Somali relationship with the authorities this has serious implications in the long term. Khat, then, sits at the heart of a number of discussions relating to the welfare of a particular minority group, over the cultural politics of assimilation versus integration, and the negotiation of identity by a dynamic group of immigrants.

Part I
Khat in the Horn

–2–

Devil's Cud or Farmers' Boon?

The Ethiopian khat industry has grown significantly in recent years, despite increasing controversy surrounding the plant and the policy ambivalence toward its cultivation.[1] For instance, farmers in Ethiopia do not receive direct support from government institutions, nor do producers and exporters receive special treatment such as subsidies and tax incentives. Even under this policy of oversight, the khat industry has become the second largest foreign exchange earner nationally, and the first in eastern Ethiopia. Between 1990/91 and 2003/04 Ethiopia earned over US$413 million from exporting 86,625 metric tonnes of khat. Over 10.7 billion birr was collected in revenue between 1980 and 2002 from taxing domestic and export trade. Khat tax revenue as a share of GDP in Ethiopia averaged 1.7 per cent for the 1990s, while public health expenditure as a share of GDP averaged 1.2 per cent, which means that khat revenues more than finance national expenditure on health. Nationwide, the contribution of khat to development finance and employment opportunities cannot be overemphasized. The interesting question is: how has khat become such an important cash crop?

Among other agricultural produce, such as fruits, coffee, vegetables, spices, maize, wheat and barley, khat has been cultivated in Ethiopia, particularly in the eastern regions, Harerge province and now Oromia region, for many centuries.[2] The Eastern and Western Oromia areas are notable for their quality khat, from Awedaay and Kombolcha, mostly destined for the export market. Khat cultivation, consumption and marketing are also spreading in the northern and southern regions. Two of these are the Southern Nations, Nationalities and Peoples Region (SNNPR) in the south, and the Amhara Region in the north. In the south, the main khat-farming areas are Sidama and Gurage zones, while one of the cities in the Amhara region where khat cultivation and consumption is becoming widespread is the city of Bahir Dar and its surrounding districts. Khat from Wendo Gent in Sidama, and Bahir Dar, known as *Beleche* and *Colombia* respectively, are reputed for their quality. Improvements in transport in the twentieth century, mainly the railway extension in 1902, road transport in the 1920s and 1930s, and air transport in the 1940s, facilitated the growth of khat as a major cash crop in Ethiopia. It is noted in the literature that land fragmentation and state control of agricultural marketing contributed to the growth of khat cultivation. Farmers, mainly reacting to fluctuations in international coffee prices, have also switched their time and resources to khat cultivation. These and other issues related to khat production, marketing and consumption up to 1991 have been thoroughly discussed in Ezekiel Gebissa's (2004) book *Leaf of Allah*.

The agrarian context since 1991 is the focus of this chapter. National agricultural productivity has continued to decline in recent years, despite the success of some aspects of Ethiopia's agriculture-based development strategy, known as the Agricultural Development-Led Industrialization (ADLI). This strategy, initiated in 1991, is essentially a mechanism to increase land productivity through improved extension services (construction of rural roads, fertilizer inputs, subsidized credit, improved seeds and water management). Increased inputs have led to improvements in the yield of annual cereal and food crops. However, prices of these crops have been falling in the face of fixed demand associated with modest urbanization, underdeveloped agro-processing industry and limited export markets. The terms of trade have moved against the agricultural sector, where input prices have grown faster than output prices. At the same time, acreage and yield for khat have increased precisely because domestic and export demand are rising rapidly. The knowledge, expertise and material gained through the extension programmes of the ADLI are devoted to the growth of khat production in response to decline in price of cereals (domestically) and coffee (internationally). Besides this trend, khat was also attractive because of its resistance to crop diseases, its durability and adaptability to growth in marginal land, the requirement for low labour inputs, and the advantage of frequent harvests (and therefore regular cash incomes).

The domestic khat market in Ethiopia has been rising as consumption of khat is crossing age, gender, social status, income and geographical boundaries. The export market is growing in line with mass consumerism in neighbouring countries (Djibouti and Somalia), as well as consumption among the large diaspora population – Ethiopian, Somali and Yemeni migrants to mainly Europe and North America. The khat distribution network involves domestic, regional and international trade routes, including transportation over roads, by train, by air, on foot and using beasts of burden. Production and consumption of khat are aided by significant intermediate activities, such as packaging, branding, retailing and transport. Farmers, traders, retailers and exporters have developed considerable entrepreneurial skills in creating a comprehensive and generally highly efficient commodity chain. While farmers supply the khat as individuals and through cooperatives, the agents and brokers work on commission basis to facilitate transaction among farmers, traders and exporters. The traders are mainly engaged in purchasing the khat from farmers and conveying it to wholesalers and retailers in the domestic market, and the exporters who supply international markets. The exporters often employ the agents, and monitor the quality, quantity and packaging of the khat provided by the trader. Exporters in Ethiopia require licences to move khat overland to neighbouring Djibouti and Somalia, and by air to the rest of the world.

Despite the obvious importance of the khat industry, successive Ethiopian governments have declined to support khat farming, sometimes even publicly denouncing the shrub, at other times remaining ambivalent, mainly in fear of lost income and public outrage. The Ethiopian government is of course aware of international pressures against the khat industry. Anti-khat campaigners show little awareness of the character and importance of khat to the Ethiopian economy. The growth of the khat industry in Ethiopia is a factor of the lack of alternative livelihoods in the growing areas, and reflects the unsustainability of crops that have previously supported the rural economy. The discussion on khat, therefore, needs to place the industry within a development framework.

The first part of this chapter places Ethiopian khat farming within the agrarian context since 1991. Next, we will survey khat production in the main Ethiopian growing regions. The final section presents data on foreign exchange earnings and tax revenues, to show how important khat has become as the basis of development finance.

Diversifying in the Dollar Leaf

Coffee was for many years Ethiopia's principal export cash crop. Much has been written about the 'curse of the green gold', with the volatility of coffee prices placing farmers in the developing world at the mercy of the vagaries of world demand and supply. According to Oxfam's campaigns to highlight the inequities of the international coffee market, the 'Big Four' coffee companies – Sara Lee, Kraft, Nestlé, Proctor and Gamble – have done little to address the issue of falling coffee prices. It is the policies of these companies that has provoked farmers in eastern Ethiopia to uproot coffee trees and replace them with khat (Oxfam 2002 and 2003). Ethiopia's coffee earnings dropped from 2.1 billion birr in 1999/2000 to 1.9 billion birr in 2003/04, while khat-export earnings rose from 618.8 million birr to 758.9 million birr for the same period. Of total value of exports, khat earnings now make up 15 per cent. This shift is mainly attributed to significant decline in coffee prices. As shown in Figure 2.1, both domestic and international coffee prices have fallen sharply since the brief boom experienced between 1993 and 1995. The price of coffee per lb fell from US$123.41 in 1995 to US$26.88 in 2002. This boom and bust cycle was very destructive to Ethiopia's farmers and traders, who accumulated debt during the boom years, borrowed for the purchase of inputs and payment for labour (picking and washing coffee beans), that they have subsequently struggled to repay. Ethiopia's coffee trees have also increasingly fallen prey to berry diseases, often worsened and intensified because farmers find themselves unable to pay the high costs of essential pesticides.[3] In contrast, while coffee has become significantly less profitable for Ethiopia's farmers, khat prices climbed from 12.86 Br per kg in 1990/91 to 28.73 Br in 1999/2000, and to 38.28 Br in 2003/04.[4]

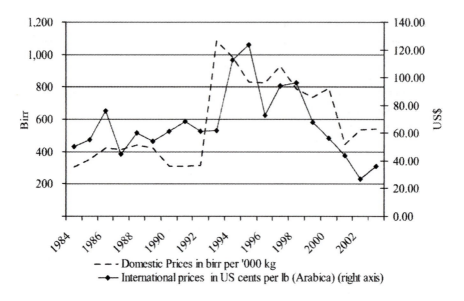

Figure 2.1 Domestic and international prices for Ethiopian coffee. *Source*: Coffee and Tea Authority (CTA), Ethiopia and International Coffee Organisation (various years).

However, the substitution of khat for coffee that these figures imply is not a new phenomenon. It can be readily explained by a series of interventions in farming practices spanning the past two hundred years. Gebissa (2004) succinctly outlines the reasons behind the shift in cultivation patterns. First, in the nineteenth century the Emirates and Egyptians, the then rulers of Harerge (the Eastern Ethiopian region), taxed farmers very heavily. When Harerge became part of King Menelik's crown territory in 1887, new agricultural land-holding and taxation systems were introduced to maintain the Crown's troops and administrative bureaucracy. By these means the state extracted further agricultural surpluses to sustain the gentry and the clergy who came from the northern highlands to settle in the east. Emperor Haile Selassie continued this pattern, awarding usufruct rights to the elites. Changes in the land-holding system under these successive regimes resulted in a higher concentration of land ownership among the aristocrats and the Church, but this land was not always used for cultivation.[5] A corollary of this was that the landholdings of the peasantry became increasingly fragmented owing to demographic pressures. Over the same period, the Oromo peoples of the east steadily converted to Islam, and many more of their number moved from pastoralism and livestock rearing to sedentary farming. These social transformations were accompanied by increasing family size, with the consequent division of landholdings upon inheritance causing further fragmentation.[6]

According to Gebissa, land fragmentation and higher population densities in agricultural areas meant that the 'bush fallowing' system of cultivation was no longer efficient. Farmers accordingly moved into marginal areas, clearing scrub and forest land to establish cultivations. This strategy could not be maintained, as population rises swiftly outpaced the availability of cultivable land, while the underdevelopment of the urban economy and the non-farm sectors meant that labour remained attached to land. Those farmers who could do so responded to these pressures by cultivating perennial crops, mainly coffee. The quantity of coffee being farmed increased, but the quality of production at the same time became more variable. These factors had an impact upon the local market, but it was price fluctuations in the global coffee market, especially in the aftermath of the Second World War, that drove farmers to seek an alternative solution. It was in this period that khat began to emerge as the 'cash crop of choice'. In eastern Ethiopia, farmers found it relatively easy to add khat to the traditional sorghum-maize-coffee intercropping pattern, and many farmers were able to experiment with khat without disrupting their food security or other income-generating activities. The next significant development came in 1975, when the Derg military government introduced a sweeping and ill-fated land reform, followed by the institution of a state monopoly over agricultural marketing. Between 1975 and 1991, Ethiopia's agricultural strategy thus focused on controlling producer prices and imposing quotas on production. However, this strategy ignored khat, the government taking the view that the social consequences of khat consumption were unwelcome. The scarcity of farm inputs at this time, however, especially the poor availability of pesticides, had serious adverse affects upon cash crops, notably coffee. According to Gebissa (2004: 153–4), 'coffee farmers made a conscious decision to increase their khat plantations rather than continue to plant a cash crop that got diseased, fetched low prices and whose marketing was monopolised by the government.'

The reasons for the longer-term pattern of increasing khat cultivation is therefore clear, but one might have expected more recent policies aimed at fostering the agricultural sector to have brought about a decline in farmers' enthusiasm for khat. This has not been the case. In May 1991, the government of Ethiopia, led by the People's Revolutionary Democratic Front (EPRDF), introduced its economic strategy under the title *Ethiopia's Economic Policy During the Transitional Period.*[7] This national strategy focused on the objective to increase productivity of peasant agriculture. The reasons for this focus are stated in numerous policy statements. The ADLI is accordingly

> based on agriculture, … makes an extensive use of the country's natural resources and … contributes to an independent development of the agricultural and industrial sectors. Because of its manpower requirements, this industrial development strategy will open up employment opportunities, in addition to expanding the domestic market for goods and services thereby creating an enabling environment for the attainment of long-term economic objectives. (MPED 1993: 1–2)

Operationally, the strategy is essentially a mechanism to increase land productivity through extension services (construction of rural roads, fertilizer inputs, subsidized credit, improved seeds, water management). The first phase of the strategy is focused on improving traditional farming techniques through provision of improved seeds. The second phase has introduced small-scale water management schemes, and improved rural infrastructure and the provision of fertilizers and pesticides. The third phase, which is under implementation, aims at releasing farm labour to be absorbed by the non-agricultural sector. In June 2002, the strategy was augmented by the implementation of a Poverty Reduction Strategy (PRS), known as the 'Sustainable Development and Poverty Reduction Programme (SDPRP)' (MOFED 2002). Under this initiative, 'development cadres' are trained to provide agricultural extension, advisory services to farmers and support access to farm technology. The SDPRP policy document notes that

> [f]or agriculture to continue serving as an engine of growth in the coming years, through the domestic economy and international trade, there has to be progress in terms of commercialisation, with more intensive farming, increasing proportion of marketable output and correspondingly decreasing ratio of production for own consumption. Aside from deepening technological progress, it will mean greater market interaction on the part of the farmer. Thus research and extension will be enhanced, application of inputs will be increased and diversified, new products will be introduced, irrigation will be expanded ... and rural roads will be constructed. At the same time commercial farming will receive more emphasis and support. (MOFED 2002: 37–8)

About 45,000 para-professional ('barefoot') extension workers currently live and work in more than 15,000 villages across the country to implement the ADLI. More than one-third of the farming population is therefore covered by these extension services (EDRI 2004).

One important impact of these initiatives has been the increased use of farm inputs to lessen crop disease and improve yield. As Figure 2.2 shows, fertilizer use has been rising steadily since 1980, but increased significantly from 1994 onward, reaching 298,000 metric tons in 2000 from 107,000 metric tons in 1993. Table 2.1 also shows that the use of two key types of fertilizer, DAP and UREA, has nearly doubled between 1993 and 1997. DAP use increased from 300,000 metric tons in 1993 to 566,513 metric tons in 1997, while for the same period UREA use increased from 160,000 metric tons to 293,257 metric tons. Total fertilizer use increased by 87 per cent between 1993 and 1997. Pesticide consumption has also risen, from 351 metric tons in 1995 to 436 metric tons in 1998 and to 674 metric tons in 2001.

The availability of credit to farmers has also been of great importance. The government has provided micro-credit to more than 4.5 million smallholder farm families. As Table 2.2 shows, between 1996 and 2002, more than 3 billion Br worth of input credit was approved and more than 2 billion Br was disbursed. However,

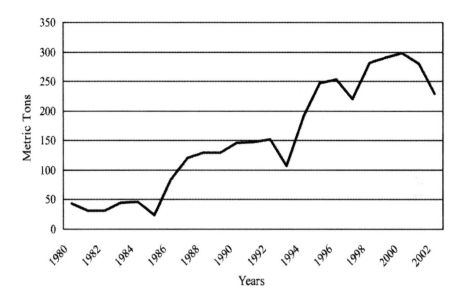

Figure 2.2 Fertilizer use in the agricultural sector, Ethiopian (1980–2002). *Source*: National Fertilizer Industry Agency (various years).

Table 2.1 Fertilizer Use by Type (Metric Tons)

	Type of Fertilizer		
Year	*DAP*	*UREA*	*Total*
1993	300,000	160,000	460,000
1994	453,370	236,685	690,055
1995	494,429	257,215	751,644
1996	519,606	260,803	780,409
1997	566,513	293,257	859,770

Source: Ministry of Agriculture (various reports).

the proportion of input credit disbursed has not improved. On average 73.4 per cent of the approved input credit is disbursed. Actually the proportion of credit disbursed declined from 77.7 per cent in 1996/97 to 71.5 in 2001/02, except for the single year in 2000/01 when the proportion of input credit disbursed reached 81.6 per cent. Access to credit has been found to be a major supply-side constraint, for the purchase of fertilizer and other inputs (Croppenstedt et al. 2003).

Since the introduction of the agricultural strategy described above, production of annual cereal and food crops has increased (EDRI 2004). As Figure 2.3 shows there has been an increase in both areas cultivated for major crops and output, especially

Table 2.2 Total Agricultural Input Credit Approved and Disbursed, 1996–2002

Year	Amount Approved (000s birr)	Amount Disbursed (000s birr)	Amount Disbursed (per cent)
1996/97	318,610	247,432	77.7
1997/98	422,946	306,971	72.6
1998/99	602,914	407,848	67.6
1999/2000	677,805	484,829	71.5
2000/01	593,963	484,698	81.6
2001/02	641,924	459,050	71.5
Total	3,258,162	2,390,828	73.4

Source: Commercial Bank of Ethiopia, 2002 and FAO, Ethiopia, Special Report, 30 December 2002.

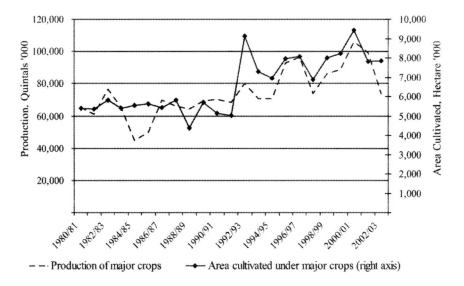

Figure 2.3 Production and area cultivated for major crops. *Note*: Quintal = 100 kilogram. *Source*: Central Statistical Office (CSO), Ethiopia (various years).

since 1992/93. Between 1992/93 and 2002/03, area cultivated averaged 7.9 million hectares compared to 5.4 million hectares between 1980/81 and 1991/92. For the same period average production of major crops increased from 64 million kg to 85 million kg. The increase in output might suggest that the extension services under the ADLI have been successful, but the gains come not from productivity but from the expansion of farming into fallow and forest land.[8] In fact, stagnating yield figures as well as declining productivity paint a grim picture. As shown in Table 2.3, the rural labour force has been growing by an annual average of 3.7 per cent between 1981 and 2003. Yield per hectare of major crops has been fluctuating, but exhibits a

Table 2.3 Yield and Productivity in the Agricultural Sector, Ethiopia, 1980–2003

	Yield per Hectare of Major Crops	*Productivity per Worker (Quintals)*	*Agriculture Value Added per Worker (birr)*	*Rural Labour Force (millions)*
1980/81	12.1	4.7	390	13.8
1981/82	11.4	3.8	327	15.9
1982/83	13.2	4.3	329	17.9
1983/84	12.1	3.5	279	18.5
1984/85	8.0	2.3	423	19.1
1985/86	8.9	2.6	246	19.3
1986/87	12.8	3.6	290	19.4
1987/88	11.3	3.3	273	20.0
1988/89	14.7	3.1	269	20.5
1989/90	12.1	3.3	276	21.1
1990/91	13.7	3.3	283	21.6
1991/92	13.7	3.1	269	22.1
1992/93	8.8	3.7	293	21.5
1993/94	9.7	3.2	273	22.3
1994/95	10.1	2.9	258	24.4
1995/96	11.7	3.7	289	24.9
1996/97	11.9	3.8	290	25.7
1997/98	10.7	2.8	251	26.4
1998/99	10.7	3.2	253	27.2
1999/2000	10.8	3.2	251	28.0
2000/01	11.2	3.7	272	28.8
2001/02	12.7	3.3	258	29.7
2002/03	9.4	2.4	219	30.6
Averages				
1980/81–1989/90	11.7	3.5	310	
1991/92–2002/03	11.2	3.2	266	

Source: National Accounts Department of MOFED for agricultural value added and CSO (various years) for the population, labour force and area cultivated, and production data.

declining trend throughout the last quarter of the twentieth century with pronounced falls during drought years and politically unstable periods (for instance during the famine of 1984/85 and transition during 1991/92). Yield per hectare averaged 1,170 kg in the 1980s compared to 1,120 kg for the 13 years between 1990/91 and 2002/03. For the same period, productivity per worker averaged 350 kg in the 1980s compared to 320 kg between 1990/91 and 2003/03. Agricultural value added per worker also declined from 310 Br in the 1980s to 266 Br between 1990/91 and 2002/03. (See Nega 2003 for similar findings.)

Even ADLI's achievement in the provision of fertilizer inputs has not been without problems. The cost of fertilizers has been rising while the price of major crops has been declining throughout the 1990s. The price of one widely used fertilizer, for example, has increased by 55.3 per cent from 289.10 Br per 100 kg in 1993 to 448.90 Br in 2001. For the same period, the average price of cereals fell by 26 per cent from 116.66 Br to 86.57 Br, with maize declining by 38 per cent to a low of 54 Br in 2001. The deterioration in the terms of trade between crop values and fertilizer prices is clear from Table 2.4. In 1993, 2.5 units of cereals were necessary to purchase 1 unit of fertilizer while in 2001, 5.2 units of cereals were required to obtain one unit of fertilizer. In a more disaggregated level, in 1993 3.3 units of maize were needed to purchase one unit of Urea, and by 2001 8.3 units of maize were required. The story is the same for the other crops.

Despite the energy with which the government has addressed the agricultural sector through the ADLI, the trends are therefore not yet positive. What impact, then, does this national picture have upon khat cultivation? The ADLI explicitly does not cover khat production. No extension services – such as credit, improved seed, fertilizers – are provided to khat farmers. Under the Derg government, the policy in Eastern Ethiopia was in fact to uproot khat and plant coffee and potato instead.[9] The current policy is also ambivalent: no support has been earmarked for khat cultivation, and no research is carried out on khat farming. This attitude is mainly the result of opposition to khat within domestic and international circles. Government policy has always been to quietly reap the foreign exchange and tax revenues without being seen to actively encourage the production of the plant. Despite khat's increasingly obvious economic success in a sector that is struggling to deliver returns, the government's current policy ignores khat in favour of diversification into high-value commodities, for instance horticulture and floriculture.

The reality, however, is that farmers are responding to the agrarian debacle without any policy inducement by diversifying into khat cultivation. This is because khat farmers seem not to have suffered the same fate as cereal and coffee producers. Here, both the inherent characteristic of khat and its market are important. In Ethiopia, khat can be planted all year round. It grows in a wide variety of soil, although the best climatic condition for its cultivation is highland areas at 2,000–3,000 feet (600–900 metres), and within moderate temperature ranges between hot lowlands and cold highlands. Khat is mostly planted on terraced hillsides and marginal land, without competing with other vegetation, while flatter lands are devoted to sorghum, maize, vegetables and grazing (Getahun and Kirkorian 1973). In some areas khat is typically planted in spaced-out rows, intercropped with sorghum and corn. As Eastern Ethiopia is mountainous and most of the land is steep and exposed, khat cultivation suits the environment exceptionally well (see Weir 1985, Lemessa 2001 and Gebissa 2004). Khat is relatively strong and resistant to disease and insect attack.[10] It needs little maintenance, and does not draw labour away from other crops, although guarding the trees against theft of leaves can be an issue (Kennedy 1987). Returns on the farmers' limited investment come quickly with khat, and is sustainable. The tree yields within two years of its planting and remains productive for up to 75 years.[11] In Eastern Ethiopia, farmers have started installing irrigation

Table 2.4 Agricultural Terms of Trade: Fertilizer Input (Urea Prices)/Output Prices

	Prices (birr/100 kg)								
	1993	*1994*	*1995*	*1996*	*1997*	*1998*	*1999*	*2000*	*2001*
Cereal	116.66	132.31	120.90	103.78	119.99	136.25	147.98	115.04	86.57
Urea	289.10	284.80	365.20	413.00	522.80	425.00	373.90	421.70	448.90
Product Prices/Urea Prices (Terms of Trade)									
Teff	1.7	1.6	2.0	2.8	3.4	2.7	2.0	2.5	3.6
Barley	2.4	2.1	3.1	4.0	4.5	3.1	2.4	3.7	5.3
Wheat	2.2	1.9	2.6	3.4	3.7	2.7	2.2	3.5	4.7
Maize	3.3	2.7	4.9	4.9	5.8	4.5	3.6	6.3	8.3
Sorghum	3.3	2.4	3.5	4.6	4.6	3.7	2.9	4.9	5.5
Millet	2.9	2.0	3.2	4.5	4.5	3.5	3.1	2.9	5.5
Oats	2.6	2.9	3.2	4.7	5.1	2.4	2.2	4.2	5.3
All Cereals	2.5	2.2	3.0	4.0	4.4	3.1	2.5	3.7	5.2

Source: Calculated from FAO (2004) and CSA (various years) data.

systems to increase yield from twice per annum with rainfall to four times with irrigation, but inputs and improvements are not necessary to maintain productivity. Khat requires minimal inputs, and is therefore ideal for farmers who have no access to credit. And, aside from its consumption as a stimulant, khat has other uses, as summarized by Lemessa:

> The wood of the plant is commonly used for fuel and due to its resistance to termite is used in the construction of houses and fencing. It is also used for making rafters, handles of farm tools (hammers and chisels) and handles of household articles such as pots and pans, rolling pins, and to make forks, combs, spoons and for rulers ... Processed leaves and roots are used to treat influenza, cough, gonorrhea, asthma and other chest problems. The root is used for stomach ache and an infusion is taken orally to treat boils. (2001: 3–4)

Khat cultivation is also part of risk-spreading and diversification strategy. In most instances, net return per acre from khat is greater than that from coffee. It only takes 13 per cent of cultivated land, and it accounts for 30–50 per cent of the total cash income per year or 40–60 per cent of the total value of home-produced food used by the farm household.[12] As Table 2.5 shows, nearly 8 million kg of khat was produced in Ethiopia during 2001/02. Oromia region ranks first with production of 451 million kg followed by the Southern region with more than 206 million kg of khat production. In Somali region, production amounted to 96 million kg, followed by 9 million kg in Amhara region. The figures for utilization of khat show that, of the total production, on average 27.5 per cent is cultivated for household own consumption and 67 per cent for sale, confirming its cash-crop status. By far the largest khat consumption by the producer is registered in Oromia region with 38.5 per cent of the khat used for own consumption. In contrast, 88.7 per cent of Tigray region's production is devoted for sale, followed by 78.5 per cent in SNNPR (southern Region), 77 per cent in Addis Ababa and 75.7 per cent in Amhara region. We now look at khat's significance in each of these production regions.

Ethiopia's Khat Farmers

Oromia Region

According to Gebissa (2004), by 1961 there were 7,009 hectares devoted to khat cultivation in eastern Ethiopia, then named the province of Harerge. By the early 1970s the area devoted to khat cultivation had increased to 26,800 hectares, and by 1983 to 96,445 hectares. For the same region, khat-export earnings in 1999/2000 stood at 618.8 million Br, from a volume of 15,684,000 kg. As Table 2.6 shows, figures from local government attest that the area of land covered by coffee increased

Table 2.5 National Khat Production and Utilization, 2001/02

Region	Total Production (tons)	Utilized for (percentage)					
		Household Consumption	Seed	Sale	Wages in Kind	Animal Feed	Others
Tigray	–	10.6	–	88.7	–	–	0.7
Afar	–	–	–	–	–	–	–
Amhara	9,674	17.2	1.4	75.7	0.1	0.0	5.6
Oromia	451,890	38.5	0.6	54.4	0.4	0.1	6.0
Somali	96,836	27.9	0.6	64.4	0.2	0.0	6.9
Benishangul-Gumuz	1,089	41.8	2.5	52.4	–	–	3.3
SNNPR	206,712	18.0	0.4	78.5	0.3	0.0	2.8
Gambela	–	19.0	–	78.3	–	–	2.8
Harari	27,337	29.7	1.2	61.3	0.0	0.0	7.4
Addis Ababa	–	23.0	–	77.0	–	–	–
Dire Dawa	–	49.5	0.8	39.4	0.8	0.0	9.5
Total and Averages	793,538	27.5	0.8	67.0	0.2	0.1	4.5

Source: (CACC 2003b).

Table 2.6 Land Cultivated and Production for Coffee and Khat in East Harerge

	Coffee			Khat		
	Area (hectares)	*Production (100 kg)*	*Yield*	*Area (hectare)*	*Production (100 kg)*	*Yield*
1996/97	12,245.00	55,102.50	4.50	62,204.00	766,353.34	12.32
1998/99	15,458.02	60,836.08	3.94	62,200.00	766,304.02	12.32
1999/2000	15,460.99	61,480.04	3.98	62,200.00	607,229.00	9.76

Source: East Harerge Zone Finance Office Statistical Abstract (various years).

in the 1990s, while khat cultivation remained constant. However, in Eastern Harerge yield is three to four times higher for khat than it is for coffee. For the period 1996–2000, yield for khat was about 1,200 kg per hectare, compared to 400 kg for coffee. The economic importance of khat is therefore apparent.

East Harerge has a population of 2.3 million with the average family size of 8 per household and 0.5 hectare landholding. From their small plots of rain-fed fields, farmers here generally grow less than what they need to feed the family.[13] On the other hand, with population pressure and land shortage, cereal production is neither profitable nor efficient. Cereal production on 0.5 hectares will not even feed the household for three months.[14] In response, farmers rear cattle, but with the collapse of coffee prices many farmers sold cattle as a short-term strategy to sustain livelihoods. Khat quickly came to be seen as a more sustainable insurance against such risk, with the proceeds used to purchase basic foodstuffs, including salt, sugar and oil, as well as paying for schooling and health.[15] Khat farmers here have also generated sufficient surpluses for consumer goods, such as satellite dishes – items which are becoming common in the larger towns here but are rarely seen elsewhere in rural Ethiopia.[16] Getahun and Kirkorian (1973: 370), have noted this association between prosperity and khat:

> Whenever farmers realise economic improvement, they are quick to point out that it is due to chat [khat]. Thus chat is the bridge and highway whereby many a farmer moves from grass thatched to tin roof, from tenant-ship to landlord-ship and perhaps to building a house in the nearest town and eventually owning an automobile.

Khat increases purchasing power, but farmers in the Oromia Region express a clear sense of priorities about their patterns of expenditure. Our informants generally used incomes from the first khat harvest to purchase foodstuffs, before assigning money to expenditure on clothing. Repairs and improvements to the household come next in the scale, and it is notable that corrugated iron sheets are now widely used for roofing in this region – a sure sign of rural prosperity. In a study of 196 randomly selected households, Kirsten et al. (2003) have also empirically attested these findings, confirming that farmers will only resort to additional purchases of fertilizer and pesticides once other household requirements have been covered. This study reported that coffee farmers in Harerge earn 11,000 Br in gross annual income, while khat growers earn 23,000 Br. As Gebissa states:

> The common theme in both large and small holdings' cropping system is that most farming families subscribed to the notion of maintaining food self-sufficiency and avoiding monoculture. Diversification was adopted as an insurance against land scarcity, disease and pest infestations, but it was also evident that, the smaller one's holding, the greater the tendency to increase the production of khat. Cash was needed to cover the household's expenditure on capital goods (tools, seeds, livestock), consumer products (fuel, clothing, household utensils) and taxes. (2004, p. 134)

This picture is confirmed by other sources. According to a study conducted by the Ministry of Trade and Industry, Dire Dawa Office, during 2000, Harerge farmers dedicate on average only one-eighth of a hectare to khat. Cash-crop farmers will typically hire labour every two months or so for heavier work, and they will use approximately 100 kg of fertilizer each year (50 per cent DAP and 50 per cent Urea). Where they can, farmers will use irrigation during the dry season.[17] A typical farmer produces 34 kg of khat per 0.125 hectare, of which 40 per cent is destined for export and 60 per cent for domestic consumption. The total cost of production per annum is around 2,330 Br (US$283.45). If we take the average three harvests per annum – one on the rainy season and two using irrigation in the dry season – the total annual produce will be 102 kg. Out of these 40.8 kg will be for export and 61.2 kg for domestic consumption. The cost of production per kg of khat is 22.85 Br (US$2.78). The total income obtained from khat would be 64.06 Br or US$7.83. Therefore, khat farmers earn 41.21 Br or US$5.05 over the cost of production per kg of khat.[18]

The Harari Region in Eastern Ethiopia also produces khat. The region's total land area is 343 square kilometres, with 14,518 hectares under cultivation, of which 3,298 devoted to khat and coffee production. The region is relatively small, with a population of not more than 500,000. Khat cultivation here in 2000 amounted to 4,600,000 kg, decreasing to 3,840,000 kg by 2002. For the same years acreage for khat plants increased from 2,300 hectares to 2,400 hectares, while yield decreased from 200 kg to 160 kg per hectare (HREFB 2004). Officials from the region's Economic and Finance bureau note that khat from Harari cannot compete in terms of quality and price with khat from Eastern and West Oromia.[19]

Southern Region

The Southern Region has a total area of 113,539 square kilometres. The region is made up of nine zones and five special districts. Of the total area, 23 per cent is cultivated, a further 13 per cent is cultivable and about 20 per cent is grazing land (BOPED 1998). As elsewhere in the country, the region suffers from fragmentation of holdings.[20] The rural population totals 10 million, with an average of 91 persons per square kilometre. But this average disguises huge differences between localities, with densities of 394 in Gedeo, 295 in Sidama, 258 in Hadiya, 197 in Guraghe and only 14 in Bench-Maji. It is estimated that between 2000 and 2004, some 1,130,250 people were affected by drought in this region. About 72 per cent of family heads own less than 2 hectares, while 43 per cent do not own oxen for farming and 27 per cent own only one ox per family. Subsistence is around rain-fed farming, and low oxen ownership, but with low productivity and poor quality (BOPED 1998). As a result the region faces food shortages. The food production gap is about 8 billion kg of wheat annually, which is satisfied by purchases from other regions and by food aid.[21]

While *enset* remains a staple food and production is mainly destined for local consumption, the region is known for producing export commodities, mainly coffee and hides and skin. Khat production is now increasing significantly here. The two major khat-cultivating areas of Southern Ethiopia are in the Sidama and Gurage zones. The town of Wendo Genet, which is located in Sidama, produces good-quality khat in several varieties already established in the market – *Beleche, Gulba, Anno, Chenege, Nole and Sike*.[22] The khat produced in Sidama is mainly sold to consumers in nearby towns, such as Shashemene to the north, and Mojo and Nasereth in the south. Wendo Genet khat also reaches the khat market of Addis Ababa. Although not as well organized as the eastern Ethiopia export trade, khat from Sidama is shipped to Kenya, particularly the varieties known as *Aposto* and *Alata*. The Gurage khat is mainly destined for local consumption and the Addis Ababa market. Provisional figures indicate that the region produced 6,524,421 kg of khat during 2004. In Gurage zone 15,180 hectares is devoted to khat cultivation and about 35 per cent of households produce khat (PEDD 1998 and GZAD 1998). Major khat producing areas are Enemor and Ener, Meher and Aklil, Kokir, Abeshege (Goro), Cheha, Endebir, Gunchere and Esia, each producing varieties known by the name of the locality. The Gurage khat is considered of relatively lesser quality in terms of taste, and has short shelf-life, wilting and decaying rapidly. Farmers in Gurage zone have recently taken to spraying pesticides to exterminate a worm which attacks their khat and depreciates its yield and value. However, this innovation has caused outrage among consumers as many have complained of stomach aches and a rather 'strange euphoric effect' that they are inclined to attribute to the chemicals.[23] After a spate of similar complaints in the early 1980s in Yemen, producers there retreated from the use of pesticides and fungicides for fear of contaminating the khat (Kennedy 1987).

The policy ambivalence toward khat is starkly demonstrated here by the fact that it is not covered by the government's flagship agricultural strategy. The story is the same as in eastern Ethiopia: khat farmers do not receive fertilizer, irrigation, credit, seed or any other farm inputs.[24] As depicted in Table 2.7, on average, between 1999 and 2004 the total cultivated area and production covered under the extension programme in the southern Region were 2,042,211 hectares and 52,968,667 kg of

Table 2.7 Area (Hectares) and Production (kg) under Extension Programme in Southern Region

	Khat		Total Agriculture		SNNPR as % of Total	
	Area	*Production*	*Area*	*Production*	*Area*	*Production*
1999/2000	1,781	252,560	1,875,146	47,574,366	0.0009	0.0053
2000/01	1,828	254,680	2,039,864	49,556,260	0.0009	0.0051
2001/02	1,798	256,241	2,068,464	51,672,523	0.0009	0.0050
2002/03	1,806	257,510	2,088,485	53,758,967	0.0009	0.0048
2003/04	1,815	258,710	2,139,097	62,281,219	0.0008	0.0042
Averages	1,806	255,940	2,042,211	52,968,667	0.0009	0.0049

Source: Agricultural Bureau, Awassa, SNNPR (various reports).

agricultural produce. The areas covered with khat which fell under the extension programme were 1,806 hectares on average and the total khat production for this area was 233,940 kg. A meagre 0.0009 per cent of the total agricultural land covered with khat fell under the government's agricultural extension programme. However, farmers in Sidama clearly identified their improved living standards with khat farming, while non-khat farmers in Sidama and Gedeo are still in receipt of food aid following the collapses in coffee prices. Like their fellows in Oromia, farmers here use khat proceeds to purchase foodstuffs and consumer goods.[25]

One particular feature of the southern-region khat industry is the tendency of the government to discourage khat consumption, and by implication its farming. This sharply contrasts with the Oromia region, where the khat industry is larger and more established and government officials are more reluctant to speak out. In the Southern Region, officials do not shy away from condemning the khat industry, speaking openly of future strategies to encourage farmers to switch to other produce. Recently the local government considered providing tax incentives for non-khat products, encouraging farmers into areas such as poultry farming, silk farming and livestock rearing. Over 11,500 farmers have been engaged in silkworm production and over 200,000 pieces of raspberry seeds have been distributed to farmers in 30 districts. Farmers who were engaged in the silkworm production in Wolayta, Sidama and Gedeo zones have earned 3,000 Br each through the sale of silk thread in 2003. The price of one kilogram of raspberry silk in the current world market is US$40, while that of castor plant is worth US$30 per kilo.[26] The local government is also experimenting with production of high-quality and economically high-return fruits such as strawberries, apple, mango, avocado, papaya, sugar cane, banana and sweet potato. Government official also argue that annual crops need to be substituted for perennial crops such as khat, partly because the latter provide poor nutrition.

The agricultural bureaux are enticing farmers to new products with various incentives, such as credit and quality seeds. The Gurage zone is a good example. Supported by Irish Aid, a five-year strategy was introduced to encourage farmers to switch from perennial crops such as coffee, *enset* (false banana) and khat to annual crops, fruits and vegetables.[27] Khat production slowed down – for instance, in the famous Guchere market where seven Isuzu trucks used to transport khat daily, but where there is currently only one truck operating. (One Isuzu truck carries up to 3,000 kg of khat.)[28] Khat farmers here may well be tempted by these initiatives, especially given the relatively poor quality of catha edulis in this area and the difficulty they experience in competition with growers of Harerge and Sidama khat.

Amhara Regional State

The Amhara Region, situated in the northern part of Ethiopia, has a population of 16.8 million. Population density averages 104 per square kilometre. In 2002 it was estimated that 2.2 million people were affected by drought (ANRS-BOFED 2002). Out of the 17 administrative districts of Bahir Dar city, 14 now cultivate khat – Bure, Finoteselam, Dangla, Merawi, Mota, Meshenti, Hamusit, Adet, Delgi, Zenzelma, Kinbaba, Tekle Dengay, Zeghe and Endasa. All these districts send khat to the market in Bahir Dar city, and much also goes to Addis Ababa. In places such as Bure, Finoteselam, Mota, Tekle Dengay and Zeghe, khat is intercropped with coffee. Recent shifts toward khat cultivation here are mainly due to coffee diseases which have had a very detrimental effect on production in this area, coupled with adverse price fluctuations. Traditional crops such as corn, wheat and *teff* are also being replaced by khat. Khat seeds, of the *Colombia* and *Zemet* varieties, are now sold at the city market in Bahir Dar and attract a brisk business.

The Amhara region presents an interesting case in the recent expansion of the crop, for this is an area where khat has traditionally been viewed as a 'Muslim habit' and therefore alien to the Coptic Christian society of the highlands. Despite the cultural and social barriers that have so long kept khat out of this region, the trade is now growing significantly – though whether this region will move toward the scale of production and consumption of khat as witnessed in eastern and southern Ethiopia remains to be seen. Officials at the agricultural bureau note that khat cultivation first emerged here significantly between 1982 and 1987, while a more recent report confirms the dominance of coffee as 'a major foreign exchange earner' in the Amhara Region, but highlights that 'khat farming is becoming a rapidly expanding phenomenon ... because of its economic importance' (CACC 2003a: 6).

All the ten zones of the region are cultivating khat, farmers invariably intercropping with wheat, *teff*, fruits and vegetables. Experts at the region's Finance and Economic Bureau comment that farmers are responding to the fragmentation of land caused by population pressure, and to declines in cereal prices.[29] Government statistics show that average landholding here is 0.5 hectare, while household size is 5. The regional government here is in policy dilemma: it wants the revenue from khat, but at the same time attempts to discourage its production by extending extension services to all farm produce *except* khat. For instance, farmers have undergone training in alterative livelihoods funded by bilateral development agencies and international NGOs, including the Swedish International Development Cooperation (Sida), Deutsche Gesellschaft für Technische Zusammenarbeit (GTZ), and the International Fund for Agricultural Development (IFAD), all aimed at steering them away from khat and into alternatives.[30] The initiatives have included the distribution of 10,000 mango seeds to woo farmers away from khat, the introduction of legislation to encourage the fishing industry, the engagement of 260 experts to train 4,680 farmers in bee keeping, dairy farming and poultry; as well as other schemes in water management, fruit-seed improvement, and pest-control measures.[31]

Despite all of this, a visit to Zenzelema (a town at the outskirts of Bahir Dar) confirms that khat is becoming a significant cash crop. Farmers here explained that they were inspired by the experience of one of their neighbours, who took up khat production and quickly raised the money to buy a car and improve his home and farm. The image of improved welfare is confirmed in a 1997 report, which identified a small number of Bahir Dar farmers in the khat business who were earning up to 3,500 Br per annum from the crop. In Bahir Dar alone the total acreages dedicated to khat were estimated at 62,950 square kilometres even in 1997 (CBDSZ 1997). More recently (2002), the total khat farming community is estimated to be 1,259 (of the total 138,672), earning an average of 664 Br per annum from khat. Of these, 20.3 per cent relied on khat as their primary source of income, supplementing salary and pensions (BFED 2002).

In a region where water scarcity is a serious issue, the watering need of khat has been a controversial topic. Government officials have noted that the use of well water for khat irrigation may have contributed to an increased incidence of scarcity (though this is inconclusive). Shortages of drinking water in Bahir Dar have also been blamed on khat farming. In 1997, a volume of 157,067 cubic metres of water is said to have been 'wasted' on khat, at a price of 1.25 Br per cubic metre (although, of course, the farmers benefited from the sale of their khat). The accusation of 'wastage' is linked to allegations that khat farmers are illegally taking water from pipes supplying other areas, and officials have even tried to evict khat farmers who are accused of 'abusing' water resources in this manner. The concern over water use is real enough, and has been reported in other khat-producing zones also. In Yemen, it is estimated that about 40 per cent of the total water resources used in the agricultural sector is consumed by khat cultivation, and that 80 to 90 per cent of new wells in the highlands are used to sustain khat production (Varisco 1986).[32] Like the farmers in Amhara Region, Yemeni khat growers have been blamed for shortages of water.

The comparison with Yemen offers a suitable way to end this discussion of khat in the context of Ethiopia's current agricultural policies. According to Kennedy (1987), khat in the Yemeni economy contributed 50 per cent of agricultural output in 1973/74, from 43,000 hectares or 2.8 per cent of the cultivated land. By 1987, the crop occupied about 5 per cent of the arable land in Yemen. It is mainly cultivated in the Tihama plane, along the Red Sea. As in Ethiopia, cultivation is primarily intercropped, on terraces and steep slopes, and on marginal land. Yemen khat also takes a significant amount of water, however. Khat from the growing areas goes to markets all over the country, in Sada, Sanaa, Ibb, Taiz, Rawda and Amran, for example, as well as some going to Aden and a portion being exported. In the Wadi area of Yemen, it was estimated that in 1975/76 a 15-metre-square plot with trees 10 or more years old yielded an annual gross of 1000–2000 YER, and old trees could reach 10,000 YER. In 1987, the net profit for farmers reached 109,375 YER or US$24,038. Farmers in Yemen often say that 'khat is our oil'. Khat growing areas also have the lowest migration rates and the highest wages for workers of any districts in Yemen. Even the roads are better repaired in these areas, to ease the movement of khat to the market (Kennedy 1987). 'Khat is an extremely profitable product at all levels', writes Kennedy (ibid.: 146), 'to the farmer, the distributor, and the merchant. The taxes upon it constitute an important source of revenue to the government too.'

As in Ethiopia, producers in Yemen have weighed the value of khat against that of another established cash crop and foreign-exchange earner, coffee. Producer prices for coffee, in the mid-1990s, averaged 350 to 400 YER per kg. In contrast prices of medium-quality khat averaged 250 to 450 YER, while highest-quality khat was sold at 1,000 YER per bundle (Milich and Al-Sabbry 1995). Yemeni farmers have responded to these price differentials by moving steadily toward khat. As in Ethiopia, fluctuating coffee prices, disease and falling yields have hit coffee production hard. Cereal crops, too, have been less rewarding for the Yemeni farmer. For instance yields of sorghum are declining and, with the conversion of sorghum fields to khat, there is a decrease in the amount of fodder produced for livestock. Coffee trees have not been uprooted in Yemen, but land, labour time and resources have been diverted to khat cultivation and marketing. In fact, cash-crop production of khat increased steadily throughout the 1980s and 1990s in Yemen, while grain production declined. What seems to be happening here is that khat is being substituted for annual crops, and especially cash crops, but not for perennial crops.

Foreign Exchange, Taxation and the Khat Economy

In addition to its production for local consumption, the khat grown in eastern Ethiopia is destined for export markets. The policy dilemma for the government emanates from the gains in foreign exchange and tax revenues, which we might call khat's 'benefit trap'. For the Ethiopian government, the notion of a 'benefit trap' can be defined simply as *high dependency on khat as source of development finance*. This dependency is to be measured by the growing share of khat-related income within overall export earnings and tax revenues.

Table 2.8 Value of the Five Major Exports of Ethiopia and Volume of Exported Khat

| Period | Value (000s birr) | | | | | Volume Khat (metric tons) |
	Coffee	Khat	Oil Seeds	Hides and Skins	Pulses	
1984/85	466,269	15,903	15,640	95,408	16,875	1,380
1985/86	664,790	8,477	7,686	119,459	12,635	711
1986/87	524,348	28,677	9,793	108,291	8,481	2,931
1987/88	439,181	21,323	22,015	133,004	16,093	3,363
1988/89	626,448	7,906	11,029	123,528	16,317	537
1989/90	405,103	21,024	8,387	134,049	35,961	1,816
1990/91	268,451	20,422	3,633	92,206	15,716	1,469
1991/92	168,324	5,073	383	58,645	386	251
1992/93	536,982	65,727	1,186	134,515	4,050	1,936
1993/94	718,019	107,932	44,187	203,610	27,704	2,808
1994/95	1,799,034	172,339	50,130	373,549	103,287	4,073
1995/96	1,724,008	174,444	41,938	309,701	77,224	3,698
1996/97	2,307,394	199,533	74,239	372,253	87,854	5,031
1997/98	2,889,531	272,355	314,660	347,699	102,953	5,981
1998/99	2,112,713	444,988	271,462	243,052	101,658	9,702
1999/2000	2,133,646	618,772	255,329	286,459	80,021	15,684
2000/01	1,520,101	510,506	269,598	633,752	72,800	11,982
2001/02	1,393,809	418,674	278,738	474,426	281,409	9,377
2002/03	1,418,324	497,866	395,565	448,003	171,244	6,106
2003/04	1,926,679	758,878	712,738	375,844	194,679	7,825

Source: National Bank of Ethiopia Quarterly Bulletin (various issues).

Table 2.8 ranks Ethiopia's most significant export commodities. Coffee exports still make up the largest proportion, earning 1.9 billion Br, but khat exports have increased significantly over the past 25 years, in terms of both volume and value. Khat overtook oil seeds and hide and skins in economic importance at the end of the 1990s, becoming Ethiopia's second most important export earner. This transformation was as rapid as it has been spectacular. Looking back to only the mid-1980s, earnings from export of pulses were higher than those from khat. In 2003/04, however, export earnings from khat were equivalent to four times the earnings obtained from pulses. The figures produced by the National Bank of Ethiopia show that the volume of khat exported from the country reached 7,825,000 kg in 2003/04, an incredible fivefold increase over the figure of only 1,380,000 kg in 1984/85.

And in terms of value, the increase is considerably more significant: khat exports in 1984/85 were valued at only 15.9 million Br in 1984/85, whereas in 2003/04 the country earned 758.9 million Br from this trade. These figures tell the story of khat's rising status in the Ethiopian economy, and explain why the khat 'benefit trap' is very real indeed for the Ethiopian government.

Over the country as a whole, khat-export earnings are steadily overtaking those of more traditional export commodities, but in the areas of relatively recent khat production this trend is not yet totally dominant. In eastern Ethiopia, however, khat is the mainstay of the region's economy. Table 2.9 provides evidence of the economic importance of khat: between 1990/91 and 2003/04, there was a volume of 86.6 million kg of khat exported from eastern Ethiopia, earning more than US$414 million. Over these years the unit price on the international market averaged US$5.48 per kg. The incentives to export have been very considerable over the years, with a steadily increasing market driven by the demand of the diaspora communities. By 2003/04, a volume of 13 million kg of Ethiopian khat was being exported annually, at a value of US$58.2 million.[33] The overall trend disguises some fluctuations in khat prices, but there has been a very clear improvement in the real value of exported khat. However, some of this apparent gain is offset by shifting currency values, since the dollar equivalent declined from the early 1990s to 2004 as a consequence of the

Table 2.9 Khat Exports from Eastern Ethiopia in Volume and Prices, 1990–2003

	Exported Khat (tons)	*Total Export Value (Br)*	*Total Export Value (US$)*	*Unit Export Price (Br)*	*Unit Export Price (US$)*
1990/91	1,184	15,228,000	7,356,522	12.86	6.21
1991/92	208	3,952,000	1,410,169	19.00	6.78
1992/93	2,783	82,186,000	16,437,200	29.53	5.91
1993/94	3,496	114,200,000	20,896,615	32.67	5.98
1994/95	4,255	163,100,000	26,484,453	38.33	6.22
1995/96	4,035	169,700,000	26,717,341	42.06	6.62
1996/97	3,659	171,800,000	25,606,095	46.95	7.00
1997/98	3,677	132,600,000	18,634,300	36.06	5.07
1999/2000	11,748	337,500,000	42,494,255	28.73	3.62
2000/01	16,033	546,000,000	66,445,506	34.05	4.14
2001/02	11,648	438,900,000	51,894,829	37.68	4.46
2002/03	10,850	438,500,000	51,346,604	40.41	4.73
2003/04	13,049	499,500,000	58,216,783	38.28	4.46
Total/Average	86,625	3,113,166,000	413,940,672	33.59	5.48

Source: Dire Dawa Foreign Trade Office (2004).

depreciation of the Ethiopian birr against the US dollar. This has diminished the real gain in the international market, but in the regional market it has had the impact of increasing demand from consumers in some neighbouring countries, notably Djibouti and Somaliland, where Ethiopian khat is now perceived as representing exceptionally good value.

The value of khat exports from eastern Ethiopia overtook that for coffee in 2000 (see Figure 2.4).[34] Some 60.2 per cent of foreign earnings in the region came from coffee in 1992, but by the end of the decade this had declined to 47.2 per cent, while those for khat climbed from 12.7 per cent of foreign exchange in 1992 to 49.3 per cent by 2000. Over the same period, export earnings from pulses and cereals have all but disappeared, falling from 11 percent to 0.7 per cent. The figures confirm the structural changes in the export economy of the region being brought about by the strength of the international market for khat.

As well as foreign-exchange earnings, the khat industry generates important tax revenues. Table 2.10 shows the revenue flows from export tax, and from taxes levied on domestic consumption. In 1980/81 total tax revenue from khat was 362.47 million Br, and by 2001/02 this had more than doubled to reach 746.60 million Br. By far the larger proportion of these revenues derives from taxes on domestic consumption, at some 95 percent of the total, while the export trade remains very lightly taxed. The high earnings from the industry within the domestic economy indicate the role of khat a major source of development finance within Ethiopia, but

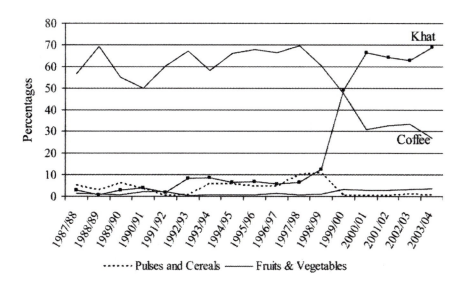

Figure 2.4 Exports from earnings from eastern Ethiopia, 1987–1999. *Source*: Dire Dawa Foreign Trade Office (2004).

Table 2.10 Tax Revenue Obtained from Khat (Birr millions) Nationwide

	Total Tax Revenue from Khat	*From Domestic Khat Consumption*	*From Khat Export*	*Khat Revenue as a Share of Total Tax Revenue*	*Khat Tax Revenue as a Share of GDP*	*Health Expenditure as a Share of GDP*
1980/81	362.47	349.12	13.34	20.6	3.6	–
1981/82	364.50	350.27	14.24	19.4	3.4	–
1982/83	399.97	379.92	20.05	18.4	3.4	–
1983/84	385.18	369.83	15.35	16.8	3.5	–
1984/85	355.70	347.42	8.28	15.3	2.7	–
1985/86	368.07	363.80	4.27	13.1	2.7	–
1986/87	419.60	402.02	17.59	14.3	2.9	–
1987/88	424.57	404.39	20.18	12.2	2.8	–
1988/89	412.88	409.66	3.22	10.6	2.6	–
1989/90	437.00	426.10	10.90	13.9	2.6	0.9
1990/91	450.49	441.68	8.81	16.6	2.3	0.7
1991/92	449.55	448.05	1.51	20.4	2.2	0.9
1992/93	488.86	477.24	11.62	15.5	1.8	1.0
1993/94	485.55	468.71	16.85	12.3	1.7	1.2
1994/95	511.04	486.60	24.44	8.6	1.5	1.4
1995/96	564.42	542.23	22.19	8.1	1.5	1.5
1996/97	585.36	555.18	30.19	7.4	1.4	1.3
1997/98	566.97	531.08	35.89	6.8	1.3	1.4
1998/99	620.97	562.76	58.21	6.5	1.3	1.3
1999/2000	667.23	573.14	94.10	7.1	1.3	1.1
2000/01	685.28	613.73	71.56	6.7	1.3	1.4
2001/02	746.60	690.34	56.26	7.2	1.4	1.4
Total/ Average	10,752.26	10,193.27	559.05	12.63	3.78	1.19

Source: Calculated from Ministry of Finance and Economic Development (MOFED), Ethiopia National Accounts and World Bank *WDI* 2003.

it is a situation that presents the government with some difficult choices. To illustrate the point, Table 2.10 shows khat tax revenue as a share of total tax revenue and GDP. Both the share in total revenue and in GDP exhibit declining trends. In 1980/81 khat tax revenue as a share of total tax revenue and GDP were 20.6 per cent and 3.6 per cent, respectively. By 1990/91 the figures had fallen to 16.6 per cent and 2.3 per cent; and by 2001/02 their decline was to 7.2 per cent and 1.4 per cent. The decline is mainly as a result of the liberalization of the Ethiopian economy. Privatization and foreign investment have been fostered to increase general economic activity, and new taxes such as VAT were introduced to strengthen the fiscal base, while measures to improve tax-collection methods were implemented. At the same time GDP has been growing, at a rate of about 6.8 per cent between 1992 and 2004. The decline in the share of khat tax revenue therefore indicates a structural change in the economy, *not* any fall in khat revenue. To further illustrate the importance of khat-related income, Table 2.10 includes health expenditure as a share of GDP, which on average was 1.2 compared to 3.8 for khat tax revenue as a share of GDP between 1989 and 2002. Revenues from khat have thus more than covered Ethiopia's total expenditure on the health sector. While the khat controversy in Ethiopia is therefore largely promoted by international concerns over the status of the commodity, debates about its resolution therefore inevitably revolve around the general importance of the crop to the domestic economy and to development financing in particular.

As an agricultural product, affected by the seasons and the climate, tax revenues from khat naturally fluctuate with the shifting harvests. Thus, in 2001 tax revenue from khat was 488 million Br, but only 363 million Br in 2002 (Kirsten et al. 2003). Even allowing for such fluctuations, the importance of khat in the core growing regions is undiminished from year to year. East Harerge zone of Oromia region collected 55,303,476 Br in khat earnings from taxes of various kinds during the first quarter of 2004, for example, amounting to around 85 per cent of the total tax revenue. According to the Planning and Economic Development Bureau of Harari Region, income from khat accounts for about 40 per cent of the total tax revenue each year. A good proportion of this is from direct taxation gathered at trading checkpoints on the roads, such as Amberess and Deker. In eastern Ethiopia, the tax regime for khat was changed in 1992 after high-level meetings between leading traders, the larger exporters and senior public officials. Tax on domestic trade was accordingly raised at this time by 50 per cent, rising from 2 to 3 Br, and by 20 per cent on the export trade, from 5 to 6 Br. The justification for the higher rise in domestic rates was based upon the costs to municipal authorities of cleaning the khat markets and other areas where traders operate, as well as clearing away the debris of twigs and discarded khat left on the streets by consumers. Service fees have also been introduced: a 0.25 cents per kilo as X-ray fee; a quarantine fee of 20 Br per daily shipment; and a customs' stamp duty of 20.50 Br for weight under 2,000 kg and 21 Br for weight between 2,000 and 3,000 kg.

Dire Dawa city is a good example of a municipal authority that has come to depend upon the khat industry for its revenues. The officials of the Dire Dawa Planning and Economic Development Office reckon that around 7,000–10,000 Br is raised each day from the Genet Menafesha checkpoint on the boundary of the city, with about the same sum being gathered at the Dengego checkpoints on the other main highway.[35] A record of Dire Dawa's revenues from khat is shown in Table 2.11. By 2003, the khat industry accounted for 60 per cent of the total municipal revenue of Dire Dawa city.

Even though khat is a less dominant crop in the Southern Nations Nationalities and Peoples Region of Ethiopia (SNNPR), here too the crop is important. Overall,

Table 2.11 Municipal Revenue Collected by Dire Dawa City Administration

Type of Revenue	Year of Revenue Collection (birr)			
	1999/2000	*2000/01*	*2001/02*	*2002/03*
Municipal trade licence fee	522,456	406,461	540,886	497,378
Loading/unloading	402,243	213,443	448,881	311,374
Urban land rent	545,431	783,826	1,222,806	177,890
Urban house tax	269,819	214,521	293,414	300,080
Sanitation fee	290,089	310,187	229,107	127,296
Khat tax	5,929,704	6,550,507	7,023,461	7,416,835
Urban and lease	77,909	329,531	294,692	709,185
Transportation service fee	98,251	71,031	80,435	68,502
Horse cart service	10,431	15,920	22,284	106,156
Cattle market service fee	104,552	51,081	47,823	52,829
Cattle market barn rent	18,909	15,316	22,422	28,442
Abattoir service	122,961	185,004	190,398	258,390
Civil engineering service fee	320,334	520,508	490,398	703,584
Open market rent	127,234	268,420	356,821	393,444
Kebele house rent	517,018	840,866	894,360	740,294
Municipal house rent	396,711	275,789	412,562	474,141
Penalties	7,885	22,869	28,212	18,637
Others	70,126	1,145,534	149,490	17,201
Total	9,832,063	12,220,814	12,748,452	12,401,658

Source: Dire Dawa Planning and Economic Development Office (various reports).

the SNNPR generates inadequate tax revenues to cover its provincial expenditure, and with a deficit running at around 70 per cent the province receives a large annual subsidy from the federal government.[36] Khat is therefore of major importance in this region, and so the authorities here have been energetic in seeking ways to maximize their revenues from the khat industry. During 1997, legislation was approved in this region to repeal the 2 Br per kg instituted in 1987 and replace it with a 3 Br per kg tax on khat for domestic consumption, and a 5 Br rate for khat destined for export.[37] In introducing the new tax regime, the regional government was evidently aware of wider public opinion over khat consumption and the implications of the khat 'benefit trap'. A statement accompanying the bill implementing the tax change explained the position of the government thus: 'given its harmful effects khat is not to be encouraged; however, it is the policy of the state to tax the trade and improve social services … at the same time the government imposes tax to discourage substitution of traditional crops with khat' (Finance-Bureau 1996). As a revenue-raising move, the increased tax on khat was highly successful. Table 2.12 shows that revenue obtained from khat in SNNPR increased by 300 per cent between 1985 and 2002, by which year the regional government obtained 33,238,851 Br from taxing the trade. By this year, more than 11 million kg of khat was being taxed in the Southern region.

Table 2.12 Taxed Khat and Revenue, SNNPR

	Total Taxed Amount (kg)	*Total Revenue (birr)*
1985/86	2,808,947	5,617,894
1986/87	4,391,855	8,783,710
1987/88	4,462,243	8,924,486
1988/89	6,056,405	12,112,810
1989/90	4,346,374	8,692,748
1990/91	5,311,772	10,623,544
1991/92	7,025,096	14,050,192
1992/93	6,101,524	12,203,048
1993/94	7,086,257	14,172,514
1994/95	10,469,137	20,938,274
2001/02	11,079,617	33,238,851

Source: Awassa Finance-Bureau (1996).

This figure compares with 2.8 million kg in 1985/86 and 5 kg in 1990/91. Even if the regional government had expressed no wish to encourage khat production, they were certainly doing nothing to discourage it. By far the greatest taxed amount of khat came from Gurage, which traded 6.5 million kg in 2001/02, with Sidama Zone at 4.3 million kg of khat. Awassa district, the largest producer of khat in the region, collected total tax revenue of 11,900,066 Br in 2002/03, of which 72 per cent (8,572,324 Br) came from khat taxes. The local government is extending its checkpoints all the time, and introduced a new one in 2004 on the outskirts of Awassa, where in just one week 30,000 Br was collected.[38] Hadiya and Gedeo zones have also emerged over these years as significant producers of khat in the region, 185,811 kg and 30,556 kg, respectively, being traded and taxed here by 2002 (Table 2.13).

With the bulk of these tax revenues deriving from tariffs applied to khat being transported on the main roads, there are ample opportunities for petty corruption among the officials administering the checkpoints. The government explicitly acknowledges that such corruption is widespread. A recent decision (2005) was made to rotate customs officials from one checkpoint to another, in order to diminish the likelihood of longer-term relationships developing between them and the main traders on any particular route. The customs department has also instituted an internal investigation wing, to oversee the work of officers and with powers to 'raid' customs posts and checkpoints without warning. According to the Revenue officials, these measures are said to have increased revenues at some checkpoints by as much as 60 per cent.[39] However, khat smuggling remains a very real problem and the government is constantly exploring new mechanisms to try to limit its impact upon revenues. Another new directive (2005) stipulates that khat confiscated for offences against the customs regulations will be sold and the money taken by government. If no buyer comes forward, the government has declared that the khat will be burnt. As

Table 2.13 Taxes from Khat and Total Tax Revenue for 2001/02, SNNPR

Zone	Khat Revenue	Total Tax Revenue	Khat as % of Total
Gurage	13,052,291	33,970,697	38.4
Sidama	8,674,209	35,794,993	24.2
Hadiya	371,621	13,992,337	2.7
Silti	168,052	7,744,526	2.2
Derashe	100,186	1,252,455	8.0
Gedeo	61,112	11,806,666	0.5
Amaro	9,214	1,257,543	0.7
Gamo Goffa	730	15,976,714	0.0
Bench Maji	830	7,826,517	0.0
Total/Average	22,438,245	129,622,448	8.5

Source: Awassa Finance-Bureau (1996).

an incentive, the legislation also allows any person who informs on khat smuggling to obtain a 50 per cent discount if they wish subsequently to purchase the confiscated product themselves.

In the Amhara region, where the volume of khat grown and traded is less, the tax system involves levies against retailers, rather than at road checkpoints aimed at wholesalers and traders. In 2003, the Amhara region collected 110,065,708 Br from khat taxation, amounting to 8 per cent of total tax revenue. South Wallo zone of the Amhara region is the largest contributor to this tax revenue, and in the first eight months of 2004 175,226 birr was collected here from taxes against the khat industry (Finance-Bureau 1996; CBDSZ 1997). As Table 2.14 shows, revenue from khat has been steadily rising in Bahir Dar. However, the levels remain surprisingly low, given the steady increase in production and trade in this region: by 2003 the sum raised in khat taxes was still only 128,208 Br. The low level of tax revenue in Amhara region is certainly due to the absence of customs checkpoints, which were abolished throughout the region in 1993 to allow a freer flow of goods.[40] This liberalization measure has restricted the ability of the municipal authorities to capitalize upon the success of khat, however, and it is significant that during 2005 the regional government in Amhara began discussing the possible reintroduction of road checkpoints as a more efficient means of tax collection.[41]

The quantities of khat moved by road transport into neighbouring Djibouti from Ethiopia is very small compared with the amounts moved by rail and air, but the total trade on this route is highly significant economically. Between 1990 and 2000, Djibouti spent on average US$180,679,333 per annum on khat imported from Ethiopia. This startlingly large trade has provoked a heated debate within Djibouti over the foreign exchange 'loss' this represents, but it is often forgotten

Table 2.14 Bahir Dar: Tax Revenue from Khat

Year	Revenue from Khat Tax (birr)
1992/93	70,359
1993/94	85,491
1994/95	102,177
1995/96	113,090
1996/97	113,980
1997/98	116,942
1998/99	120,511
1999/2000	141,697
2000/01	126,346
2001/02	149,992
2002/03	128,125
2003/04 (July–January)	128,208

Source: BFED (2002).

that the trade also generates important tax revenues for the Djibouti exchequer. As in Ethiopia, the taxation of khat is an important source of domestic finance for the tiny port enclave of Djibouti.[42] Customs officials in Djibouti suspect that 5 per cent of the khat entering the country from Ethiopia is illegally smuggled through the district of Ali Sabieh in Galileh, and they report a fall in market price at times when the contraband trade is thriving. In the Djibouti trade, therefore, legitimate traders who are registered importers are keen for customs officials to strengthen control of cross-border trade as a means of protecting their market.[43] As Table 2.15 shows, khat revenues in Djibouti reached DJF 3.5 billion by 2002 and made up 16 per cent of total tax revenue. In this busy trading city, revenue from khat tax is equivalent to 3.4 per cent of GDP – almost equivalent to total expenditure on health in Djibouti, which stands at 3.5 per cent of GDP.

A similar picture is evident in the other main regional export destination, Somaliland. With the collapse of the state of Somalia, and in light of the extent and duration of cross-border smuggling in this trade, figures of any kind are difficult to come by (Gebissa 2004). Some 8,000 kg of khat per day was reckoned to enter Somaliland from Ethiopia in 1982, raising revenues of US$30,000 per day (Araita 2004). The 65 per cent of the legitimate trade was reckoned to earn a tax revenue for the state of 65.8 million shillings from import duties, sales and business taxes, which earned the Somaliland government 21 billion shillings in duties.[44] According to another source (SOVOREDO 2002), of the 30,000 kg of khat imported daily to Somaliland by 2003, some 45 per cent was smuggled and therefore brought no fiscal revenues.

Table 2.15 Total Tax Revenue and Revenue from Khat

Year	Total Tax Revenue (Djibouti Francs)	Revenue from Khat Tax (Djibouti Francs)	Khat Tax as % of Total Tax
1970–1979	3,232,000,000	285,000,000	8.8
1980–1989	10,907,000,000	1,107,000,000	10.1
1990	11,257,000,000	1,522,000,000	13.5
2001	20,862,000,000	3,321,684,239	15.9
2002	22,164,000,000	3,540,140,953	16.0
2003	22,928,000,000	3,519,417,465	15.3

Source: IMF and Ministry of Finance, Djibouti (various reports).

As is apparent from the foregoing discussion, the khat industry in the Red Sea Littoral has significantly grown in response to various factors including policies instituted by various governments, the decline in coffee prices and the deteriorating terms of trade against rural communities. The latter turned out to be the unintended consequence of the agricultural strategy of Ethiopia, which saw increases in crop production followed by the inevitable drop in prices. Under the series of incentives to switch to growing khat, the plant itself – mainly due to its inherent characteristics that require little maintenance – provides an easy opportunity to substitute it for traditional crops.

While khat cultivation expands in areas where it has been cultivated for centuries, recent evidence in Ethiopia indicates that it is also becoming a significant source of household as well as state income for development finance. The foreign exchange and tax revenues obtained from khat in Ethiopia have reached such proportions that reversing its cultivation is no longer an issue of plant extermination or alternative livelihood projects, but a question of how the development of the country will be financed in the absence of the khat industry.

–3–

Trading in the Dollar Leaf

Ethiopian khat comes in a seemingly bewildering variety of brands and types, with price variations that reflect a highly sophisticated market in which consumers discern differences in quality, strength, taste, freshness and source. The brand names by which khat is marketed also change frequently, particularly if an agent loses a contract or if a producer withdraws from one market and shifts supply in another direction. To keep up with these changes can be a challenging endeavour even for the most committed follower of this complex market. But in the *mercato* of Addis Ababa, the largest and most important site of khat trading anywhere in the world, a legion of wholesalers, traders, retailers and exporters make it their business to know exactly what is available and what its market value really is. Consumers can be forgiven for feeling somewhat at a loss when asked to name those varieties they have sampled, or even those they have most recently purchased. Wendimu Wegayehu, a khat chewer and resident of Dire Dawa, smiled and shrugged when asked about his favourite types: 'there are so many', he exclaimed, and proceeded to list the varieties and their distinguishing qualities that came immediately to mind – *Chirra* (a short-stemmed khat), *Karabule* (freshly cut and delivered overnight), *Umerkule* (a very strong type), *Kuda* (a rich red colour, but with few leaves), *Kerti* (always neatly wrapped with false banana), and *Abba Chebsi* (typical of the many types named after the principal trader to deal in khat of distinct locality of origin).

Back on the farm, the market seems less refined. Where the trader plays his market to maximize price through the emphasis upon features such as scarcity, unusual style or distinctive taste, the farmer focuses upon the basics: is the condition of the khat suitable to maximize the harvest, and will the condition of the leaves be retained for the lengthiest period once they have been picked? Farmers thus look for the signs that their crop will fetch the premium price, distinguishing *dima*, the name given to the flush of medium-sized reddish leaves on the ripe plant, which is said to be stronger and to last longer, and hence is the best for the export market, and *dalotta*, the smaller, pale-yellowish leaves, which is preferred for its less acidic taste and its greater effectiveness.

The availability of types and qualities of khat differentiates the growing regions one from the other. For instance, in eastern Harerge four types of khat are produced in the Kombolcha and Awedaay areas. The khat from these areas is divided into four grades. First-grade khat is known as *Ureta Bukassa*, and its common name is *Abo Mismar* – a name deriving from the unusual shape of the end of the stem (it being 'like a nail'). This type of khat is exported to Djibouti, where it is popular with high-ranking officials and among high-income groups. Though less stimulating than some varieties, this khat tastes less sour than many lower-grade khat. It also requires care during packaging and shipment, as it is soft and wilts relatively quickly. While perfect for the nearby Djibouti export market, this variety would not travel well to Europe. Second-grade khat from these areas is known as *Hadera Kuda*, and is a much stronger stimulant with larger leaves. This khat is mainly exported by individual traders for consumption by middle-income groups. This variety makes up 72.3 per cent of the total export to Djibouti. Third-grade khat is called *Hedera Kerti* and unlike the preceding two, it is broken off rather than detached from the roots. Its stems and leaves are harder. This type of khat is consumed locally, being particularly popular in Addis Ababa, but it also reaches the export market in Somaliland. This third grade of khat makes up 27.7 per cent of the total export to Djibouti. The fourth grade of khat here is known as *Ureta Kuda*. This is a stronger stimulant, but with smaller leaves. It is also exported to Somaliland, and is sold for local consumption. Khat from western Harerge, in contrast, is divided into only two types, known as White and Red. The white khat is destined for the Djibouti market, mainly consumed by low-income groups. The red khat, produced in Deder district, is often combined with white khat in mixed bundles and is also exported to Somaliland.

This khat taxonomy owes nothing to regulation or legislation. The state is in no way involved in defining this market. Rather, it is the intermediaries in the market – the great number of traders, retailers, wholesalers and exporters – who work hardest to maintain the range of variety of what is available to consumers. They earn their money by understanding the market intimately, and by realizing that price will shift dramatically as quality and freshness declines. Even a prized premium brand will decline in value as it wilts and decays over time. What is sold for 30 Br a bundle at noon might be worth less than 5 Br later in the evening when the khat wilts.[1] In the many khat markets across the Horn of Africa, knowledge, skill and experience determine who can turn the most handsome profit.

Ethiopia's Khat Markets

Awedaay Market in Eastern Ethiopia

Awedaay has long been the most thriving and busiest khat market in eastern Ethiopia. Back in 1994, it was estimated that 350 traders converged in the market each day, and that even in the later evening there were still more than 200 merchants busy plying their precious commodity. At Awedaay, up to 700 kg of khat was traded daily at that time, an amount worth 218,500 Br, or about 79.8 million Br annually (Gebissa, 1997). By 2004, Awedaay was visited by no fewer than 5,000 farmers, agents, traders and exporters on a daily basis, doing business in khat valued at around 10 million Br every day.[2] This makes Awedaay the second most important marketplace next to the *mercato*. Awedaay is the hub for the eastern Ethiopian khat trade, where khat from the surrounding villages, towns and cities is brought for transaction. The khat from Awedaay is destined both for the domestic market throughout the country and for regional export, mainly to Djibouti and Somaliland. Ahmeddin Muktar, a prominent khat trader in Awedaay, who has traded in the market over the past 20 years, summed up the place of khat in the lives of those who work there: 'khat is our food, our culture and religion, we will always consume it, the market will never die, it is our life – even the state should encourage it'.

Markets such as Awedaay are at the heart of rural entrepreneurial activities. Gebissa (2004) has observed that '[K]hat-selling enabled young males to get a foothold in urban centres and look for non-agricultural opportunities' (p. 124), becoming middlemen and brokers by virtue of the trust they command among cultivators. The role of the small-scale trader in this market is to accumulate khat from various farmers and convey it to other wholesalers, retailers and exporters. The exporters line-up their Isuzu trucks to transport the khat to processing sites (for repackaging) and retail markets. The agents operate as intermediaries between farmers and traders, sometimes bringing the crop to market on behalf of the farmer. These individuals usually take a 10 per cent commission. Farmers, some of whom might only provide very small amounts (perhaps as little as 3 kg) to the market, are often bound to the agents by trust – the agents are often from the village and rural growing areas, are thus known to the farmers and have established longer-term relationships with them. Agents are the link between the farm and the town market. Trust and loyalty are crucial to the khat trade, and those who break trust take a severe risk. According to informants in Dire Dawa, one supplier who cheated the farmers was killed, and his body chopped into pieces and sent in a sack to the retailers whom he had supplied.

Trust does not necessarily mean that it is the farmer who reaps the maximum benefit from the trade. Indeed, farmers are well aware that they often suffer from a lack of information on market prices and quality. A good agent will thus protect them from underselling their khat, and in doing so he is also protecting his commission. Interviews with farmers revealed that they do not fully benefit from the khat trade, as agents and traders appropriate a much higher share of the profit. There have recently been some attempts to address this problem by organizing cooperatives for the marketing of khat, for example in Deder and Kombolcha towns, but the system of agents still very much dominates the trade. For their part, traders are generally content to deal with agents because it reduces the negotiation process. Relatively wealthy farmers, whose khat is in demand and who cultivate larger acreages, reap the benefits of lower transaction costs by using agents. (See Figure 3.1 for the Khat Chain, from the farmer to the consumer.)

Aside from the farmer–agent–trader–exporter chain, Awedaay market hosts numerous individuals, both men and women, who are engaged in a great variety

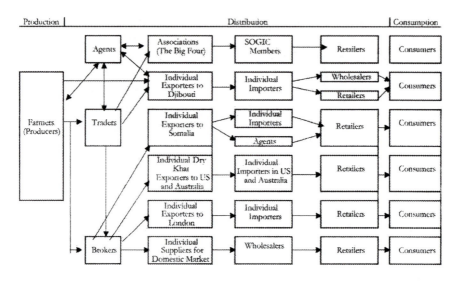

Figure 3.1 The khat chain – from farm gate to consumers.

subsidiary activities. Many of these individuals eke out a living, and the market is in fact flooded with persons offering adjunct services. This is partly a function of the very high levels of unemployment in the Dire Dawa area, and the relatively low entry costs involved in servicing the khat industry. The textile factory in Dire Dawa which used to employ 7,500 staff has undergone restructuring and numerous workers have been made redundant. Dire Dawa was also a major trading city throughout the last three decades, mainly related to transaction of contraband goods – mostly clothing and electronics brought in by the Ethio–Djibouti railway. However, since the late 1990s tighter government controls, coupled with the liberalization of formal trade, has killed off much of the contraband trade which had previously accounted for 67 per cent of employment in Dire Dawa. The unfortunate result of these developments was that many urban traders and retailers lost their employment.[3] Many of these individuals have drifted into the khat industry, involved in processing, packaging, transportation and distribution.[4] There are businesses that sell carrier sacks, banana leaves for wrapping khat, ropes for binding the bundles and for strapping khat to the vehicles, grass for padding the khat bundles to protect the leaves. Others man the stalls which sell khat, and some sell large banana leaves used for covering the khat and keeping it moist. Even water is sold, which is sprinkled on the grass padding to help keep the khat at a cool temperature. There is also a vibrant service sector, with restaurants, hotels and tearooms entertaining those who come to town to deal in khat. Another important subsidiary activity is transportation, with Isuzu trucks and their drivers available all day for hire by traders and wholesalers who wish to move their purchases or deliver to their buyers. Local youths are also engaged in washing the trucks and in packing, loading and unloading the khat. The Isuzu drivers are known for their furious driving to reach the market ahead of everyone else in order to deliver fresh khat in urban centres (Carrier 2005b for Kenya parallels). Pedestrians flee in front of the hurtling vehicles as they leave the market, loaded with khat intended for Addis Ababa, Djibouti or some other centre of consumption. Speed is of the essence. The key is khat's perishable nature: the price falls as freshness declines.

The experience of one small khat farmer, Omar Abdulali, is typical of many. He came to Awedaay on 29 September 2004, carrying 3 kg of khat. At Awedaay he looked for his agent, a man well known among the farming community in Abdulali's home area. He travels to the Awadaay frequently. The 3 kg khat he carried was harvested from nine rows of trees on his own farm. Abdulali had no idea how much his khat was worth and gave the crop to his trusted agent, who managed to sell the crop at 90 Br for the whole 3 kg harvest. All of Abdulali's seven children go to school, mainly financed by the surplus cash from khat. Depending on the market, he spends 20 Br per half kilo for poor-quality and 40 Br for good-quality DDT, which he uses to spray the khat trees and protect his crop from pests. Abdulali has thought about planting more khat, and replacing other crops on his farm, but price fluctuations made the market unpredictable. He continues to cultivate peas, beans, sweet potato and sorghum, mainly for the subsistence of his family. Ziad Jibri, the agent who brokered Abdulali's khat, also said his two children went to school only because of the extra money he gets from brokering. Jibri also owns a farm, cultivated by his close relatives. Hussein Abdurahmen, another agent, brokers on behalf of both the traders and the vehicle owners. He gets a commission by connecting the transporters and the traders. At the same time he also mediates between loaders and traders, who come with their own vehicles (some own up to 3 trucks) and purchase up to 500 kg of khat at a time.

The story of the retailers is equally fascinating. Phosia is a respected female trader in Awedaay. She buys up to 40 kilos of khat every day from distributors in Dire Dawa. She retails directly to her customers. Phosia employs more than 10 people, including the bodyguard who protects her and her money, the wrapper who bundles the khat for customers, the water provider, and the banana-leaf provider. She buys the banana leaves, costing 60 Br, and the twine for binding the bundles, costing 3 Br. Phosia pays 3 Br per kilo at the customs checkpoint from Awedaay to Dire Dawa, a journey of about 38 km. As most traders do, Phosia admits that she often attempts to dodge the checkpoint, and is sometimes successful in disguising the true quantity of khat she is carrying. Muhammed Remedan, whom Phosia employs as a retailer, sells the many varieties of khat that Phosia buys from Awedaay, including *kuda, chira, ubeta, mercule, uberta,* and *bedessa.* She has many loyal customers, who attest that she retails the best khat in Dire Dawa City. Phosia has been enterprising in other ways, too – she was the first trader in Dire Dawa to establish designated chewing rooms for the use of her customers, after noticing such facilities during a visit to Addis Ababa. She charges 10 Br per person for admission to her chewing rooms, and employs five waiters who provide cigarettes, water, tea and music. She is quite certainly the pioneer of the Dire Dawa khat service sector, and typical of those in the khat industry who are responding to new opportunities in what is a vibrant market.

Tula and Teffera Night Markets, Southern Ethiopia

One of the most fascinating aspects of the khat trade in Sidama is observing the night markets at Teffera, near to the Wendo Genet growing area, and at Tula, on the road to Yergalem. The sight is quite astonishing, especially at Tula, where the market is conducted under torch- and candlelight. The night markets were devised so that the khat can be moved to market in the freshest possible condition, and to maintain its moisture for the longest possible time. Teffera market opens at 10:00 pm, and Tula at 7:00 pm every evening, both staying open for around six hours. Officials estimate that 300,000 Br changes hands in Teffera each night, and more than 500,000 Br in Tula. Farmers bring their produce directly to these night markets, and stand in perfect line waiting for their agents. Only those farmers with the very largest plots here engage agents who go to the farms to collect the khat. Traders from Shashemene, Mojo, Nasereth and Addis Ababa come nightly to these markets with their pickup trucks to purchase the fresh khat. Negotiations take place on the roadside, and the khat is bundled, packed and loaded on the spot, or taken into local houses, where enterprising residents have rented rooms to traders and wholesalers. In these neighbourhoods, too, as in Awedaay, local youths make a living as car washers, security guards, packers and loaders.

The highly organized and commercial night markets contrast markedly with distribution systems in the more outlying production zones. In Gurage, for example, the crop is directly traded by the farmers on an ad hoc basis without resort to local agents. Some sell in the urban centres, while others engage their relatives to transport the khat directly by road to Addis Ababa. The people of the Gurage zone have a high rate of migration throughout the rest of the country, and they are renowned for their entrepreneurial flair. They have so far managed to keep the Gurage khat industry in local hands, but as their production grows and the quality improves, the commercial tentacles of the national market are likely to extend to the farms of this region.

Khat in Bahir Dar City

Most of the retail trading in Bahir Dar is conducted in the four non-agricultural districts of the city. The traders here purchase the khat from the farmer and use child labour for trimming and packing, before retailing. There are three categories of retailers in Bahir Dar City: those who vend in the streets, carrying the khat in plastic bags; those who sell khat among other consumables at market stalls; and those who retail in designated khat shops. In 1997, a municipal survey found that there were 58 retailers selling khat from stalls and in shops, but gave no estimate for the numbers roaming the streets. Khat prices here range from 3.50 Br per 100 grams in glut times, up to 7 Br during the dry season. On quality terms, *Tana* and *Colombia* are the most highly regarded, costing up to 10 Br per 100 grams (CBDSZ 1997). Most observers note that the commodification of khat in Bahir Dar is in the hands of Gurage migrants. Khat is consumed locally in Bahir Dar, and wholesalers from here also send the commodity on to outlets in Wello, Gonder and Addis Ababa.[5]

The Export Trade

(i) The Importers from Djibouti City

While Djibouti was under French rule, the importation of khat was in the hands of a group of independent traders with connections to the Ethiopian cities of Harar and Dire Dawa. In 1958, khat imports were limited to around 300 tons per year. In 1960, pressure from the French colonial administration led to the first anti-khat campaign, launched with announcements on the local radio and in newspapers. As a control measure, the authorities banned khat consumption over the first three days of the week (Monday, Tuesday and Wednesday). These regulations met with public protest, and were widely disregarded. Despite official sanctions, in 1965 khat imports from Ethiopia reached 850 tons per year, and in 1974, long after the French ban had ceased, importation reached 1,350 tons – an increase of 37 per cent (Araita, 2004). In 1977, khat consumption was again banned, this time by Djibouti's indigenous national government. Ironically, the reasoning was that their colonial masters had encouraged khat consumption in order to make the population docile and acquiescent. Though this ban lasted only a little over two years, from 1977 to 1979 the price of khat inevitably increased as the contraband trade flourished. On 27 June 1977, the new government in Djibouti, under M. Al Hadj Hassan Gouled Aptidon, decided to reverse the policy of prohibition in order to capitalize upon the revenues to be accrued from taxing khat. After lengthy negotiations with Ethiopia in 1980, the government put into effect a set of rigorous regulations to formalize the khat trade in Djibouti. One of the key initiatives, finally brought in during 1982, was the amalgamation of the various importers into an association, the Société Générale d'Importation du Khat (SOGIK).[6] For the governments of both Ethiopia and Djibouti, the establishment of SOGIK provided a means to more efficiently channel tax revenue into the state coffers.[7] This was clearly not in the interests of the smaller importers, many of whom objected to the establishment of SOGIK and tried to avoid compliance. These importers, who called themselves 'Sans Pieds' ('Without Feet') resisted SOGIK, but to no avail. Importation to Djibouti was totally dominated by the official khat association for much of the next decade.

With 240 members, SOGIK controlled and monopolized the import business until the mid-1990s. SOGIK's monopoly was challenged when the Ethiopian government opened the market for individual exporters as part of its general steps toward economic liberalization. The individual exporters, licensed from the Ethiopian side, soon began to network with individual importers from the Djibouti side. With price advantages quickly becoming apparent in these bilateral arrangements, due to competition to build partnerships, the power of SOGIK diminished. This eventually forced the government of Djibouti to capitulate and follow their Ethiopian neighbours in liberalizing the market. These importers became known as the Porte Clé, a loose association of 177 individual importers, each with quotas ranging from 40 to 250 kg per day. Prior to the liberalization of the market, SOGIK's subsidiary in Dire Dawa had negotiated directly with farmers in eastern Ethiopia to secure the supply of khat. The arrival of the Porte Clé facilitated the rapid re-emergence of independent khat traders and agents. However, SOGIK remains in the market and continues to flourish, being better organized than the Port Cle group and also enjoying cordial relations with the politically influential class in Djibouti. Liberalization of the khat market in Djibouti has not, therefore, resulted in a market free-for-all between importers, but has seen the retention of collective organizations able to better manage the movement and distribution of a perishable product.

State controls in Djibouti also set limits on the amounts that individual traders could ship. In 1991, importers' quotas were set at 10,000 kg per day, at US$10.00 per kg for good-quality khat and US$8.00 for lower quality. However, few months later it was realized that contraband prices in Djibouti for smuggled khat were considerably lower, with the inevitable consequence that unofficial trade increased while official imports declined. The state directive was accordingly revised, prices coming down to US$8.00 per kg for good-quality khat, mostly imported by SOGIK, and US$6.00 for lower-quality khat imported by Porte Clé.[8] In recent years, SOGIK has purchased khat mainly from Bedessa, while Porte Clé members import khat predominantly from Awedaay market and from Kombolcha. Khat retail prices ranged between DJF300 and DJF800 a bundle during 2005, depending on quality and freshness.

The overland trade in khat between Ethiopia and Djibouti is now augmented by the daily arrival of a cargo flight from Dire Dawa. The flight arrives at Ambuli Airport, Djibouti City, each day at around 1.00 pm. Ethiopian Airlines make the journey on three days each week, Djibouti Airways on the remaining four days. In the hour before the flight arrives, the airport becomes crowded with traders, gathered in nervous huddles, talking and smoking, and some playing traditional games such as *nsolo*. The khat from the flight is the quickest to reach the market in Djibouti, and is accordingly very highly prized for its freshness. There have been occasions when serious delay to the flight, or even its cancellation, has caused riots in the city. Squabbles have also ensued among the traders at the airport, as they compete for their fair share of the lucrative cargo. The police therefore patrol the airport concourse when the flight is due, there not only to keep the peace but to guard the khat. SOGIK and Porte Clé have their trucks ready as the plane lands, and both usually manage to get loaded in no more than 30 minutes. The cargo is then driven from the airport to the distribution compounds, located only half a mile from the airport. Here the association members of Porte Clé obtain their quota, which has already been marked with the codes of individual traders, while SOGIK also distributes to its traders.

This stage of the distribution system is chaotic and dangerous, especially that of Porte Clé. The representatives of each of the 177 members of Port Clé all wait around the crowded compound in their four-wheel-drive vehicles, taxis and pickup trucks. Speed is essential. Though it is hard to believe, the time between the trucks entering the distribution compound and being unloaded is little more than five minutes. The cargo of 4,000 to 5,000 kg on each truck literally vanishes before your eyes, as the scrum of eager traders descends upon it. The speed with which the cars leave the compound and hurtle along the adjacent roads is truly frightening. As they rush through the city, these vehicles barely come to a halt at the retail outlets, instead tossing the white sacks of khat to the street vendors who stand waiting at the kerbside.[9] According to Hassan's (2004) vivid description of the scene, 'a foreigner visiting the country must think that it's the shooting of a film where stunt men are in action. In general, stunt men risk their lives but the khat transporters threaten people's lives'.

Khat retailers are to be seen everywhere in Djibouti City. Nearly all are women, who reputedly earn between DJF1,500 and DJF2,000 per day. Having delivered the khat early in the afternoon, the traders return later in the evening to collect their money from the day's sales. In some cases, Porte Clé members are also retailers themselves, and it is not uncommon for another family member to be involved as a street vendor. Family members, and other involved in street retailing like this, might be paid on either a salary or a commission basis. The time from the landing of the plane at the airport to the first sale to a consumer in the city can be less than 40 minutes. Porte Clé members have a secure and well-established niche in the Djibouti market for the air-freighted khat, and the Bedessa varieties they deliver are considered to be relatively less perishable. This khat fetches good prices in what remains a very competitive market. The miraculous efficiency of distribution is, of course, driven by the perishability of the khat, a factor made even more relevant by hot and extremely humid climate of Djibouti City. However, these legitimate traders are also hurrying to get to market before the arrival of the smuggled khat, a race that it can be especially difficult to win in the outlying districts, closer to the Ethiopian border. By comparison with their Porte Clé rivals, the merchants of SOGIK take a more relaxed 50 minutes or so to get the khat from the airport to the street vendors.

The need for speed in the marketing of khat affects distribution in all the main consumption centres. For instance, across the Red Sea strait in Yemen, khat marketing has given impetus to the expansion of the national transportation infrastructure. Most of Yemen's khat was traded by donkey and camel until the 1970s, the crop taking as much as two days to get from the growing areas to urban consumers in cities such as Aden. Subsequently, motor transport has taken over and hundreds of roads and feeder tracks have been built into the khat farming regions (Weir 1985: 30). Another aspect of perishability is the immediacy of the trade: unlike coffee, which can be withheld from the market after picking, 'khat must remain in the trees until the last moment before marketing. It cannot be stored and withheld from the market by speculators' (Kennedy 1987: 164). Small farmers and traders in Yemen have therefore been willing to contribute to the costs of the construction of feeder roads, in order to better link their areas to the market.

Ethiopia's khat farmers and Djibouti's traders have been equally enterprising in finding the swiftest route to market. Khat reaches the northern districts of Djibouti, Tadjourah and Obock over the sea by fishing boats. Tadjourah is about one hour from Djibouti, and Obock is about one and a half hours distant. About 1,000 kg is delivered to each district every day and, here again, the speed and efficiency of the distribution system is breathtaking, with boats ready in the harbour to leave with the fresh khat as soon as it reaches the quayside. The transportation of khat to the districts to the south of Djibouti City – Arta, Ali Sabieh and Dikhil – is by road. Powerful 4×4 vehicles ply this route at tremendous speeds. This is a low-income region, and the market here is supplied only with the 'petits paquets' [small packets/ bundles] to meet the requirements of individual consumers. The higher-quality khat that will fetch exorbitant prices in Djibouti City never finds its way to the south.

The sharpest Djibouti traders are always on the lookout for new consumer groups, although in such a competitive and lively market this is no easy task. One enterprising Porte Clé member has managed to collar a new market with Ethiopian truck drivers, however. Since the recent Ethiopian–Eritrea wars, Djibouti is now the only port through which goods reach Ethiopia. It is estimated that some 800 Ethiopian trucks move along the main highway between Djibouti City and the Ethiopian border each day. The trucks have to pull up at a designated area, Pika Douze, where the loads are inspected by customs officers and the paperwork authorized. This can take several hours, especially if things are busy. The trader who has set up his stall at this truck halt sells to the drivers approximately 80 kg of khat every day, which they chew while waiting for the cogs of bureaucracy to turn.

Gender relations play a role in the Djibouti trade. Women monopolize the khat-retailing activities in the city, while men are their principal customers. The male consumers are often heard complaining that they are made 'to dance to the ladies' tune'. Indeed, a visit to the khat market exposes men who are short of disposable income to the wiles of the saleswomen. Power relations between the genders shift in this situation, with the women able to manipulate the desires of the men. Customers ready to pay cash will always get the best advantage, as will regular customers, some of whom might pay by monthly deposit to secure the best supplies. Those with little spare cash to finance their habit must go to the back of the queue, where they may find themselves at the mercy of the female retailers. Without sufficient cash to pay up front, consumers crave the indulgence of the seller, and many can find themselves entering into heavy debt. In Hassan's (2004) imaginative account of the conversation between the chewer and the retailer, he neatly captures the dynamics of their relationship: 'Hadja, I swear on my children's lives. I'm going to pay you at the end of the month', exclaims the chewer. 'Try to understand my situation – with the delay of my salary, nothing remains for me.' The lady retailer answers him: 'pay your debt and you'll be served.' But the chewer has a further retort: 'Listen, if you don't serve me you'll never get your money I owe you.' And with this, the woman curses him, but eventually allows him to take some khat and increase his debt. The scene is a public humiliation for the male chewer, and provides vivid evidence of the power of the khat retailers.[10]

The Exporters from Dire Dawa

Until the early 1990s, the Ethiopian export market in khat was monopolized by the Ethiopian Chat and Agro-Industrial Products Manufacturing Import and Export Share Company, first established in 1970, but restructured and renamed Ethiopian Chat Exporters Association (ECEA) in 1988. At this time the company held an effective monopoly, exporting 8,000 to 10,000 kg daily. It is, in effect, a cooperative of traders, with some 790 members. In the early 1990s, new legislation began to be implemented aimed at liberalizing the market and as a consequence the dominant position of ECEA was challenged. In 1991, the Khat Exporters Cooperative of Ethiopia (KECE) was allowed a quota of 3,000 kg, and the Eastern Oromo Khat Exporters Association 5,000 kg; 14 named individual licence holders were given a quota of 1,580 kg. In 1996, the arrangements were cancelled, once again in the interests of market liberalization. Four major export companies were now successful in gaining licences, while some 90 individual exporters eventually entered the market alongside them (Dire Dawa Foreign Trade Office 2002). This 'Big Four' now dominate the export trade. They are BIFTU, the old Ethiopian Chat Exporters Association (ECEA), Koulmiyeh and Berawako.

These exporting companies are all very different from one another. Berawako General Trading and Construction Works Share Company, to give its full name, has a quota of 980 kg per day for export to Djibouti. Established in 1990 the company employs 280 workers. The management of the company have expressed fears that the monopsony position of the buyer, SOGIK, might eventually drive them out of business. They have also been concerned that the international pressure to outlaw khat will ultimately destroy the business. As a result, Berawako has embarked on a policy of diversification, entering the construction sector while retaining its activities in the export business. BIFTU, established in 1994 with an initial capital of 7.9 million Br, has its headquarters in the town of Chiro in western Harerge. Dinsho Plc holds 50 per cent of the company, while the four other shareholders include Shiferaw Jarso, Ethiopia's then Minister of Water Resources, and Girma Birru, the

Minister of Trade and Industry. Both Ministers are high-ranking officials of the Oromo Peoples' Democratic Organization (OPDO), a member of the current ruling coalition in Ethiopia. BIFTU also engages in a range of development activities, such as credit schemes to farmers, and the construction of schools and clinics. With 320 employees, BIFTU handles a larger volume of the khat export trade to Djibouti than any other company. BIFTU's quota is 2,500 kg per day, having been cut back from 5,000 kg to allow other associations and private exporters to enter the market. Koulmiyeh, owned by traders who are main players in SOGIK, was set up in 1997. It employs 148 people and has a quota of 758 kg per day. Compared to the other export companies, Koulmiyeh is small and has few members.

As Table 3.1 shows, between 1990 and 2000 a total of US$180,679,33 was earned from exporting 34,674,283 kg of khat to Djibouti. Unit price averaged US$5.62. For the year 2002, of the total export volume an amount of 55 per cent was exported by the associations and of 45 per cent by individual exporters. The share of individual exporters had stood at only 10 per cent in 1991, so the balance of the market has shifted considerably. Fluctuations in the trade reflect seasonality in production. June to October, the rainy season in Ethiopia, sees growth in khat exports of up to 15,000 kg per day, while the figure falls to 8,000 kg per day during the dry season, December to May. At the peak periods, it is estimated that Air Djibouti and Ethiopian Airlines earn about US$10,000 each daily from their khat cargo shipments.

The cost of purchasing khat and preparing it for export to Djibouti, calculated by the Dire Dawa Foreign Trade Office in 2002, are indicated in Table 3.2. The costs per kilogram are related to:

1. purchase of khat from farmers, on average 27.26 Br for the Big Four and 56.00 Br for individual exporters;
2. packing costs, at 1.51 Br for the Big Four and 0.5 Br for individual exporters;
3. labour costs, at 1.85 Br for the Big Four, and 0.4 Br for other exporters;
4. transportation costs, at 1.45 Br and 1 Br, respectively;
5. khat tax levied at 8.40 Br and 5.95 Br respectively;
6. fees of various kinds, including Customs X-ray charges, quarantine fees and bank transfer fee, amounting to 0.39 Br and 0.25 Br respectively;
7. other administration costs and expenses, adding up to 1.52 Br for the Big Four and 0.75 Br for the individual exporters.

Therefore, 1 kg of khat costs, on average, 42.41 Br for Big Four exporting associations and 64.7 Br for individual exporters. At the export price of khat in Djibouti, 46.19 Br for the Big Four, and 68.35 Br per kg for individual exporters, the Big Four therefore make a profit of 3.78 Br and individual exporters 3.65 Br per kg of khat. In terms of quantity, the associations exported 1,797,000 kg in 2000 and individuals exported 2,136,000 kg, which means the associations earned 6,788,167 Br (US$825,811) and the individual exporters made 7,796,400 Br (US$948,467).

Table 3.1 Khat Exports from Ethiopia to Djibouti in Volume and Prices in US$, 1990–2000

	By Associations (Big Four)			By Individual Exporters			Total			Export Share	
	Exported Khat (kg)	Total Export Value	Unit Export Price	Exported Khat (kg)	Total Export Value	Unit Export Price	Exported Khat (kg)	Total Export Value	Unit Export Price	Associations	Individuals
1990/91	1,749,769	10,143,588	5.80	191,324	1,848,493	9.66	1,941,093	11,992,081	7.73	90.1	9.9
1991/92	26,141	111,933	4.28	181,922	1,298,334	7.14	208,063	1,410,267	5.71	12.6	87.4
1992/93	2,226,400	12,269,400	5.51	555,000	4,167,800	7.51	2,781,400	16,437,200	6.51	80.0	20.0
1993/94	2,236,105	12,526,681	5.60	1,259,638	8,377,806	6.65	3,495,743	20,904,487	6.13	64.0	36.0
1994/95	2,829,000	16,675,047	5.89	1,426,000	9,815,271	6.88	4,255,000	26,490,318	6.39	66.5	33.5
1995/96	2,458,049	14,047,499	5.71	1,576,595	12,676,310	8.04	4,034,644	26,723,809	6.88	60.9	39.1
1996/97	1,865,000	1,139,307	0.61	1,794,000	1,420,855	0.79	3,659,000	2,560,162	0.70	51.0	49.0
1997/98	1,863,000	4,958,700	2.66	1,814,000	13,683,511	7.54	3,677,000	18,642,212	5.10	50.7	49.3
1998/99	1,849,911	7,417,441	4.01	4,839,429	20,233,186	4.18	6,689,340	27,650,627	4.10	27.7	72.3
1999/2000	1,797,000	10,100,690	5.62	2,136,000	17,767,480	8.32	3,933,000	27,868,170	6.97	45.7	54.3
Total/Average	18,900,375	89,390,286	4.57	15,773,908	91,289,046	6.67	34,674,283	180,679,333	5.62	54.92	45.08

Source: Dire Dawa Foreign Trade Office (2002).

Table 3.2 Expenses Incurred by Khat Exporters to Djibouti Br per kg

	BIFTU	EKEC	BERWAKO	KULMIYE	Individual 1	Individual 2
Khat price	27.00	25.20	30.85	26.00	56.00	56.00
Packing (sacks, grass, ropes, plastic bags)	0.84	1.02	1.00	3.20	0.30	0.40
Labourers (loaders and trimmers)	1.85	0.17	4.90	0.50	0.50	0.30
Transportation	1.60	1.25	0.46	2.50	1.00	1.00
Khat Tax	9.50	6.25	5.00	12.87	5.95	5.95
Customs X-ray, quarantine, and bank transfer fee	0.41	0.43	0.42	0.32	0.25	0.25
Other expenses	0.37	3.67	1.57	0.50	0.75	0.75
Total	41.57	37.99	44.20	45.89	64.75	64.65

Source: Dire Dawa Foreign Trade Office (various receipts).

All the associations run a similar-style operation. They buy primarily from Bedessa district in West Hararge Zone, 224 km from Dire Dawa, but also from Assibe Teferi, Awdaay Habro, Kuni, Bedessa and Darolebu. Their Bedessa branches are primary processing sites, where khat is bulked and packaged before reaching the main processing establishments in Dire Dawa. At Bedessa town the khat is cut short, weighed, wrapped with grass and watered. The shipments are then moved in trucks owned by each association. If extra vehicles are needed, then these are hired. All the khat is eventually brought to the main packaging warehouses in Dire Dawa City, where it is packed to comply with the export licence requirements and inspected by SOGIK representatives. Then, according to the quota allocated by SOGIK to each of the Big Four, the khat is delivered to SOGIK at Dire Dawa airport at f.o.b. price. SOGIK has a Revolving Letter of Agreement with each association, whereby SOGIK deposits foreign currency (dollars) at the Commercial Bank of Ethiopia in Djibouti City a day before shipment. After the khat arrives in Djibouti and the quota set prior to shipment is confirmed, the money is released to the associations in local currency every 10 days.[11] In 1992, SOGIK and the exporters associations agreed to export 25 per cent first-grade, 25 per cent second-grade and 50 per cent third-grade khat to Djibouti, and this still prevails. The grading is according to established tastes in the market. Inspectors confirm the grading of each batch for export. According to the agreement between the association of exporters and SOGIK, the khat exported to Djibouti must be two-thirds of leaf, 28 centimetres long, 90 grams each, with two bundles packed in one plastic bag. Each bundle is wrapped with plastic film and tied with thin rope. When the khat is bundled, 15 bundles will be put in a white cotton sack. The sack is sewed up, and is then ready for export.

Most of the khat exported by the individual exporters is packaged at Awedaay and delivered directly to Dire Dawa airport. Individual khat exporters receive the local-currency equivalent in advance payment from the bank, which the importers have deposited in dollars in Djibouti City. The individual exporters to Djibouti have signed an agreement with the government of Ethiopia to export khat that is 35 centimetres long and 200 grams in weight (Dire Dawa Foreign Trade Office 2002). The size and weight difference between SOGIK imports and individual imports have caused variations in the Djibouti market in favour of individual exporters, which is evident from their changing market share. This is mainly to do with the initial agreement between SOGIK and the Ethiopian Khat Exporters Cooperative, which has not been changed for the past 30 years.

The market does not run as well as it should, however, and according to a study conducted by the Dire Dawa Foreign Trade Office (2002) there are major impediments to these official exports. First and foremost, there is the flourishing contraband trade to contend with. SOGIK representatives highlight the negative impact of contraband trade. For instance, SOGIK's net profit in 2000 was DJF 314,570, rising to DJF 626,142 in 2001, but falling to DJF 470,984 in 2002 (Araita 2004). The fluctuations reflect the intensity of contraband trading. According to Ibrahim Ahmedu, a senior official in the Ministry of Finance, the government reckons that between 6,000 and 8,000 kg of khat is smuggled out of Ethiopia every day. This illicit khat trade thrives in the border villages – from Dawanlé toward Galilé, through Achaa toward Dikhil; and to the north, from Manda toward Tadjourah, as well as Aisha, Aidora, Asbuli and Adigola to Djibouti, and Biyo Gurgur to Somaliland. Most of these borders are in fact highly porous, and the trade flourishes by every conceivable means of transport.

Gebissa (1997) notes that the smugglers often exchange their foreign-exchange gains from khat for other consumer goods, creating a typical parallel market. The Customs agents are very energetic in trying to contain the contraband trade. In Dire Dawa between 1992 and 2003, no less than 2.4 million kg of khat were seized by customs en route to Djibouti and Somalia. Table 3.3 shows the figures of seizures: the year 2002 saw 28,160 kg of contraband khat seized, and for 2003 the amount seized was 21,953 kg, in Ali Sabieh and Chebelleh along the Ethio-Djibouti border. Gebissa describes these and other smuggling routes across the borders between Ethiopia and neighbouring Djibouti and Somaliland, highlighting the links between shortages of consumer goods and the khat trade – 'unofficial exportation finances the unofficial importation of commodities' (Gebissa 2004: 169). Khat smuggling is 'a means to get access to hard currencies with which to import much-needed consumer commodities: the volume of the goods that were smuggled out was determined by the value of the goods that were smuggled in' (ibid.: 170–1). It has also been noted that residents near the border towns and villages have set up their own unofficial checkpoints for taxing khat, milking the trade for their own advantage.[12]

Table 3.3 Khat Seizures (kg) at Ali Sabieh and Chebelleh

	2002	*2003*
January	2,470	3,925
February	3,265	2,975
March–May	11,181	3,410
June/July	5,330	5,330
October–December	3,920	4,310
Total	28,168	21,953

Source: Djibouti Customs Authority Various Tax Invoices.

Much of the smuggling of khat is done on foot, carried in 200- or 300-kg bundles on the backs of the 'koutoubles' (khat smugglers). The Ali Sabieh district is renowned for its role in this illicit trade, with smuggled khat usually arriving here very late at night to supply eager consumers who travel out from Djibouti city. The popularity of the Ali Sabieh supply increases markedly whenever there are any hitches in the air supply route to Djibouti.[13]

A second impediment to the smooth running of the khat trade is the taxation system. The Big Four point out that while transporting the khat from Bedessa to Dire Dawa, a distance of about 200 kilometres, they encounter at least five checkpoints where the local government imposes its own taxation. Everyone, it seems, wants a slice of profit from this trade. Traders also feel that they are paying tax on the packaging of the khat, rather than the crop itself, when they are charged on the weight of the transported goods. The bulky packaging on khat can raise the weight of a bundle by around 40 per cent. Traders feel that this is unfair and onerous. They would mostly prefer to pay a flat-rate tax at the airport, net per kilo. However, any such arrangement would constrain the capacity of local government authorities to raise their own taxes against the khat trade, and none are willing to give up their tax raising powers.

Khat Exports to Somaliland

Ethiopian khat has been exported to Somaliland over at least the past 80 years. It is an old and very well established market (SOVOREDO 2002). In 2000/01, as shown in Table 3.4, the amount of 12 million kg of khat with a value of US$37.4 million was exported to Somaliland from Ethiopia. Between 1998 and 2001 a total of 22.6 million kg of khat was exported to all of Somalia, including Somaliland, earning US$68.2 million in foreign exchange. Unit price averaged US$2.98. The khat exported to Somalia comes mainly from Awedaay and Kombolcha, which is second-grade compared to the khat exported to Djibouti. There are three shipment routes to Somalia: the first is by road from Jijiga via Togochale and Teferi Ber to

Table 3.4 Khat Exports to Somalia, Including Somaliland in Volume and Prices

	Exported Khat (000s kg)	*Total Export Value (US$)*	*Unit Export Price (US$)*
1998/99	5,492,000	16,457,503	3.00
1999/2000	5,058,600	14,347,848	2.84
2000/01	12,100,000	37,481,570	3.10
Total/Average	22,650,600	68,286,921	2.98

Source: Dire Dawa Foreign Trade Office (2000 and 2002).

Hargeisa in Somaliland; the second is by air from Dire Dawa to Mogadishu and Bosaso; and the third is also by air, from Dire Dawa to Puntland.

Hargeisa is a major Somali centre for the khat trade, with up to 15,000 kg entering this city each day. The Hargeisa trade is dominated by a single woman entrepreneur, Zuhura Esmail Kehim. Zuhura's brand mark is the number '571', which appears on the sacks her agents handle and the trucks on which the khat is transported, as well as on the retailing stalls (as depicted on the cover of this book). Although she says this number has no meaning, people say it is the year Prophet Mohammed was born according to the Islamic calendar and that this is why Zuhura uses it.[14] Zuhura's business is based in Jijiga, where khat farming is negligible apart from the areas bordering Oromia region. But Jijiga is renowned for its khat consumption, and as a major route toward the Somaliland market. The best khat here fetches up to US$10 per kg, a high figure that is indicative of the town's high purchasing power linked to the flourishing contraband trade in consumer goods coming all the way from Berbera in Somaliland, through Togo Chale and Artshek in Ethiopia. *Gursum* khat is popular and mainly used for local consumption.

With no significant agricultural activity or industrial base, the residents of Jijiga rely on contraband and khat trade. With little agricultural activity (vegetables, maize, sorghum and wheat are all cultivated here, but not in significant quantities) and a weak industrial base (Jijiga has a flour mill and some textile manufacturing, but precious little else), Jijiga relies on contraband and the khat trade. In 2005, tax revenue from khat made up 28 per cent of the total tax revenue of the region.[15] Zuhura started as a street trader in 1992 and ventured into other businesses; she currently owns, with her husband, hospitals and an orphanage in Jijiga and Hargeisa. She has close relations with khat traders in Metta, Deder, Karamile and Kobo, who supply her khat of *Webera* and *Guber* types, which are reputed for maintaining moisture for a longer period. In some cases Zuhura provides her own money to start up new suppliers. The family linkages across the border in Somaliland also strengthen her market network on the import side. Her husband is from Hargeisa and he is a major investor in the city. She dominates the market along the Jijiga-Hargeisa route so much so that BIFTU withdrew from the Somali market, failing to compete with Zuhura's '571' enterprise.

The 571 business employs 300 permanent staff, and many more people on a temporary basis at the Jijiga packaging and processing station. The khat is packed in one sack (Merduf) containing three bundles (1 kg = 2.5 Merduf). Zuhura claims to export 18,000 kg per day, using her twenty-two Isuzu trucks, at a price of US$3.50 per kg.[16] She pays a tax equal to 6 Br per kg. In the late 1990s the government lacked the resources (personnel and logistics) to control the contraband trade which forced Zuhura to divert about 40 per cent of the export quantity without paying taxes, which significantly contributed to falling foreign exchange for the National Bank. With the resumption of controls on contraband, 571 became legally and fully operational in 1999. Due to the difficulty of formalizing agreements with banks in Somalia, the arrangement is that the exporter deposits – at the Commercial Bank of Ethiopia branch in Jijiga – foreign currency equal to the amount of khat exported, and then receives the birr equivalent.

On the retailing side, Zuhura supplies numerous women to retail khat in the streets from their colourful boxes. Researchers from the University of Hargeisa who investigated the municipal economy of Hargeisa found that 85 per cent of the employment in the city is related to the khat trade (SOVOREDO 2002). In this lively and strong market, the 571 brand is utterly dominant. Customers know whose khat they are buying in Hargeisa – Zuhura's branding is by far the most extensive and successful exercise in the entire khat market of the Horn of Africa. The retail price in Hargeisa is US$8 to US$15 per kg. To some extent, these purchases are financed by remittances. According to the Deputy Governor of the Central Bank of Somaliland, the country is heavily dependent on remittances transferred to Hargeisa from Somalis living abroad. This is mainly done through the *Hawala* and other related systems, over which the government has no control. Official estimates suggest that between US$80,000 and US$100,000 per day is spent on khat purchases in Somaliland, and this represents a direct transfer of funds to Ethiopia though the khat trade.[17] It is not surprising, therefore, that many in Somaliland think that the khat trade is simply a drain on the local economy.

Despite the scale of khat trading to Somalia, the profit margins earned by traders appear to be quite low, owing to the high and varied forms of taxation, currency differentials and the small scale of the activities of most individuals involved in the industry. The SOVOREDO (2002) study of the khat market found that 73.2 per cent of khat traders depended upon the trade for their livelihood. However, 29 per cent of retailers claim that they are often not paid by consumers and 32 per cent admitted that they found it very difficult to chase those who purchased khat on credit. At the same time, 70 per cent of traders said they were likely to continue retailing khat as no other source of income seemed to be feasible.

According to a BBC report, in 2005 Hussein Mohamud Jiir, mayor of Hargeisa, decided to move khat dealers to the outskirts of the city. He said that the pink, blue and red plastic khat carrier bags that they used blocked the municipal drains, clung to trees in the city centre, and generally littered the city. Government officials believe that the khat trade lowers hygiene and sanitation standards in Hargeisa. The Public Health Officer, Abdiwahab Nakruma, was quoted as saying 'it has become so cumbersome to declare every Thursday as a general clean-up exercise' in his battle to contain the mess made by the khat trade. The Rangeland Development Director in Pastoral and Environmental Ministry, Abdikarim Adan Omar, added to the criticism, claiming that khat consumers damage the environment by burning charcoal to finance their khat consuming habit – invoking a popular local saying that people would 'cut a tree to chew a twig'.[18] Even where the khat market seems at its strongest and most robust, then, the future of the trade is challenged and contested.

Khat Exports to Bossaso, Mogadishu and Puntland

In 1992, an estimated 6,000 kg of khat arrived in Mogadishu each day; this being the very worst period of the collapse of the state of Somalia. Kenya was the main provider of this supply. Even in more recent years it has been estimated that Kenya provides khat to Somalia worth about US$300,000 a day. About 57 per cent of Somalia's foreign exchange is estimated to have gone to Kenya through the khat trade in recent years (Cabdidaawuud 2004). The opening of the khat markets in Bossaso and Mogadishu has consolidated the market in Somalia, and has also ensured that some foreign-exchange earnings from this trade now find their way to Ethiopia.[19]

The Bossaso and Mogadishu market is estimated to handle up to 10,000 kg of khat from Ethiopia per day, but the contraband trade from Kenya that is not reported in these figures may be four or five times as large. The packaging and processing of the Ethiopian khat for this market is carried out in Awedaay and Kobo. Exactly twenty Merduf are packed in each sack. The export price was initially US$6.00 per kg, but in 1998 the price came down to US$4.00 f.o.b. The adjustment was in response to the cost of the air charter, estimated at US$6,000 per flight for 5,000 kg of khat (Dire Dawa Foreign Trade Office 2002).[20] The payment arrangement is that the exporter deposits foreign currency at the Commercial Bank in Dire Dawa and receives the revenue in local currency. The khat, which goes to Bossaso and Mogadishu, is taxed on gross weight with the sack and grass (Bardan) while the exporters supply only 1.6 kg to the retailer, which contains 400 gm of chewable khat.[21] Exporters to Somalia say they contribute more foreign exchange than exporters to Djibouti. But there is discussion among policy-makers on the possibility of taxing the khat at one central location, for instance Dire Dawa Airport.

The export market to Puntland began in 2004 when BIFTU entered an agreement to ship US$270,000 per day, mainly financed by remittance earnings, which are thought to be around $800,000 per day. The importing company is SOMEHT, based in Garoowe, handling around 7,000 kg of khat each day.[22] SOMEHT has agreed to transfer payments five days prior to BIFTU exporting the khat. The cash transfer is made through the Dahbshi and Amel international money-transfer companies, whose Ethiopian agent is Wegagen Bank. Djibouti Airways charter flights carry the khat from Dire Dawa to Bosasso via Garoowe. The costs of this trade operate on the same basis as the trade into Mogadishu. Exporters purchase the khat at an average price of 13 Br per kg. The brokers' fee is 50 Br per 20 kg of khat. Labourers are paid 300 Br for loading 2,500 kg on Isuzu trucks. Charter flights cost 49,320 Br per 5,000 kg, and Isuzu trucks charge 1,200 Br for 2,500 kg of khat from Chelenko to Jijiga. From Jijiga to Togochale, the cost of trucks is 300 Br for 10,000 kg. The sacks, grasses and ropes cost 0.27 Br per kg., and the labourers who trim the khat are paid 0.63 Br per kg. A tax of 3.00 Br per kg and cleaning fee of 1.70 Br are paid to the revenue authorities and the municipality. For X-ray and quarantine, exporters to Bossaso and Mogadishu pay 0.27 Br per kg. At the export price of 49.32 Br (US$6) per kg to Bossaso and Mogadishu, and Br 24.66 (US$3) for khat exported to Hargeisa, it is possible to calculate the profit for exporters. The input costs per kg are 32.35 Br for khat exported to Bossaso and Mogadishu and 22.72 Br for khat exported to Hargeisa. The profits respectively are 16.97 Br (US$2.06) and 1.93 Br (US$0.23) per kg. The khat exported to Somalia in 2000/01 was approximately 12,100,000 kg. With an average profit of 9.41 Br (US$1.15), in the year 2000/01 individual khat exporters therefore earned 113,883,990 Br (US$13,854,500).

Exports to the Rest of the World

Ethiopia exports khat beyond its immediate neighbours to Australia, Asia, Europe, the Middle East, Africa and North America. As Table 3.5 shows, the volume of khat exported to these countries increased from 5.8 million kg in 1997 to 7.2 million kg in 2002. Over 98 per cent of the khat exported to Europe is destined to the UK, which doubled from 43,671 kg in 1997 to 80,842 kg in 2002. Between 1997 and 2001, almost 100 per cent of the khat exported to North America was destined to the US. However, exports to the US declined from 31,499 kg in 1997 to 6,344 kg in 1999, and picked up to 19,969 kg in 2002. In 2002, 78 per cent of the khat was exported to the US, with the remainder exported to Canada. According to customs officials in Addis Ababa, the shift is primarily to do with the control measures introduced in the US after 9/11. Khat exports to Australia grew in line with the migration of the Somali and Ethiopian communities, from 482 kg in 1997 to 5,179 kg in 2002. The khat exported to Africa is mainly destined to Djibouti and Somalia.

In 2002 the highest export price, US$35.47 per kg, was offered by consumers in the US, followed by consumers in Australia at US$35.24 per kg and US$34.29 in Asia. Khat prices increased significantly in the US, from US$9.10 per kg in 1997, matching the decline in supply mentioned above, while export prices declined in the UK from US$35.06 per kg in 1997 to US$19.54, reflecting the increase in

Table 3.5 Khat Export by Country of Destination, Value, Volume and Prices

	1997	1998	1999	2000	2001	2002
Volume (kg)						
Australia	482	353	1,475	2,145	2,715	5,179
Asia	–	–	–	–	14	496
Europe	44,253	55,992	54,477	46,327	75,397	82,529
Great Britain	43,671	55,784	49,797	45,444	74,744	80,842
Middle East	500	–	8,685	1,245	9	301
Africa	5,822,239	6,493,189	14,042,351	13,946,615	9,654,783	7,131,023
Djibouti	5,822,233	5,745,921	5,648,516	4,359,262	5,075,764	3,926,965
Somalia	–	747,168	8,393,835	9,587,325	4,577,323	3,204,056
America	31,499	3,446	6,347	24,339	21,453	25,714
USA	31,444	3,446	6,344	24,259	21,275	19,969
Grand Total	5,898,973	6,558,953	14,113,335	14,020,738	9,754,515	7,247,242
Value (000s Br)						
Australia	112	97	409	707	801	1,562
Asia	–	–	–	–	4	146
Europe	10,408	11,740	12,469	11,631	14,734	14,023
Great Britain	10,273	11,700	12,041	11,370	14,543	13,515
Middle East	2	–	145	317	3	30
Africa	260,927	345,817	503,315	585,697	436,235	340,990
Djibouti	260,925	320,994	300,612	301,476	322,820	258,445
Somalia	–	24,801	202,703	284,214	113,291	82,544
America	1,933	721	1,734	4,170	6,410	7,290
USA	1,921	721	1,733	4,143	6,357	6,061
Grand Total	273,382	358,426	518,072	566,525	458,230	364,058
Prices (US$)						
Australia	34.73	38.55	34.90	40.12	34.88	35.24
Asia	–	–	–	–	36.32	34.29
Europe	35.05	29.47	28.82	30.55	23.11	19.86
Great Britain	35.06	29.48	30.45	30.45	23.01	19.54
Middle East	0.50	–	2.11	30.97	35.26	11.67
Africa	6.68	7.48	4.51	5.11	5.34	5.59
Djibouti	6.68	7.85	6.70	8.42	7.52	7.69
Somalia	–	4.66	3.04	3.61	2.93	3.01
North America	9.15	29.42	34.39	20.85	35.33	33.13
USA	9.10	29.42	34.39	20.79	35.33	35.47

Source: Ministry of Finance and Economic Development, Ethiopia.

supply. The total foreign-exchange earning from exports, other than Djibouti and Somalia, increased from US$3,674 million in 1997 to US$4,968 million in 2002. If we add the value of exports from Djibouti and Somalia, Ethiopia's foreign-exchange earning from official trade increased from US$40,742 million in 1997 to US$42,431 million in 2002.

Table 3.6 Total and Khat-related Income of the Dire Dawa Post Office

Year	Khat-related Income	Total Income	Khat-related Income as % of Total Income
1999/2000	317,694.95	1,676,999.64	18.9
2000/01	660,600.33	2,618,201.91	25.2
2001/02	4,994,921.70	6,194,213.51	80.6
2002/03	5,726,662.69	6,719,687.07	85.2

Source: Dire Dawa Post Office (various receipts).

These figures are impressive enough, but they do not capture the full extent of the international trade in khat. Air transportation is not the only way that khat from eastern Ethiopia reaches consumers around the world. The Dire Dawa Post Office is the hub of a thriving trade in dried khat, which is sent by mail to North America, Europe and Australia. The foyer of the Post Office resembles a khat factory, with counter assistants running around weighing the packages and ensuring they are properly sealed and addressed. The local Customs authorities take 2 Br per kg in tax, while the Post Office charges by weight. One kg of dried khat is sent at a price of US$35.[23] According to the management of the Dire Dawa Post Office, khat is exported through the post office without any hindrance, despite the ban on khat in effect in some countries. The Universal Postal Union, of which Ethiopia is among the 170 countries who are members, has not listed khat among the substances that are debarred from being sent through the mail service.[24] Business slowed down after September 11, with US Customs more suspicious of packages from strange lands. But the mailing of dried khat soon picked up again. The figures for 2002 indicate that 38,079.65 kg of dried khat was exported through the mail from Dire Dawa. As Table 3.6 shows, in 2000 the Post Office earned 1.6 million Br from khat-related activities. By 2003, this figure had increased to 6.7 million Br. As a share of total income of the Post Office, in 2003 some 85.2 per cent of the total business of the postal service was related to dried-khat export, compared to only 18.9 per cent in 2000.

As the discussion in this chapter illuminates, the trade in khat, which has come to be known as the Dollar Leaf, unleashed the entrepreneurial flairs of the community surrounding the Red Sea Littoral. Farmers, brokers, wholesalers, associations and retailers formed an industry with vertical and horizontal linkages reaching as far as Australia, Europe and America. The development of the industry took place with little support from international and domestic policy-makers, unlike other commodity agreements, for instance. It is very much the result of individuals who set up their own system of standards, grading, transport, payments and brokerage. The trade in khat is testimony to the vibrancy and flair of the community to elevate a once locally confined transaction to an international operation.

–4–

Consuming Habits in the Red Sea Littoral

> Cultural theorists of consumption [need] to take the economy seriously (and economists to do likewise for culture). There is a world out there that must be acknowledged as a source not only of the objects of consumption but also of how they are and can be interpreted.
>
> (Fine 2002: 5)

Khat chewing has long been associated with a wide and diverse range of social practices, being consumed by the pious who wish to stay awake during Ramadan or at a Mwalid praying assembly, and by long-distance travellers who need to suppress their fatigue or stave off the pangs of hunger. It is also consumed at social ceremonies and given as indication of hospitality, dowry and gift. Such uses of khat are mainly related to traditional and rural contexts, while urban consumers chew khat for social pleasure, often taking alcohol to 'break' the euphoric after-effects. The Somalis, for example, drink milk and soup while the urban youth in Ethiopia usually go for alcoholic drinks after chewing. Khat is also a means of social interaction 'that fosters amity, cooperation and sociality' (Gebissa 2004: 11). The impact of urbanization of the Somali community from their pastoralist way of life – instigated by both British and Italian occupation – was also catalyst for creation of chewing forums for social and political discussions. Today, khat consumption transcends class, ethnic, sex, age and religious boundaries. In the Red Sea Littoral all classes of society consume it – from politicians to businesspersons; women; children; poor and rich.

This chapter will place khat consumption in its broader social context, drawing upon data collected in consumer surveys conducted in Addis Ababa and Djibouti between March and June 2004. As noted by Fine (2002) the consumer revolution in the developed nations is closely related to the retail or distribution revolutions (transport and communication) followed by mass production, advertising, specialization, 'the housewife consumer, the male motor car lover'. The story of khat consumption can also be explained by similar developments.

Khatism in Ethiopia and Djibouti is marked by the rise of mass consumerism that transcends social and economic categories and by the pre-eminence of the consumer. There are various forms of khating, from the luxury or conspicuous consumption of the wealthy to display of the self and identity. This chapter reinforces the links between production and consumption recognizing the significant intermediate activities such as packaging, branding, retailing and transport discussed elsewhere in the book.

Consumers in Ethiopia

There is limited written information about the usage of khat in the Ethiopian context, although much has been said about the plant recently in the media. Khat consumption three decades ago was associated with religious practice. Today, however, its uses are widespread throughout the country. While khat is commonly grown in eastern and southern Ethiopia, other towns and cities are witnessing growth in khat consumption. At the same time, khat consumption is much despised in both Ethiopia and Djibouti, and a series of media campaigns often associate its consumption with the spread of HIV/AIDS. Khat is depicted as a major cause of reckless and irresponsible behaviour, even sometimes with temporary insanity. An informational joke broadcast on Ethiopian Television on 4 January 2004 went like this: 'Two khat chewers were at it for a while. One of them said I want to buy the world, the other said no it is not for sale because I bought it already.'

In *Leaf of Allah*, Gebissa (2004) explains the factors that led to khat's commodification in Ethiopia by making a distinction between the urban and rural consumer. The domestic market in Ethiopia grew with the expansion of salaried civil servants. From the 1940s the civil service expanded, and with higher educational qualifications being demanded of officials through the 1950s and 1960s, there was greater movement of professionals between the various regions of the country. At the same time expansion in secondary and higher education has seen movement of students and teachers. These two factors have led to the introduction of chewing habits to previously khat-free regions. One example which Gebissa cites is the literacy campaign known as the *zemecha*, which started in 1975–77 and continued in various forms up to the mid-1980s. These campaigns sent students from urban centres to various rural towns and villages. For Gebissa the absence of parental guidance and community values inevitably resulted in the students picking up alcohol, cigarettes and khat chewing. The students frequently chew khat when they gather together to discuss politics. Having gained the habit of chewing, they then continued to consume khat when they returned to their home areas. These factors all had a part to play, but Gebissa recognizes that the 'reasons for the phenomenal expansion during the Derg years are complex and not always easily explicated' (p. 13).

A study carried out on a sample of 123 male Addis Ababa University students by Mohammed (2003) shows that 60 per cent are khat users and 89.8 per cent of them joined the university with the habit. About 47 per cent of the khat-chewing group are also combined users of khat and alcohol. What is evident from various research and studies as well as anecdotal evidence is that khat consumption has been growing significantly. Khat consumption in Bahir Dar is traced back 30 years; residents of Bahir Dar assert that up to the mid-1990s mainly Muslims in Eastern Amhara region consumed khat. Now it is pervasive among Christians, young, old, male and female. Religious people chew for religious reasons, students to study, civil servants and young people as entertainment, the unemployed and street children to forget their 'misery', prostitutes and housewives to 'pray' for a better life. The local consumers are students and civil servants. Again this is attributed to migration. The Amhara State University attracts students from all over the country. Similarly, people from various ethnic backgrounds, assigned outside of their birthplace, have always staffed the Ethiopian civil service. The argument is that students and workers from khat-consuming regions of the country imported the habit. The youth make up the majority of consumers, often explained by lack of entertainment, sports facilities and youth clubs.[1]

As Table 4.1 shows, khat consumption in Ethiopia has grown considerably throughout the 1980s and 1990s. In 1980/81 an amount of 116,376 tons of khat was consumed locally. By 1990/91 the amount consumed had reached 147,224 tons, and by 2000/01 it had reached 208,332 tons (a 79 per cent increase between 1980/81 and 2000/01).

As we have seen in our discussion of the marketing of Ethiopian khat, the bulk of the crop grown in eastern parts of the country is intended for export. However, khat from Awedaay is distributed throughout the country. Dire Dawa city is the centre for the export market as well as for local consumption. The retailing market known as *Chat Terra*, is where all the action takes place. The women retailers and their customers have unique relationships, and the customer receives excellent service if he remains loyal to a particular vendor known as the Mamila. The Mamila keeps the best and freshest khat for her regulars in return for brand loyalty. The customer in return offers a stem or two to his best friends and company commonly referred to as Rebsas. Therefore, the consumer-retailer relationship is very personal and involves constant interaction (Abebe 2004). Jimma, in western Ethiopia, is also reputed for having among the largest numbers of khat consumers, and Mains found that between 70 per cent and 85 per cent of the youth in Jimma chew khat. The khat consumed in Jimma grows in and around the city, as well as coming from Gurage areas. Most consumers have confirmed that the *Merkana* (the euphoric state after chewing) 'generates dreams that allow an escape from depression' (Mains 2004: 9).

Ahmed notes an interesting consumption ritual in Wallo, located in northern Ethiopia. There are five chewing practices dichotomized along age and gender: *ya wand wadājā* (attended by men); *ya dubarti wadājā* (attended by women); and *ya lej wadājā* (attended by young boys). A further two chewing practices involve *ya tolfannā wadājā* (during which locally brewed alcohol is consumed) and *ya lej wadājā yāwatāl hajā* (for the fulfilment of wishes, especially those of children). In Wallo, as succinctly explained by Ahmed, khat was mainly grown wild and the owners gave it away as gift and gesture of some kind. The commodification of khat

Table 4.1 Khat Consumption in Ethiopia

Years	Khat Domestic Consumption (000s kg)
1980/81	116,376
1981/82	116,757
1982/83	126,640
1983/84	123,278
1984/85	115,807
1985/86	121,270
1986/87	133,981
1987/88	133,189
1988/89	136,556
1989/90	142,033
1990/91	147,224
1991/92	149,478
1992/93	159,082
1993/94	156,237
1994/95	162,202
1995/96	180,743
1996/97	185,059
1997/98	177,027
1998/99	187,586
1999/2000	191,045
2000/01	208,332

Source: CSA (Various Years) Household Income, Consumption and Expenditure Survey, Central Statistical Authority, Addis Ababa, Ethiopia.

in this area started following the migration of Yemeni traders and the subsequent rise in demand and its planned cultivation:

> The *jafjif* [a type of khat tree] was replaced by several types with smaller and more tender leaves and slender stems whose high stimulating power was appreciated by the Yemenis, particularly by the older members who could not chew the coarser leaves (some had the tough leaves pounded in a mortar). The names of these new varieties reflect the influence of the Yemeni Arabs: *nāshif, ratib, bustānī*. (H. Ahmed 2004: 9)

A survey conducted among 391 street children from Adis Ababa, Awassa and Dire Dawa found that 24.8 per cent and 33.2 per cent were found to be light and heavy users of drugs, alcohol and khat. The survey also found that children from broken families (divorce, physical separation and death) were found to make a larger proportion of those who used drugs, alcohol and khat. Peer pressure is found to be a major contributor to taking up the habit.[2] According to the study: '[d]rug use behaviour is found to be associated with the physical setting in which the children are living. Therefore, an ecological milieu might have a share in suppressing or intensifying the flourishing of multi or poly drug use behaviour among the street children' (FSCE 1998: 85).

A consumer survey was conducted as part of the research for this book, mainly to find out basic characteristics of khat consumers in Addis Ababa. According to official figures, the estimated consumption of Addis Ababa's 2.79 million inhabitants amounts to a total of 3,071 tonnes per annum (CSA 2000). The survey was carried out in the city's hub for khat consumption, namely Arat Kilo, Bole, La Gare, Mercato, and Sidist Kilo areas. Khat consumers were randomly selected and questioned about their consuming habits, khat-related activities and their perception of khat itself (see Table 4.2). The results show that all age groups consume khat in Addis Ababa. Out of the 212 consumers surveyed, 46.2% of the consumers fall within the 17–24 age group and 43.9% of the consumers are within the 25–39 age group. Males, constituting 84% of the consumers, are habitual khat users. The majority, 77.8% of the consumers, are single or unmarried, and 79.7% have no children. Contrary to popular beliefs that link idleness and khat consumption, the survey found that a significant number of khat consumers are employed (52.8%) and 59.4% have attained higher education (12.7% and 23.6% completing primary and secondary education, respectively). A more revealing picture emerges when the data is disaggregated by gender. Of the total male consumers 92% are employed, while out of the total female consumers only 8% are employed or own their own businesses.

A large number of consumers, 57.6%, earn less than 300 Br per month, which is less than US$2 per day, used by the development community to measure head-count poverty (8.6 Br = US$1 at the time of writing). Given the price of khat is 3.48 Br per kg at the lower quality range, a typical consumer spends 104.4 Br per month. This amount is 69.6% of the income for those 37.3% who earn less than 150 Br per month and 46.4% of the income for those 35.4% who earn less than 500 Br per month. These findings show that low-income groups spend a large proportion of their income on khat. The survey also found that 76.5% of the consumers spend up to 10 Br per day on khat consumption and 52.4% spend 5–10 Br per day. If one takes the average spending per day of 7.50 Br, a typical consumer spends 225 Br per month on khat consumption. Taken together, these figures confirm that those earning less than 300 per month or US$1.16 a day make up 57.6% of the sample and spend up to 75% of their income on khat.

The behavioural indicators show that 42% of consumers chew khat seven days a week and 51.4% spend 3–5 hours chewing khat, 61.3% chewing in the afternoon. Morning chewers make up 19.3%, chewing during the session commonly known as '*ye jebena*' (for the kettle). Place of chewing varies as 33% chew in their own houses, 19.3% in the work place and 21.2% in khat houses (especially prepared and rented). There are places where chewers can hire a space or room to chew khat where food is prepared, beverages are served and even entertainment such as films and music videos is provided. Those who chew at work places tend to be self-employed, mainly shop owners. Most khat chewers, 52.4%, engage in reading

Table 4.2 Addis Ababa Khat Consumers Survey, 212 Respondents (178 Male and 34 Female)

Personal Details			*Income Status*		
Age group	No.	%	Income	No.	%
17–24	98	46.2	<150	79	37.3
25–39	93	43.9	150–300	43	20.3
>40	21	9.9	300–500	32	15.1
Marital status			500–800	28	13.2
Single	165	77.8	800–1200	19	9.0
Married	40	18.9	1200–2000	10	4.7
Divorced	5	2.4	>2000	1	0.5
Separated	1	0.5	*Income spent on khat*		
Widowed	1	0.5	<5	51	24.1
Number of children			5–10	111	52.4
0	169	79.7	10–20	38	17.9
1–2	22	10.4	20–30	7	3.3
3–4	6	2.8	30–60	3	1.4
5–6	5	2.4	60–100	1	0.5
>6	10	4.7	>100	1	0.5
Educational background					
No Schooling	9	4.2	*Personal Activities*		
			Any entertainment facilities?	No.	%
Primary	27	12.7			
Secondary	50	23.6	Yes	77	36.3
Higher Education	126	59.4	No	135	63.7
Employment			*Club membership*		
Unemployed	100	47.2	Yes	67	31.6
Male	75	75.0	No	145	68.4
Female	25	25.0			
Employed	112	52.8			
Male	103	92.0			
Female	9	8.0			

Khat-related Activities			*Perception on Khat*		
No. of days spent chewing	No.	%	Is khat bad for health?	No.	%
1	29	13.7	Agree	78	36.8
2	25	11.8	Uncertain	65	30.7
3	29	13.7	Disagree	69	32.5
4	18	8.5	*Does khat disrupt family life?*		
5	13	6.1	Agree	77	36.3
6	9	4.2	Uncertain	49	23.1
7	89	42.0	Disagree	86	40.6
Hours spent chewing			*Does khat affect productivity?*		
1–2	25	11.8	Agree	65	30.7
2–3	40	18.9	Uncertain	34	16.0
3–4	52	24.5	Disagree	113	53.3
4–5	57	26.9			
>5	38	17.9			

Part of day spent chewing		
Morning	41	19.3
Afternoon	130	61.3
Night	20	9.4
Any combination	21	9.9
Place khat chewed		
Own house	70	33.0
Friend's house	32	15.1
Workplace	41	19.3
Khat house	45	21.2
Other place	24	11.3

Should khat be banned?		
Agree	53	25.0
Uncertain	33	15.6
Disagree	126	59.4
Activity after chewing		
Sleep	31	14.6
Work	41	19.3
Read	111	52.4
Drink	18	8.5
Other	11	5.2

after chewing, while 19.3% and 14.6% work and sleep, respectively. These findings are in line with the fact that most chewers reached higher education and chewing khat is functional – students chew to increase level of concentration, civil servants work during or after chewing and shopkeepers close deals and work on accounts. A number of consumers, 63.7%, pointed out that lack of pastime and entertainment facilities drives them to engage in khat chewing, while 68.4% confirmed that they are not members of social, community or professional clubs.

The survey also tested the perception of consumers about khat. When asked what they think about the statement that 'khat is very bad for health', 36.3% agreed, 32.5% disagreed and 30.7% were uncertain. When asked whether khat disrupts family life, 36.3% agreed, 40.6% disagreed and 23.1% were uncertain. To the question of whether khat lowers productivity, 53.3% disagreed, 30.7% agreed and 16% were uncertain. These percentages are not surprising, given that khat is commonly chewed for functional purposes and that people believe that khat is anti-fatigue and enhances memory capacity and concentration. Finally, consumers were asked whether khat should be banned or not. Most – 59.4% – said it should not, 25% voted for a ban and 15.6% were uncertain. What we conclude from the consumer survey is that a typical consumer is young, single, educated, low-income, either employed or a student who uses khat to enhance productivity in work or study.

While consumption in Ethiopia is growing, a fierce debate is taking place on the harmful impacts of khat. In Addis Ababa there is a larger anti-khat camp, including Rouh Anti-Khat Association established around *Mercato* area in 2003 by a group of young ex-chewers.[3] According to the founders of Rouh their habit negatively impacted upon their health and destroyed their family life. Members of Rouh state that the major motivation for them is to stop the 'scourge of khat grazing', mainly to control the spread of HIV/AIDS. According to Rouh among the causes of HIV/AIDS infection is khat, through its euphoric effects that lead to irrational behaviour and poor risk assessment. Rouh members acknowledge that their task requires a 'revolution', given the rapid spread of khating among young people. They organize awareness campaigns through theatres and literary and music clubs as well as through use of public promotion (banners and leaflets). By 2005 the association registered 700 members. Volunteers run the association and they have been given support from local government and the business community.

Khat Consumers in Djibouti

Alongside those in Ethiopia, Kenya, Somalia and Yemen, Djiboutians form part of the hardened consumers of khat.[4] The population of Djibouti consisted of nomads from neighbouring regions as well as Yemeni labourers and businessmen who spread the use of khat in the first half of the twentieth century. Khat consumption has developed in a context of social and economic transformation through urbanization and the constraints of modern life for which the nomad population was not quite prepared (Araita 2004). At that time, the first khat users at Djibouti were the great *sheikhs* of the Issa nomads who came to the region from Seyla (Somaliland), and those coming from towns crossed by the railway like Aichaa and Hadagala, and afterward the Afar *sheikhs* from the Islamic 'Sufi' sect. According to Araita (2004) there is a very well known legend among the Muslim Ethiopians that an angel revealed khat to two Muslim saints to allow them to fight sleep and fatigue during their nocturnal meditation. A saint of khat by the name Abadir is believed to have existed, whose tomb is said to be located in Ethiopia's eastern region.

In Djibouti, from the end of the 1950s until independence in 1977, the consumption of khat formed a constant topic of interest, particularly over its health and social impact (Warsama 1973 and WHO 1984). Currently, the debate in Djibouti on khat is alive with headlines such as 'Djibouti Says No to Drugs'. The government appears ambivalent: officials have the intention of limiting the import of khat on the one hand, and an interest in maintaining the trade as the source of tax revenues on the other. Top Djiboutian officials, met on condition of anonymity, attest to the fact that besides the impact of consumption on the health status of the population, khat has been the cause of continued foreign-exchange outflows. But in the face of protests, notably from khat importers and consumers, prohibition had to be scrapped.

Official importation of khat by plane to Djibouti dates from 1949, and official taxation started in 1952. In 1957, the French government brought out a decree forbidding the importation and cultivation of khat in France and in its colonies. But this decree could not be applied in Djibouti because of the many pressures of the Afars and Issas as well as neighbouring Ethiopia. During the armed clashes between the army and FRUD (Front de Restauration de l'Unité et de la Démocratie) in 1991/92, the leaders of the rebellion tried to ban khat in their area of occupation, but did not succeed. The lack of alternatives to the habit of 'khat grazing', and the lack of preparation for this all too abrupt change, explains the failure of this initiative. Ironically, when in December 1994 the signing of the peace accord with FRUD took place, it was over khat-chewing sessions. The enemy brothers also held negotiations under the 'tree of peace'. In April 1999 Mr Ismail Omar Guelleh was elected President of the Republic of Djibouti and instituted an afternoon work schedule on three days a week (Saturday, Monday and Wednesday from 4.00 pm to 6.00 pm) intended to limit khat chewing by civil servants, but the attempt failed to inhibit consumption. On 12 May 2001 another peace accord between the FRUD army was followed by demobilization of former combatants who entered into the daily distribution and consumption of khat (Araita 2004). Today khat has reached the status of an institution and has its own Yellow Page telephone number, exactly like the police or fire brigade. ['Le Khat s'est hissé à la hauteur d'une institution jusqu'à posséder son numéro de telephone à la même enseigne que la Police secours les Pompiers' (Hassan 2003).]

Consumers in Djibouti can be divided into three groups. First on the top of the pyramid we have the affluent consumers, whose ration is delivered to their house on a daily basis. They are politicians who consume first-grade Bukassa khat from Fedis or Kombolcha towns in Ethiopia, delivered by SOGIC. This khat is shipped in well-marked sacks and is the first to get unloaded and put on an ever-ready 'presidential' vehicle. The second level of consumers are civil servants and business people consuming a second-class khat from Awedaay, which makes up 72.3% of the import from Ethiopia. The third group are low-income consumers who purchase third-grade white khat from west Harerge. This type of khat makes up 28% of total import of khat from Ethiopia.

Interviews for this book gathered various explanations for why in fifty years khat consumption exploded in Djibouti. According to Araita (2004) and Hassan (2004) at least three factors are said to have contributed to the spread of the khat-consumption habit in Djibouti. First, the political theory says that the French tolerated it because it kept the population too drugged and dormant to express anti-colonial movements – hence why it took so long to gain independence in 1977. Since then indigenous governments used the same tactic in the name of stability and peace between the Afar and Issa. The French, anxious about eventual demands for independence, had favoured the spread of the Mabraz where agents of the state could easily act as informers. However, the Mabraz is and remains a place of conviviality where bonds of friendship are tightened and where the sense of collective identity develops, thus responding to the demands of African solidarity.

Second, according to the social theory, without khat people have no social status. Religious ceremonies, marriages, funerals, engagements, traditional debates all revolve around khat. A study carried out by the WHO (1984) among 500 Djiboutian households concluded that the essential factor pushing Djiboutians to buy and consume khat is, without doubt, its social role. Traditionally khat consumption served particular purposes. For instance, during the course of marriage negotiations, the parents of the boy offer khat to the parents of the young girl. It is said that the parents of the young girl taste the khat delivered by the fiancé, which is an indication of respect on both sides. The payment of dowry is accompanied by a gift of khat.

During Ramadan, khat is not consumed during the day, but from the prayer-call announcing the end of the fast, khat chewing is authorized, and the khat session lasts until dawn.

Third, the economic theory says that the population under 20 years old is nearly 60%, the unemployment rate is also 59%, the unemployment rate for those less than 30 years old is 87% and for women the rate is 66%. Hence the khat trade provides alternative employment, escape from misery and indolence,[5] as well as being a major source of government revenue. Many among the young have devoted themselves to khat from, on average, the age of 14, especially those excluded from schooling. The poor rate of literacy – 42.8% – greatly influences khat consumption among uneducated youths. Effectively, the rate of schooling at the primary level being in the order of 39%, with 44.5% for boys and 33.2% for girls, youths who have no chance of going to school or continuing their primary education easily fall into khat-chewing habits. This situation is reinforced by the importance of the school dropout rate, which is estimated at 58.1% in primary school and 51.3% in secondary school.

The young take refuge in khat 'to escape themselves', as some youths interviewed at Fukuzawa de Balbala High School tended to say (April 2004). Anti-khat campaigners claim that it is a drug craze of the masses. They see khat at the heart of many social problems, relational conflicts in households, separations, the maladjustment of some youths and the degradation of moral values, etc. A survey on this subject among 40 consumers carried out by Absieh (1973 quoted in Araita 2004) gives the following results: To the question as to whether khat is an aphrodisiac, 34 responses were positive, 6 negative. Out of 35 subjects, 29 of them stated khat is bad, while 6 had a contrary opinion.

A survey of consumers in Djibouti City, Randa and Tajoura, conducted for this book, shows that 75% of the khat imported from Ethiopia is consumed in Djibouti City (see Table 4.3). It emerges from the interview that 72% of consumers chew daily, while 16% chew two or three times a week. 'Grazing' sessions last on average five and a half hours. Thursday is the favoured day for consumption as this is the weekly day of rest in Djibouti. The survey also found that 64.4% of the consumers are aged 17–24, and 56.8% fall within the 25–39 age group. The figures indicate that 45.9% of the consumers are single and 48.6% are married. A larger number, 68.9% of the consumers, have completed secondary school. Only 2.7% reached higher education. This is not surprising, given that higher education in Djibouti is still in its infancy. If we recall the results above for Addis Ababa, the majority of consumers are in higher education or among those who completed high school.

Of all consumers covered by the survey 62.5% earn less than DJF70,000 per month, which is US$384. It is also found that 67.5% of the consumers spend DJF750 or US$4.10 per day on average for purchasing khat, and a significant number of consumers spend 35% of their income on khat. Concerning the frequency of consumption, it emerges from the survey that 72% of khat consumers chew

Table 4.3 Djibouti Khat Consumers Survey 74 Respondents (34 Male and 36 Female)

Personal Details			*Monthly Income*		
Age group	*No.*	*%*	*Income*	*No.*	*%*
17–24	13	17.6	<30,000	10	13.5
25–39	42	56.8	30–50,000	14	18.9
>40	19	25.7	50–70,000	22	29.7
Marital status			70–100,000	16	21.6
Single	34	45.9	100–200,000	9	12.2
Married	36	48.6	>200,000	0	0.0
Divorced	4	5.4	*Income spent on khat*		
Educational background			<500	1	1.4
No schooling	7	9.5	500–700	18	24.3
Primary	13	17.6	700–1,000	32	43.2
Secondary	51	68.9	1,000–1,500	13	17.6
Higher education	2	2.7	1,500–2,000	6	8.1
Number of children			>2,000	4	5.4
<2	16	21.6			
2–4	20	27.0	*Personal Activities*		
4–6	10	13.5	*Any entertainment facilities?*	*No.*	*%*
6–8	3	4.1	Yes	29	39.2
>8	3	4.1	No	40	54.1
			Do not know	5	6.8
			Club membership		
			Yes	26	35.1
			No	45	60.8
			Do not know	3	4.1

Khat-related Activities			*Perception on Khat*	
No. of days spent chewing	*No.*	*%*	*Is khat bad for health?*	*No.*
1	3	4.1	Agree	21
2	7	9.5	Uncertain	33
3	28	37.8	Disagree	20
4	17	23.0	*Does khat disrupt family life?*	
5	9	12.2	Agree	26
6–7	10	13.5	Uncertain	20
Hours spent chewing			Disagree	28
1–2	0	0.0	*Does khat affect productivity?*	
2–3	0	0.0	Agree	45
3–4	6	8.1	Uncertain	16
4–5	35	47.3	Disagree	13
>5	33	44.6	*Should khat be banned?*	
Place khat chewed			Agree	16
Own or friend's house	45	60.8	Uncertain	38
Khat house	25	33.8	Disagree	20
Other place	4	5.4		

Table 4.3 Djibouti Khat Consumers Survey 74 Respondents (34 Male and 36 Female) *(Continued)*

Activity after chewing	No.	%
Sleep	36	48.6
Work	12	16.2
Read	16	21.6
Drink	6	8.1
Other	4	5.4

khat daily. About 60.8% of the consumers spend 3–4 days per week and 91.9% of them spend more than 4 hours a day consuming khat. The Mabraz (a special room furnished with mattresses and cushions which each consumer uses to lean on) are popular in Djibouti for khating, and 33.8% of those interviewed said they frequent them, while 60.8% consume at home or at friends' houses. Owners of the Mabraz provide beverages, for instance tea with spices (cinnamon, cloves and cardamom), which, according to chewers, stems the thirst provoked by the mastication of the leaves. An interesting finding is that, while most consumers in Addis Ababa said they read after chewing, in Djibouti, 48.6% stated they usually sleep after chewing khat, followed by 21.6% reading and 16.2% working. Most of the interviews refer to the hot and humid climate for the sleeping patterns post-chewing. Khat consumption is also becoming visible among taxi and bus drivers.

The survey solicited responses for the statement 'khat is very bad for health'. About 21% agreed, 20% disagreed and 33% were uncertain. Consumers confess that only certain factors could persuade them to cease consuming khat: illness, a dramatic hike in the sale price or a straight ban on the trade. When asked whether khat disrupts family life, 26% agreed, 28% disagreed and 20% were uncertain. This is not surprising as the whole family including children commonly chew khat. To the question of whether khat lowers productivity, 45% disagreed, 13% agreed and 16% were uncertain. Consumers were also asked whether khat should be banned or not: 16% said it should not, 20% voted for a ban and 38% were uncertain. Similar to the results found in Addis Ababa, 54.1% of khat consumers have said there are no entertainment facilities and 60.8% are not members of any professional or social club.

The life of Djiboutians, without overstatement, revolves around khat. The debate over khat in Djibouti is skewed against the anti-khat camp, which happens to be a real minority. It is highly sensitive as influential people are either in the importation business or consumers themselves.

Khat Consumers in Somaliland

The history of khat in Somalia is associated with various restrictions that emanated from political considerations. Siyaad Bare's regime banned khat on 19 March 1983 because anti-government sentiments were expressed during group khating sessions.[6] Gebissa's archival studies reveal that the British colonial authorities were alarmed by intensified independence aspirations discussed over khat-chewing sessions among the Somali community. Following the 1964 border conflict between Ethiopia and Somalia, the Ethiopian government banned the export of khat in the hope that 'shortages would lead to internal discontent and instability' (Gebissa 2004: 98). Later, as the ban failed to work as planned, trading resumed in the hope that Somalia will turn into 'physically unfit and psychologically incompetent addicts who could not be able to field an effective fighting force' (ibid.: 104). During the civil conflict in Somalia in the 1990s, various groups controlled the import and distribution of khat. In the 1970s, the Government of Ethiopia nationalized khat-exporting businesses to develop infrastructure in the Ogaden area.

A study on khat consumption in Somaliland was conducted by the Somali National Well Doing Organization (SOVOREDO 2002). The study interviewed 10,000 residents of Hargeisa randomly and found that 29.8% chew khat. According this study the first time khat was used in Somaliland was in 1910, imported from Ethiopia and Yemen. The study shows that khat consumption has grown significantly between 1991 and 2003. As Figure 4.1 shows, the number of khat consumers has been steadily rising from 33 in 1991 to 3,000 in 2003. A typical khat consumer spends US$1.54 per day, and about 75% consume between 1 and 2 bundles per day (approximately 1 bundle is 400 grams). The study also found that 43% consume khat seven days a week, 24% three days a week and 23% 4–6 days per week. About 65% of the consumers also spend 7 hours per day on chewing khat. Of the total khat-chewing population, the majority, more than 95% are men. About 75% of the chewers are between the ages of 21 and 40. The increases in consumer numbers, according to the study, are attributed to the influx of nomadic people from the countryside, as a result of disrupted life due to civil conflict since 1991.

However, when the SOVOREDO (2002) study asked consumers whether they will stop chewing khat or not, 40% said they will likely stop chewing in the near future; 10% said they will definitely stop; and 20% said they are unlikely to stop chewing. As to the reasons for chewing khat, 69% said they do so to 'kill time', 21% due to their job, 5% because they 'love khat', and 4% because they like taking 'narcotic'. Of those who do not consume khat, 30% are not sure if they will start or not and 51% said they will not pick up the habit. Of those who used to consume khat, 74% confirmed that they are unlikely to pick up the habit again. Of those who do not consume khat, 60% said they simply disliked the shrub, 13% said they couldn't afford the habit, 12% said they were afraid of the health effects and 9% said they did not have the time. One interesting finding of the SOVOREDO study is that about

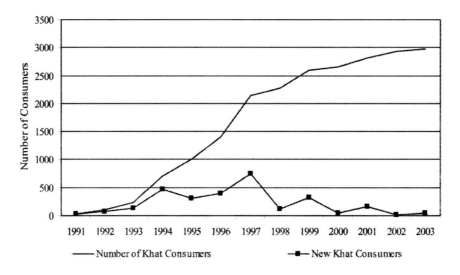

Figure 4.1 Number of khat consumers 1991–2003. *Source*: SOVOREDO (2003).

61% of those who chew khat see those who do not as 'good people', while 50% and 41% of those who do not chew khat see those who do as 'bad people' and 'crazy people', respectively.

Anti-khat groups currently highlight that TB transmission is facilitated through khat as people gather to chew in enclosed spaces, and where Shisha and cigarettes are shared. Another finding by SOVOREDO (20023), based on statistics from the courts, is that 90% of family breakdowns are caused by khat. Meanwhile, academic and students from the University of Hargeisa argue that the positive aspects of khat are neglected. These include poem recitals and resolving community disputes over khat-chewing forums.[7]

In 1983, the number of Somali men who consumed khat was estimated to be 84% in the city of Hargeisa and 39% in Mogadishu. The number of Somali women who had started to consume khat reached 7–10%. Recently, there have also been reports on an increase in the number of children under the age of 15 who start consuming khat. Moreover, there is more frequent use due to the introduction of the *ijabane* and *qarjin*, which are chewing sessions in the morning and the evening, respectively. It is also estimated that consumers, usually fathers, spend over 50% of their daily income on khat. In one case it has been reported that a father with three children has not seen them for five years because he would come home very late at night after the *qarjin*, when the children are already sleeping, and then he would be sleeping when they leave home for school. Many students are also said to turn up to classes in *Mirqaan* (in euphoric state), while the teachers also chew and more often than not miss lectures (see Cabdidaawuud 2004).

Concluding Remarks

Khat production, marketing and consumption are increasing rapidly. Production is mainly in response to declines in productivity and prices of major agricultural produce. Marketing of khat is becoming sophisticated, in some cases aided by khat itself causing the expansion of transport infrastructure including air, road and sea. Consumption is reaching hitherto khat-free areas within the Red Sea littoral as well as major cities in Africa, Europe, Australia and America. It is mainly consumed by people from the regions and the countries in which khat grows. The resettlement of Somalis throughout the region as well as internationally, and the growing diasporas of Ethiopians, Kenyans and Yemenis who have taken the khat habit abroad with them, have contributed to the spread of chewing. Unlike other stimulants such as opium or coca, khat remains confined to the Diaspora, which make up the same communities from the Red Sea Littoral. The questions are about what makes khat culturally unique to these communities: in other words, why is there no consumption crossover to the host community in the developed countries? Weir attempts to answer these questions by stating:

[i]mproved infrastructure and marketing were not the sole causes of increased khat consumption in Africa or Arabia. Their effect was only to make khat more readily available in areas where it was already consumed or where there was a local cultural potential for khat consumption. The demand that already existed could be more easily met but new demand was not created. That in fact was created, or increased, by changes in economic and social conditions, which *coincided* with improvements in transportation facilities. This needs stressing because the diffusion of khat consumption and analogues consumption practices are often described as though they were diseases which only require carriers in order to spread widely and indiscriminately in any population. But the host culture must be receptive to the adoption of such a complex practice as khat chewing. It is hard to imagine that it would catch on, say, in Edinburgh parlours or Paris salons, however many planeloads of khat leaves were imported. (1985: 30)

Part II
Khat in East Africa

–5–

Made in Meru
A Market History

Most of the khat, or *miraa*, produced in Kenya is produced in the lush Nyambene Hills situated between Mount Kenya and the arid plains that are the gateway to northern Kenya. This is the country of the Igembe and Tigania clans of the Meru. Goldsmith has described the mixed agricultural system that now has khat as its main cash crop and the ways that these Meru clansmen, from the nineteenth century onward, have marketed and distributed khat to an ever widening market, first within Kenya and then beyond (Goldsmith 1994: 101). Drawing on their age grade system and regulated by their traditional council of elders, the Igembe and Tigania succeeded in developing khat use from being the preserve of elders and an integral part of ritual connected with marriage and dispute settlements, to being a national pastime (Carrier 2005a). However, the production remains family-based, with households maintaining khat trees on their mixed farms using a sustainable agricultural system that allows continued high production of both cash and food crops, while the intensive farming system allows more people to stay on the land. Although practising a farming system that developed long before the British colonialists or Kenyan government agricultural extension workers, the farmers are sensitive to changing markets and in recent years khat has started replacing tea bushes, as it yields far greater profits (UNDCP 1999).

Hence, environmentally friendly farms produce *miraa* to sustain families on the land. Such a picture of a rural idyll, however, is a highly misleading portrayal of the khat industry in Kenya. The marketing of khat is now a multi-ethnic enterprise with customers drawn from a wide range of social groups across the country and beyond. It is the Somalis, however, who are prominent as both consumers and traders of khat in Maua, the major hub for the khat industry and the administrative centre serving the Nyambene Hills. Goldsmith has observed the development of the town over recent decades.

Maua, on the edge of the traditional *miraa* zone, developed as the main commercial centre of the Nyambene Range. In 1980 the town was one wide boulevard of shops, restaurants, and butcheries. There is a Methodist church, a hospital, and a miniature Barclays Bank symbolizing the rural prosperity of the area. Electricity reached the town by 1987, followed by an automated telephone exchange in 1992. (Goldsmith 1994: 107)

In the 1990s Maua has started to develop into a boom town, and Goldsmith described it as it was at that time:

Fleets of new pickups and cruisers grace the main road, the on-going building boom proceeds unabated, and a crowd of Somali casuals attracted to the *miraa* itself and Maua high life as much as employment are a new addition to the town's informal service sector. (Goldsmith 1997: 477)

By 2004, a visit to Maua revealed that the town comprised a couple of streets that alternate between mud and dust, and still had the air of a frenetic boom town. Small cafés, bars and cheap lodgings abounded and the open-air market was thriving. From dawn until mid-morning scores of Meru men bring *miraa* into town from their smallholdings, head-loading supplies wrapped in the leaves of the false banana plant. The Meru farmers sell their wares to Meru agents and wholesalers, but also fulfil orders to the Somalis who control the markets to north-eastern Kenya, Somalia and Europe. In the afternoon there is a slight lull in the trade, while people draw breath ready for the night shift. In the early evening, rickety Land Rovers carrying *miraa* purchased from nearby farms by Somali agents converge on crude corrugated shelters strung along the main road of the small town. More Meru farmers arrive on foot with their stock balanced on their heads. This is khat destined for Somalia, packaged in the evening and dispatched overnight by road to Wilson Airport in Nairobi, where it arrives in the early hours of the morning.

Many Somalis have moved to Maua in the last decade to work in the *miraa* industry. Cheap lodgings and cafés cater to Somali men who have come to Maua without their families, while others have set up permanent homes with their wives and children. For example, one clerk – whose job is to check the stock and see that it is packed correctly, to pay the suppliers and then receive more money when the vehicles return from Nairobi the next day – uses the income earned to sustain his family, his wife and children. He came to Kenya as a refugee from Somalia and does not speak English or Swahili. His wife runs a coffee stall and sells clothes offering, credit to Somalis working in the *miraa* trade. Her customers are not wealthy, and some men come to Maua in search of labour, most of them refugees originally from Somalia.[1] The wealthy *miraa* dealers, the employers of the clerks, drivers and packers, remain in Eastleigh, Nairobi. Only a part of the Somali-controlled stock goes by road direct to places such as Garissa, Wajir and Mandera. Vehicles also leave Maua daily, heading for the three main Somali-controlled markets: the international trade from Jomo Kenyatta International Airport to Holland, Denmark and London; to Eastleigh for the Nairobi market; and to Wilson Airport in Nairobi for air-freighting to Somalia and northern Kenya.[2] At Wilson Airport the khat is loaded onto small aircraft for transport to Somalia. The leading exporter is a man called Duale, who also controls a large chunk of the European export market. The largest carrier of khat to Somalia is Bluebird Aviation, with approximately 250 flights each month to Somali destinations; next is Knight Aviation with sixty to seventy flights per month, followed by Capital Airlines with 50–60 flights. According to informants in Eastleigh, in 2004 Kenya exported between 5,000 and 7,000 tons of khat a year to Somalia. Most of this khat passes through Maua.[3]

Competition and Cooperation

Stories of Somali businessmen buying up farms in Meru circulate in Nairobi, but this has not occurred. Despite Somali incursions into the *miraa* industry, all farms producing *miraa* are still Meru-owned and run. Some farmers do, however, sell their crop a week or two in advance to Somali agents who then employ experienced farm labourers to help with the harvesting of the crop. The emergence of Somali traders as a force to be reckoned with in the khat industry, and in particular their dominance of the international trade, has not been without tensions and occasional violence. As Carrier notes.

> Somalis have much control over the international trade, exporting the commodity to Somalia and the diaspora in Europe and beyond. Somali control has created much tension, as some Meru see themselves as exploited by the Somali network: this tension was most evident in 1999, when a Tigania who had started to trade a little *miraa* died in London. Suspicion that he had been killed by Somalis jealous of their monopoly led to clashes between Meru and Somalis back in the Nyambenes and in Nairobi. (Carrier 2005b: 541–2)

Tensions were again high in 2002 over the increasing Somali control of vehicles to transport khat in Kenya (Carrier 2005a, 2005b). Notwithstanding these tensions, the Kenyan distribution system of khat is primarily a story of cooperation and trust between different ethnic groups and entrepreneurs who operate a complex logistical operation with the minimum of commotion. Visits made to different markets across Kenya point to a thriving industry that has long been either ignored or reviled by many government officials.

Indeed with no central marketing system and no public body overseeing the khat industry, estimating the volume and value of the Kenyan trade is difficult. The official approach to khat consumption so far has been that it is a harmful substance, which also goes to explain the government's neglect of the production. The use of child labour to pack *miraa* and the devotion of Meru farmers to khat are routinely deplored in the national press and in general discussion on drugs issues in Kenya. The fact that khat is both a valuable domestic cash crop and an export earner is often overlooked.

Production and marketing is to some extent self-regulated. The Meru elders who make up the membership of Nyamita, the Nyambene Miraa Traders organization, deal with matters relating to whether it is acceptable to spray *miraa* trees with insecticide and the encroachments of Somalis on the industry (Carrier 2003). If Nyamita or anybody else knows how much khat is produced daily in Nyambene, they are not disclosing any information. The Somali agents and brokers who control the export trade and northern Kenyan markets are equally tight-lipped about the volume of the trade. Of course, seasonal variation in both wholesale price and output further complicate matters, but the observations by informed market participants allow for some rough estimates. According to one Meru farmer, a former town councillor, interviewed in February 2004,[4] the total value of the trade was KSh15m per day. (Assuming that khat was traded to this value every day of the year, and calculating on the basis of exchange rates prevailing at the time of the interview,this amounted to an annual value of US$68.5 million.) Another farmer and trader estimated that forty pick-ups loaded with *miraa* leave nine Nyambene wholesale markets daily.[5] A Somali man working in the khat industry in Maua also estimated that 30 planeloads a day transport *miraa* within East Africa and beyond.[6]

The Export Market

Since the 1990s, when many Somalis fled the civil war in their country and settled in Europe as refugees, there has been a significant rise in the consumption of khat in many cities across the world. Nuur Sheekh interviewed khat exporters based in the Somali-dominated area of Eastleigh in Nairobi in April and May 2004. He found that in the late 1970s and early 1980s, less than 400 kg of khat was exported from Kenya.[7] Since then the business, fuelled by the increased demand for khat by Somali refugees, has grown enormously. Supplies for the Kenyan export market come from the Nyambene Hills, but the Meru have failed to make an impact on the export market of their product. The virtual Somali monopoly on handling the khat export can be attributed to three major factors: knowledge of international trade, availability of funds, the large khat-chewing Somali diaspora population.

By 2004, between 1,000 and 1,800 boxes of khat were exported every evening to Europe. UK-bound *miraa* was leaving Nairobi on Mondays, Tuesdays, Thursdays and Saturdays, while khat for the Netherlands market was going out on Wednesdays and Fridays. Other supplies travel even further and one Eastleigh-based exporter claimed that khat is clandestinely exported to the US through Europe on Tuesdays. Arriving in London, a box of 40 *kilos* of khat is purchased by the wholesaler at £50 while it costs the exporter less than £25, thereby making a profit margin of 80–100 per cent.[8] Most exporters were then using British Airways to transport khat consignments to Europe, and a company called Air Connections was the sole agent for British Airways.[9] Somalis dominate the export market both in Eastleigh, where supplies are packed and dispatched, and at the receiving end of the operation. This domination of the khat trade is closely linked to the dispersal of Somalis all over the world and to the informal financial arrangements that facilitate the movement of money and khat.

Ever since the collapse of the Somalia state in the early 1990s, there has been a massive capital flight to safer countries, especially to Dubai and Kenya. However, Somalis in the diaspora are well organized in terms of business development, and an informal finance system, *hawala*, oils the wheels of trade. Hence, millions of US dollars, UK pounds sterling and other hard currencies are remitted annually from around the world to Somalis and Somali businesses in Kenya, Dubai and elsewhere, promoting the development of Eastleigh as a commercial centre and contributing to the stability of the Kenya Shilling (Lindley 2006).

Payments from Europe and elsewhere are sent through Somali remittance firms such as Olympic, Dalsan, Dahab-Shil and the now defunct Al-Barakaat. *Hawala* is very efficient in that money is transferred instantly by either fax or e-mail. Mainstream banking is not mainly related to high transaction costs. The commission charged on *hawala* is 2–5% depending on how much is sent: the more the money amount the less the commission. *Hawala* agents can even deliver cash to the door of the recipients. No passports or identity cards are required, as the sender is given an identification number that is passed on to the receiver. The system is widely used to receive money in Somalia, Ethiopia, Kenya and Uganda, and these firms operate in most cities of Western Europe, North America and the Middle East. They are mostly Somali-owned, and a cross-clan network – showing that the Somali clans can work together – runs the network.

Yet, despite the existence of effective money-transfer systems, many smaller Eastleigh-based exporters are at the mercy of distant importers who do not pay on time and sometimes completely default on payment. The business remains risky and disorganized and is based on the same notions of trust that work well in the domestic khat trade. Prospective importers based in distant European cities telephone the Nairobi exporters and place orders, without providing verification of identity. Often the exporter dispatches a consignment to the prospective customer solely on the basis of a UK telephone number. In the absence of a written agreement traders have no recourse to the courts when payment is withheld. Many exporters do still take such risks because of the high potential return if the deal is successful.

An Ethiopian trader, Tesfaye, the only non-Somali engaged in the Eastleigh-based export business to the UK, says that he usually makes up to 100 per cent profit from his export business.[10] Indeed, he has bought a bungalow in South C, a middle-class area of Nairobi. However, Tesfaye says that some UK-based retailers occasionally default on payments, and he claims to have lost £23,000 over a period of two years to unscrupulous retailers. Other exporters told similar stories. Mbithi, a Meru trader, who used to supply Somali exporters, explained how UK retailers exploit the competition between exporters. A telephone call from the UK or the Netherlands is all it takes to procure a supply of khat from Nairobi. Sometimes retailers in the UK tempt Kenyan-based exporters by making prompt payments in the first three to four transactions, only to disappear and play similar tricks on another exporter by 'bad mouthing' the other supplier.[11] Most Eastleigh exporters running large-scale operations therefore work with reliable, long-term contacts and are unlikely to be caught out in the way that Mbithi and Tesfaye were.

Miraa destined for Europe reaches Nairobi in the early afternoon, having been packaged in sacks in Maua and driven at great speed to Eastleigh. The khat is rushed to a workshop where it is then repackaged in ventilated boxes suitable for the export of perishable vegetables. Each repackaged box weighs between 7 and 8 kg, and contains forty *kilo* bunches. As in Ethiopia, the workshops provide sorely needed employment for the people of Nairobi. In Yasmin's workshop, up to 120 people – a mix of Somali refugees and non-Somali Kenyan's – earn up to KSh400 (approximately £3) a day. Yasmin is a pioneer of the khat-export business. Originally from Somalia, she migrated to Kenya in the early 1970s, first settling in Garissa town where she started a retail business. It was only after she moved to Nairobi in the late 1970s that she moved into the khat trade, buying supplies from Nairobi-based Meru traders. Initially, she exported small quantities to the UK, between five and ten boxes each containing the standard forty *kilo* bunches. Yasmin, together with her son now export an average of 200–250 boxes daily and, like other established traders, she relies on regular suppliers in the Nyambene Hills.[12] Yasmin is obviously a force to be reckoned with, and a woman able to succeed in a male-dominated culture. One man expressed the view that it was because of her beauty, charm and entrepreneur skills that local Somalis invested in the khat industry.[13] Yasmin is now the third biggest exporter of khat – and one of about six women traders – and operates alongside about twenty competitors, who export between six and 400 boxes daily.

In 2004, a Kenyan Somali named Duale was the largest exporter. Duale is from the town of Mandera, close to the borders of both Somalia and Ethiopia. He exports 350–450 boxes of khat to the UK on most evenings of the week, and also supplies khat to the Netherlands and to Somalia.[14] Like Yasmin, Duale maintains a host of brokers and agents in Maua town and rumour has it that he owns a share in one of the aircraft companies that covers the Somalia and northern Kenyan routes. Duale's closest rival is another Somali who has the honour of being Yasmin's first husband. Hashim exports 250–350 boxes to the UK and has a fair share of the Dutch market too. He has recently completed a shopping mall in Eastleigh that consists of more than 100 shops let out to Somali businesses, and he also owns property in the UK and other parts of Nairobi.

Meru Marketing

While the *miraa* trade in Maua is increasingly Somali-dominated, other smaller markets remain the preserve of Meru agents and wholesalers. In addition to Maua, *miraa* is also traded and packed onto pickups in seven rural markets, as well as from minor roadside collection points. Various types and grades of *miraa* are produced in different locations within the Nyambene Hills (Carrier 2003; Goldsmith 1994) and are sold in local markets for specific consumer groups. Hence, much of the *laare* type of *miraa* on sale in Ifo camp and across North Eastern Province is grown around the village of Laare and is either sold to agents in Laare market or transported ten kilometres down the road to Maua. *Miraa* from Laare comes from more recently planted farms and is considered to be of low quality. *Laare* commands far lower prices than *gisa* from Murungene market. In these markets Meru men and boys bring pre-packed supplies direct from their farm to the market. They deal with the same agents on a regular basis. Hence, an agent in Murungene supplies high-quality, expensive *gisa* to a successful Meru retailer operating in Malindi on the Kenya coast. The *miraa* is labelled and sent from Murungene to Kongowea wholesale market in Mombasa where it is collected by the retailer, who sends back cash with the driver or conductor to cover the costs of the previous day's supply (Carrier 2005b).

Both Goldsmith (1997) and Carrier (2005b) highlight the differences in the variety and range of different types of *miraa* grown in Nyambene, and stress the importance of age of trees in producing high quality products. According to Goldsmith:

> [T]he quality and strength of *khat* varies according to climate and ecological conditions, the variety (many consumers are poor at distinguishing among the three main varieties of *Catha edulis*), and the age of trees. The best *miraa* harvested from hundred year or more old trees of the slow-growing 'dark' variety cultivated in Kenya's Nyambene Hills is the metaphorical equivalent of a fine cognac. The 'white' *miraa*, especially when harvested from young trees, is more akin to cheap brandy. (Goldsmith 1997: 475)

The Meru have been very skilled in marketing *miraa* to different consumer groups. The same, or a similar, tree can produce many different types of *miraa* depending on the timing and style of pruning and/or whether the leaves are removed. For example, *kangeta miraa*, much favoured by Somalis, retails at KSh500 a *kilo* in prosperous Malindi, while a *kilo* of woody but potent *matangoma* type sells for KSh100 or less to the pastoralist Turkana community living in northern Kenya around Isiolo. Consumers usually say that the cheaper types are more powerful, whereas the expensive types have more subtle effects and allow sleep after use (Carrier 2003). Nevertheless, the main difference – apart from the prestige value associated with certain brands from certain locations – appears to be whether the product is tender or woody and the effect it has on the mouth. Stimulant effects are known to be the product of the expectations of the user, the environment in which the drug is used and the actual active ingredients. To some extent it would appear that the same substance can be packaged and promoted in one way to, for example, the Turkana and in a different way to the Swahili, with slightly different expected – and therefore perceived – effects. Similarly, Meru producers and retailers make much of the subtle superiority of *miraa* from older trees. Yet they are not the sole producers of *miraa* in Kenya, and other newer products are acceptable and desirable to a growing number of khat users. For example, consumers said that *makokaa miraa* grown by the neighbouring Embu people from bushes less than five years old was stronger than *miraa* from Nyambene. For those who want to achieve a *miraa* high or *handas* at a reasonable cost, talk of superior trees becomes irrelevant.

From the late nineteenth century, Meru men of the Igembe and Tigania clans pioneered the distribution and marketing of *miraa* (Goldsmith 1994). *Miraa* is not only graded and named according to where it is grown, but is packaged in a standardized fashion. Goldsmith attributes the metric packaging system to 'the famous *miraa* dealer Samwel' who popularized the '*kilo*', the main unit of consumption:

> One *kilo* consists of two halves, each half consisting of ten small bundles of ten sticks each. The measure has nothing to do with weight; also the growing popularity of the shorter '*giza*' variety of *miraa* led to variations in which fewer but larger bundles of the twigs make up a *kilo*. (Goldsmith 1994: 108)

The small bundles making up a *kilo* are often called *durba* or *zurba*. However, despite the metrication of *miraa* there is considerable variation in packaging and portioning. For example, by the time a *kilo* reaches Malindi, a few *durba* may have been removed from *kilo* units by retailers stretching their stock, while some types of cheap *miraa* are sold in roughly tied bundles.

Prices of retail *miraa* in any given town depend on a combination of distance from the growing area and the overall prosperity of customers, combined with seasonal variations in the volume of supply that are closely linked to rainfall. In 2004 the drought in the Nyambene Hills led to a shortage of *miraa* and very high prices throughout the country. In August 2004 the top price for *miraa* in Malindi was KSh700 (approximately £5.40) a *kilo*, although the usual price for high-quality miraa in the town was KSh500 (£3.80).[15] The price in Malindi appears to be high year-round compared with that in other towns, because the customers are willing and able to pay such prices. Price variations are a function of purchasing power, supply factors and transportation costs. The result is that there is no set price even for the *miraa* of the same type and quality. Thus, in July 2004 *miraa* cost more in Malindi (KSh500), a town easily accessible from the wholesale market in Mombasa, than in the remote village of Kisingitini situated on Pate Island (KSh300). The justification of the traders for this price differential is the quality of the product. On the other hand, transportation costs do also sometimes affect price. Hence, *miraa* destined for Kisingitini starts in the wholesale markets of Nyambene, is sent by road to Mombasa and then north to Lamu, where it is collected by Meru retailers and carried by ferry to the consumers. The Lamu price is KSh200 and this jumps to KSh300 in Kisingitini.

Networks, Cooperation and Trust

Through the operation of numerous personal business relationships that are based on trust, *miraa* is sent to cities, towns and villages throughout Kenya. *Miraa* passes through wholesale markets in Nairobi and Mombasa and into the hands of young Meru men who retail *miraa* far and wide (Carrier 2005a). In many places they work alongside traders from other ethnic groups, with whom they may develop good business relationships. As the *miraa* business has come to dominate life in the Igembe and Tigania areas, young people of these clans have little alternative but to become *miraa* traders. The Meru have the advantage of being part of the ethnic-based network that links farmers, agents, wholesalers and retailers. A typical Meru retailer runs a kiosk or small shop far from home, often sleeping on the floor of the business premises. Their aim is to acquire capital in order to move into *miraa* wholesaling or to diversify into other business ventures (Goldsmith 1994: 110). In many towns, such as described in Lamu, the Meru traders are organized into welfare societies that help members with the cost of burials and medical fees.[16] Mutual support extends to the actual business arrangements. Hence, 'traders provide for each other, and if one does not receive *miraa* one day, someone will share their consignment with him' (ibid.).

In many places in Kenya, such as in Nakuru, a large Kikuyu-dominated town in the Rift Valley, the Meru are the only retailers of *miraa*. Yet, times are sometimes hard. In August 2004 kioskholders near the bus-booking offices said that a few months earlier there were about 200 Meru trading *miraa* in Nakuru. Now in a time of drought leading to a reduced supply and high prices, about half of them have returned home to farm until the retail business picks up.

Our travels around Kenya revealed cooperation and competition between distributors and retailers. The current arrangements are mostly peaceful and allow many people in diverse settings to make a living from *miraa* produced in the Nyambene Hills. One of the first areas to benefit from the Meru marketing drive was Isiolo. Through interviews with Igembe elders, Goldsmith (1994: 101) dates the marketing of *miraa* in Isiolo back to 1885. The trade to Isiolo remains brisk and the town is noted as a major centre of consumption with many young people chewing khat for recreational purposes (Carrier 2005a: 213).

Many Borana people live in the town of Isiolo, the 'gateway' to northern Kenya. Like Somalis the Borana are Muslim pastoralists. The origins of the Borana lie in Ethiopia and they are related to the Oromo of Ethiopia. Although khat is not part of their culture and plays no part in their rituals, the Borana are avid chewers. Isiolo is about two hour's drive from Maua. On the day we visited the area, a pick-up truck dropped off 20 sacks of khat on the main street of Isiolo at about midday. Another 30 or so sacks were loaded onto another vehicle for onward transport north to Wamba, in Samburu country. The Isiolo supply was moved to a line of shops and received by about fifty waiting traders, about two-thirds of whom were Somali or Borana men and women and the remaining one-third Meru men. In Isiolo, the leafy *miraa* is known as *bogwa*. It is not subdivided into *durba* and is tied with a twig. One Somali man was selling *bogwa* for KSh250 per *kilo*. The majority of traders were small-time and selling mostly *bogwa*, although *gisa* and *kangeta* were also available.[17] In the nearby Isiolo municipal market, two groups of Turkana women were selling loose miraa sent from Nyambene by Meru agents. This was called *matangoma* or *matahedi* and consisted of woody and green twigs with the leaves and small white blossoms still attached. The traders count out the twigs into a plastic bag, charging KSh20 for twenty twigs. There are an estimated 300 women in the trade. They supply small places outside Isiolo where Turkana people live. *Matangom*a is considered very strong, and much more potent than *bogwa*. It is popular among Turkana men and women who chew at any time of day, or smoke it or drink it as an infusion, or tea.[18]

The Gateway to Tanzania

In Namanga, a small town in Maasailand that straddles the Kenya–Tanzania border, *miraa* arrives from Nayambene via the wholesale market in Nairobi. In Namanga the retail trade is divided between Meru men and Somali women and men. One Somali woman trader described how she had her Meru agent in Nyambene build up trust over a long period of time.[19] However, she thought that no Somali nor anybody outside Nyambene could ever grow *miraa* because she had been told that for the stems to have any potency the trees must be more than 200 years old. This view provides a good example of how successful the marketing of the Meru has been with their emphasis on the superior quality of old trees (Carrier 2005a). Many of the Somalis in Namanga are 'British' Somali, but there are also Somalis originating from within the borders of modern Kenya as well as some refugees. About half the Somali in Namanga were highly visible chewers, while the other half opposed chewing on the grounds that it is un-Islamic. The Somali and Meru retailers agreed that the customers came from all the different tribes, including Tanzanians who walk over the border to purchase *miraa*.

In the dead of night *miraa* is also driven in pick-up trucks over the border, where it immediately becomes contraband. By asking around in Namanga, we located the Meru people who operated the export market. Twenty-four sacks of khat from Nyambene were offloaded from a pick-up vehicle at about 2.00 am. Three-quarters of this load was put onto another pick-up by Tanzanians and taken across the border. Even the presence of the research team made the Tanzanians so nervous that they had to be assured about our objectives by the Kenyan customs officers. Khat trafficking can carry a heavy prison sentence in Tanzania. A Somali informant said that if the smugglers were caught they paid '*hongo*' (a bribe) or simply abandoned the stock to rot.[20] Informants confirm that it is Chagga people who run the trade on the Tanzanian side of the border.

The Marketing of Other Types of Khat

Although the Meru marketing and distribution system is formidable, other types of khat are successfully distributed and marketed within Kenya. Notably, *makokaa* grown around Embu in the central highlands has captured some of the market share from the Meru distributors of Nyambene-grown khat. Thus, in Embu town itself there are no Meru traders; only *makokaa* sold by men of the Embu or Wabeere ethnic groups. In other areas *makokaa* competes successfully with Nyambene *miraa*. For example, in Thika, a few hours' drive from Embu, Borana and Somali market-women sell a mixture of textiles, *makokaa* and Nyamabene *miraa*. They easily outnumber the handful of Meru traders selling khat from Nyambene. The market-women said that *makokaa* is more popular than Nyambene khat because it is strong and cheap.[21] *Makokaa* is sold by the handful, at a starting price of KSh20 (approx. £0.15) and going up to KSh100 worth. The short (approximately 6 cm) loose shoots are put in small plastic bags. In Mwingi, about three hours to the south-east of Embu, *makokaa* is sold by Meru and Kamba men in shops and kiosks that line the highway. Retailers in Mwingi said that *makokaa* was more popular than Nyambene *miraa*. *Makokaa* also reaches Nairobi and Mombasa using a transportation system similar to that employed by the Meru. One box of *makokaa* is sent from Embu to Mombasa daily on the Sunbird bus, and picked up from the booking office by the traders who ordered it.

In northern Kenya khat is imported from Ethiopia. For example, in the town of Moyale that straddles the Kenya-Ethiopia border, khat from Nyambene is not available, and most khat consumed on the Kenyan side is brought over the border on wheelbarrows.[22] Although they live in a remote part of Kenya, Moyale communities have three different kinds of Ethiopian khat from which to choose. Men and women traders positioned on verandas outside shops sell Ethiopian khat. According to Amina, a *miraa* trader, three kinds of khat are usually on sale on the Kenyan side of Moyale.[23] These include

Garfur: about twelve inches long – similar in appearance to Yemeni qat. The wholesale price is KSh60 (£0.4) and it retails at KSh100. Amina, when preparing the khat for sale, breaks off the tender shoots from the woody stems and puts them in a plastic bag. As she discards the waste material, a young man and woman sitting next to Amina pick up the discarded leaves and start to chew, while storing the rest in their pockets.
Seike: this type is longer and wholesales at KSh200 (£1.30), and commands a retail price of KSh250.
Fisa: is rare, and was not available for sale at the time we visited Moyale.

Amina explained that the khat she retails comes from 100 km inside the Ethiopian border, from an area with a good paved road. The khat is brought to the border by

Ethiopians and distributed on the Kenyan side by Kenyans. As described by Amina, the system seems to be similar to that of the domestic Kenyan trade – based on personal contacts, with suppliers putting in orders and with some credit arrangements in place for long-term traders. Amina confirmed that in Moyale there were about 200 women selling between 10 and 20 kg per day. A point noted by the retailers is that there is no traders' association and everybody is 'on her own'. The infrastructure on the Ethiopian side is more developed. At 12.30 pm the khat usually arrives to the Kenyan border by wheelbarrow, packed in white sacks. The retailers, mostly young men and women, spread across the busy market selling a variety of wares, including five types of khat: *eddy*, *ganfur*, *sikei*, *garbicho* and *entess*.

The Khat Trade in Chyulu

Midway along the road from the coastal Mombasa to Nairobi, where people of the Kamba ethnic group predominate, the Chyulu Hills are visible. Turning eastward off the main road, the paving disappears and the saloon car bounces along a forested track, through and around pools of water. It is February 2004 and has been raining, so that supplies of khat are abundant. After about half an hour we reach Dongoni, a trading post with a vigorous market. Beans and chapatti are on sale in one café and young Kamba men, agents in the *chyulu* khat trade, join in for a late lunch. In the past, according to these young men, *chyulu* was used to stave off hunger and its consumption is part of Kamba culture in this area. They explain that harvesting *chyulu* for commercial sale started in the 1970s, and now a few farmers have started cultivating *chyulu* khat.[24]

Nevertheless, most *chyulu* is wild khat poached from the Chyulu Hills, a forest reserve. The informants explained that the wardens used to make it very difficult for the harvesters, but now there is a better understanding and the Wardens have become more accommodating. The traders describe the harvesters as 'like animals' because they lead a precarious existence in the forests, sometimes sleeping there and rarely bathing or changing their clothes. They bring the *chyulu* down from the hills to packing stations. The main packing station for *chyulu* is only accessible by a 30 minutes' walk.

The packing station, constructed of wattle and daub walls with a thatched roof, is situated in the foothills among scattered farms, and doubles as a bar selling sachets of cheap spirits and local beer. Ragged youths sit on rough wooden benches in the dim interior of the bar. They take loose *chyulu* from the canvas bags they carry, sort them by size and tie them into small bundles, chewing the stock as they work. They eye visitors suspiciously, refusing to be drawn into conversation. After a while some of their colleagues arrive from the mountains bearing their freshly harvested stock. Brief negotiations take place with the agent whose base is the bar, and the stock is added to the pile for sorting and packing.

From the packing station the *chyulu* is sent to the towns and markets on the main Mombasa–Nairobi road by male Kamba agents and wholesalers to be retailed by Kamba women and men. In Mtito Ndei, on the highway midway between Nairobi and Mombasa where buses and trucks make rest-stops, most of the khat on sale is *chyluu*, but *miraa* from Nyambene is also available. The main customers are travellers, many of whom buy *chyulu* because it is cheaper than Nyambene *miraa*. Moving north and south along the road, the distribution of *chyulu* peters out within 100 kilometres either way. In February 2004 there were three grades of *chyulu* selling at more or less set prices:

1. Top grade, simply called '*chyulu*': sent by order to Mombasa and not available in kiosks. It retails at KSh150 (£1.15) per *kilo*.
2. *Gisa*: it retails at KSh100 (£0.77) per *kilo*
3. *Gat*: low-grade woody stems, like the *kata* of Nyambene *miraa*. Retails at KSh50 (£0.38) a *kilo*.[25]

Most towns and villages in the Chyulu Hills along a large stretch of the Mombasa–Nairobi road from Voi to Salama display large banana leaves selling *chyulu* khat. In August these are absent. The whole of the Kamba area of Kenya, including the Chyulu Hills, is in the grip of a severe drought and emerging famine. By 2004, in Mtito Ndei most kiosks closed and there was virtually no *miraa* of any kind on sale. The municipal council had closed many kiosks that were considered to be on squatted land. Winnie, a *miraa* retailer who was interviewed in February, had on sale two tired *kilos* of *chyulu* from the previous day. According to her, supply was very much reduced because of the sun and lack of rain, but the price had not gone up because consumers would not bear this extra cost.

Along the road in the trading post of Missionary there is one young Kamba man selling a few *kilos* of *chyulu* wrapped in leaves similar to those of cabbage. According to him, the price has increased from KSh10 (£0.07) a *durba* (one-tenth of a *kilo*) to KSh15 a *durba*. He expects the supply of khat to recover from the month of September, the supply of which is also affected by the widespread drought affecting much of Kenya. The Kamba traders are selling low-grade Nyambene *kata* and *gisa*, which they get every morning from Majengo wholesale market in Nairobi. The price of *gisa* had risen from about KSh200 per *kilo* to KSh350, because of the drought and resulting shortage in *miraa*. Over the road Fatouma, a Somali woman, has been trading in Missionary for three years, selling to truck drivers who are mostly fellow Somalis. She usually sells *gisa asli* for KSh250 a *kilo*, but at the time of our visit the price was KSh400. Fatouma travels to Majengo to buy supplies and was paying KSh3,700 per *bunda*.[26]

Production: Beyond Nyambene

For most Kenyans *miraa* production is synonymous with the Meru of the Nyambene Hills. As part of their attempt to maintain a monopoly and promote their product, the Meru are quick to talk down the poor quality of *miraa* from other areas. But the wild *miraa* (or *murungi*) from the Chyulu Hills appears to be indigenous to that area, and is now cultivated on a small scale. Other new producing areas reviewed here, around Embu, Taita Hills and Timau, have been established with *miraa* plant tubers from Nyambene. It is likely that over the next 10 years, the sale of *miraa* produced in other areas will spread so that *miraa* production and marketing is poised to become a multi-ethnic business within Kenya.

On the north side of Mount Kenya, the village of Timau is dominated by Meru people of the Imenti clan. The Imenti have no long-standing tradition of khat production. We observed some mature plantations and others with new shrubs, and visited one farm with about 300 trees planted in 1968 with stock from Nyambene by the current farmer's father.[27] The visit took place on a Sunday and a group of five or six young men were sitting in the plantation awaiting the farmer to harvest *miraa* that they would consume fresh on the farm. A large bunch costing KSh800 would be shared among them. Some of the miraa is sold in Timau market where it competes with Nyambene *miraa*. The local Timau product is sold in bunches tied with a twig and put in a plastic bag. It goes under a number of names: *skemu* (because it is grown on an agricultural scheme area), *gisa*, *matangoma* and *chelewa* ('late' in Swahili). There is no special price, but a decent *kilo* retails at about KSh200, according to our informant, Harrison.[28]

Another area of localized production using seedlings imported from Nyambene is the Taita Hills of the hinterland of the Kenya coast. Following reports of khat production we went to Wundanyi, near Voi, where we found Dixon, a Forestry warden and avid chewer, who agreed to be our guide for the day.[29] He took us to several farms located in highly mountainous terrain. Dixon estimates that there are about 100 farms cultivating *miraa*. According to all informants, *miraa* was introduced to the Taita Hills by former MP Darius Mbela, who brought plants from Nyambene. There was opposition to the introduction of *miraa* by local leaders ('chiefs') who argued that *miraa* is a drug. They temporarily limited production in around 1987/88. Now the government supports *miraa* cultivation, seeing it as a valuable cash crop. Some farms have about 400 trees scattered among coffee and other crops. The farmer sells directly to neighbours especially at weekends and for celebrations. The usual retail price for this *miraa* is KSh10 (£0.07) per *durba* (small bunch), or KSh100 per the ten *durba* that make up a *kilo*. Farmers complain that recently a problem with young people stealing the crop from the fields has arisen.[30] Other farms had 100–200 trees, planted among other crops or in orderly plantations. The Taita trade is confined to the local area and the *miraa* does not find its way even to the nearest market town, Wundanyi, where *miraa* from Nyambene is sold.

Khat trees and bushes are being planted in many highland areas of Kenya. The Embu and Wambere peoples who occupy an area to the south of Nyambene produce *makokaa* khat that is marketed in a number of towns locally and as far afield as Nairobi and Mombasa. In Embu town itself, only *makokaa* is available, although supplies of Nyambene khat pass through the town on the way to Nairobi. There are an estimated 3,000 producers of *makokaa*, concentrated around the Kiritiri.[31] These farmers originally obtained khat shoots from the Nyambene region, but now cultivate shoots in nurseries and sell them for about KSh150 (£1.15). Returns for farmers are quick and plants that are only one to four years old are harvested, packed in round banana-fibre packages (*roboto*) and sent to roadside or town market locations where men wait at the roadside for supplies and buyers. Retailers purchase the *roboto* for KSh500–700, and sell in market areas or from shops and kiosks.[32]

At the other end of Kenya, in Moyale – a town straddling the Kenyan-Ethiopian border – khat from Ethiopia is the substance of choice for local chewers resident in both countries. However, on the Kenyan side farmers have started planting khat seedlings not from Ethiopia nor from Nyambene, but *makokaa* from Embu. At one farm on the edge of Moyale a man in his fifties, Abdulalihi, claims to be the first man to market *makokaa* in Eastleigh, Nairobi. (This claim was later confirmed by *makokaa* sellers in Eastleigh.)[33] Abdulalihi sprays his 3,000 trees to kill pests. He has grown the trees from seedlings brought from Mbere (near Embu) because the *makokaa* is better adapted to heat typical of the Moyale climate than Nyambene *miraa* which thrives in more temperate conditions. The Moyale trees do not produce all year round, only for a few months when it rains. Abdulalihi grows the trees on terraces with some irrigation/channelling of water, fertilizes with goat droppings and leaves the crop for two weeks after spraying before starting to harvest. Abdulalihi and his family harvest the khat and people come to buy direct from the farm, paying KSh100–150 per plastic bagful. Abdulalihi, says people in Moyale are poor and cannot afford to pay more, although his product is in high demand and sells out quickly. Nevertheless, he adds that he built his new house with *miraa* money.

The Spread of Chyulu

Khat trees grow wild in many areas of East Africa and beyond and not all Kenyan khat is cultivated by farmers. Informants often mentioned western Kenya, particularly Mount Elgon and the mountains around Kapenguria, as areas where Khat is harvested. Recently farmers have been taking seedlings of wild *chyulu* khat and starting plantations. These plantations are found in unexpected places, such as in Kimana near the Tanzanian border under the shadow of Mouth Kilimanjaro in Maasailand. Although in Maasai country, this area has been settled extensively by Kikuyu who grow onions and other vegetables to supply the Nairobi and Mombasa markets. In Kimana, the main town of this remote area, a 'British' Somali retails khat on the verandah of the shop, where four men and women sort and bunch up *miraa*. Mohamed showed us round his plantation of 1,300 trees. He also has about 300 seedlings that he will retail for KSh200 (approx. £1.35) each.[34] In order to start the plantation ten years ago, he sent Kamba men to the Chyolu Hills to bring young plants. He has recently started harvesting these plants and sells about fifty *kilos* per day, and more at weekends and holidays. Mohamed pays local pickers to harvest each tree once a week after spraying with pesticides and leaving the trees for two weeks. He sells two grades: *gisa* at Ksh200 per *kilo* and *ngata* at KSh100 per *kilo*. The customers are Kamba, Kikiyu and Maasai men and Maasai women. Customers come directly to his shop, some of them travelling from the neighbouring town of Oloitokitok. Mohamed does good business as there are no Meru retailers in Kimana and the only competition he faces is from several other small-scale growers.

Tucked away under Mount Kilimanjaro, Mohamed's plantation and the business he has built up illustrate that the *miraa* industry in Kenya is no longer the sole preserve of the Meru. Rather, it is in the process of becoming a multi-ethnic phenomenon. Mohamed, a Somali, used *chyulu* seedlings to produce *miraa* that is bought by Kikuyu, Kamba and Maasai people. With *miraa* plantations springing up all over the country and consumption on the increase, the marketing and distribution system is sufficiently flexible to allow a large number of people to enter the business and make a living from *miraa*. While the Kenyan media has focused on ethnic clashes between the Meru and Somalis for control of the industry, *miraa* is delivered daily from Nyambene to the rest of Kenya, to surrounding countries and to Europe (Carrier 2003). This operation involves cooperation and trust between retailers, wholesalers and agents from many ethnic groups.

–6–

Kenya
Culture, Controversy and Cooperation

For centuries khat production was confined to a few highland areas, notably in Ethiopia and Yemen, and the Nyambene Hills of Kenya. As cathinone quickly degrades after the khat is picked, consumption was until recently limited to people living near these production areas. As road, rail and air transport developed over the course of the twentieth century, the people of the Nyambene Hills started marketing khat outside their own district (Goldsmith 1994; Carrier 2005b). Ready-made demand came from Yemeni migrants to Kenya who settled in numbers along the coast, often intermarrying with the local Muslim communities. Small Yemeni trading communities can also be found in many towns of the interior. These migrants, coming from a country where khat, or *qat* as it is known in Yemen, has been consumed for centuries, played a pioneering role in the expansion of the khat trade.

According to Varisco, Yemeni *qat* consumption can be dated back to the late fourteenth or early fifteenth centuries (Varisco 2004: 106). Over the centuries, *qat* use has become not only institutionalized, but ritualized (Weir 1985; Meneley 1996; Varisco 2004). Varisco describes the effects of participants in classic *qat*-chewing sessions in Yemen, where single-sex groups sit together in the afternoons to consume the drug:

> As the bitter juice descends into the stomach, a heightened sense of mental alertness begins within quarter of an hour. The result is stimulus to conceptualization and conversation, which can become animated or remain at a minimum, depending on the individuals present and the news of the day. After two hours a more reflective mood sets in, a state of euphoria or well-being that is sometimes called *kayf.* (Varisco 2004: 108)

The Yemeni migrants, therefore, came to Kenya with a memory of *qat* consumption as a deep-rooted culture practice that appeared to be largely compatible with Islam. By the mid-twentieth century, in Kenyan towns, Yemenis were able to buy khat grown in the Nyambene Hills. Slowly the people among whom the Yemenis lived, the Swahili at the coast and people of all ethnic groups in the highlands, also started chewing khat. A khat subculture emerged with local names for khat such as *murungi*, *veve* and *gomba*, as well as terms for describing different grades of khat and its effects. In the coastal town of Malindi, for instance, Yemeni street-corner coffee sellers had initially introduced *miraa* to their Swahili customers. By the 1980s, *miraa* chewing was part of the daily routine of many young Swahili men in the town of Malindi (Peake 1989). But in this new setting, consumption lacked the ritual and cultural finesse of Yemen. It has been associated with a range of emerging problems even though khat production, sale and consumption have always been legal, apart from a short period during the 1970s (Carrier 2003), there is a growing and increasingly organized opposition.

Many government agencies and civil society organizations view khat as a harmful substance. Some officials claim that it exacerbated the civil war of the 1990s in Somalia and that it impedes development in Somali-dominated areas of Kenya. There have been sporadic efforts at local level to limit the spread of khat. For example, in 2004 in Bungoma, western Kenya *miraa* could not be purchased in shops or kiosks within the town because the municipal council had banned its open sale. But the main battle of the war on *miraa* was fought in the town of Lamu. A coalition of local activities in Lamu on the north Kenya coast made great efforts to ban the local sale of khat by attempting to pass a by-law. The arguments against *miraa* that the campaigners used echo those of the national debate, just as the views of khat consumers and distributors echo those heard all over Kenya.

Khat Use in Lamu

The town of Lamu is situated on an island of the same name just off the north Kenya coast. The town is well over a thousand years old and is one of the old Swahili city-states that dominated the east coast of Africa between the fifteenth and nineteenth centuries (Allen 1993). Within East Africa, Lamu is an important Islamic centre and the focus for the annual *Maulidi* celebrations marking the birthday of the Prophet Mohammed. In 2001, Lamu was declared a UNESCO World Heritage Site and the main industry is tourism. All these aspects of Lamu's history and culture were cited in the anti-miraa campaign.

Miraa chewing in Lamu is said to date to 1968 when a bus driver on the Mombasa–Lamu route started chewing with two Yemeni friends. A few of the locals followed the habit until it gradually gained some popularity. The first agent was Ali Fahri who bought supplies of *miraa* in Mombassa and brought them by bus to Lamu.[1] As demand grew through the 1970s, other Swahili agents who imported supplies from the wholesale *miraa* market in Mombassa joined Ali. The wholesalers paid their Meru suppliers by Postal Order sent the next day.

By 2004, there were 300–500 *miraa* consumers in Lamu town, the majority Swahili men and youths, but including a growing number of Swahili women. While the women tend to chew at home, some with their husbands, the men usually chew on street corners at *baraza*, the meeting places that are an important feature of Swahili daily life. In Lamu, as elsewhere, consumption levels vary. Khat prices fluctuate, depending on availability, which in turn is determined by supply from and production in the Nyambene growing region. In July 2004 when a drought had severely limited supply, a bundle of *miraa* was selling between KSh150 (£1.15) and KSh350 (£2.70). There is no fixed price for *miraa*, and in order to get a good deal customers need to know about type, quality and supply in order to haggle effectively. For example, as *miraa* should be consumed while fresh, it is important not to buy day-old supplies at full cost.

The retailing operation has changed significantly over the past 20 years, with young Meru men displacing local *miraa* traders. Many are young, unmarried men who eke out a living selling ten to twenty bundles of khat a day. Leaving home to work in the *miraa* trade has become a rite of passage that replaces older Meru traditions of warriorhood for circumcised youth (Goldsmith 1994). Some Meru had ventured even further and set up business at the remote villages on the islands to the north of Lamu. The small village of Faza on Pate island, for instance, is home to two Meru traders, who bring their supplies by ferry from Lamu. In 2004 there were about sixty Meru *miraa* traders operating in Lamu and only a handful of retailers from other ethnic groups. The trade-licensing system of Lamu County Council does not discriminate against outsiders, and levies a daily charge of KSh30 on each street trader, shop- or kiosk-owner for the right to trade in *miraa*. The only other fee is a KSh40 (£0.34) charge by the Kenya Port Authority for each sack landed on Lamu seafront. With such a presence in this distant market, the Meru traders have organized themselves into a Welfare Association, comprising around forty members. According to the Treasurer, many members saw Lamu as alien and far from home, like 'the end of the world'.[2] The Association provides a safety net, paying medical bills and funeral expenses of members and their families. But they also act as a lobby for the interests of the Meru trading community, and came to the fore during the anti-*miraa* campaign.

The Anti-*Miraa* Campaign

The campaign to get *miraa* banned in Lamu started in 2001 and included representatives of Islamic groups, youth and women's organizations, the teachers' trade union, officials from the National Museums of Kenya and community-based organizations. The main objective of the campaign was to introduce a by-law banning the sale of *miraa*. They received no support from either the sitting MP or the opposition candidate, as both had used gifts of *miraa* for wooing potential supporters and would not advocate banning a substance that was legal in the rest of the country. Nor did the campaigners involve church groups as they considered *miraa* consumption to be an exclusively Muslim problem.[3]

Concerned with the consequences of the *miraa* culture, the campaigners associated rising consumption with the rising divorce rate in the community, the loose sexual morality and falling school attendance of youthful *miraa* users, unemployment and economic decline, as well as a range of medical conditions. These arguments were an echo of policy debates that have been heard in other parts of East Africa (Carothers 1945; Dhadphale et al. 1981; Ihunwo et al. 2004).

The campaign was skilfully mounted and, in a series of letters, appealed to individuals and organizations that had the power to curb *miraa* sales in Lamu. Thus, in June 2001 an appeal from the Imams of the Friday mosques was made to fellow Muslims:

> Miraa as we are all aware has been a big menace and a cause of a number of problems in our Islamic community. Some of these problems are divorce, prostitution, begging and abandonment of families and etc.
>
> It is in this regard that we are humbly appealing for your assistance in eradicating this social vice which is almost destroying our Muslim Ummah.
>
> We would like you to please assist us by not allowing your vehicles to transport *Miraa* to Lamu. By this you will be to a large extent preventing divorces, prostitution (which leads to HIV/AIDS), begging and other malpractices and we are sure Allah's reward to you will be great.

The following month, in a letter from 'Lamu District Community' to Kenya Airways, another approach was attempted:

> Our request has nothing to do with in interfering with your company business operations, but it will very much help us the entire community of Lamu District from eventual total destruction and doom. As an air service you are free to do any business and we very well know we have no right whatsoever to interfere and it is not our intention to do so but this is an appeal based on humanitarian grounds and your contribution will greatly assist in solving the valuable culture of the people of this district.
>
> Sirs, *Miraa* imported and consumed by our youths and even elders is causing the district great damages, socially, economically and culturally. Socially, it is one of the major causes of rising crime rates, it is contributing high rises of disease e.g. STDs HIV/AIDS. Our district is now experiencing high rates of thefts and prostitution as well as other sexual crimes. *Miraa* is one of the great causes of broken marriages and divorces.
>
> Economically it is draining away from our district much of our youth's earnings, hence subject us all to ever increasing trends of severe poverty.

In September 2001, the Lamu Kadhi wrote to Lamu County Council expressing his concerns:

> From my office, I can assure you that the major cause of the alarming rate of divorces is nothing else save *miraa* addiction, which leads thereafter to a lot of social problems due to the broken marriages.

On 21 November 2001, the *Daily Nation* newspaper carried a notice of a proposed by-law that: 'No person shall carry on the business or trade in *Miraa* in all areas under the jurisdiction of Lamu County Council'. This was a direct attack on the livelihood of the Meru traders who, via the Welfare Association, which enlisted the services of a fellow Meru lawyer from Nairobi. As *miraa* is a legal substance traded and consumed openly throughout the country, the objection was upheld by the court.

This legal setback did not stop the Lamu community leaders from continuing the letter-writing campaign. Over time, the campaign was becoming increasingly acrimonious and desperate in tone. In April 2002, the Kenya Assembly of Ulamaa and Imams complained to the Provincial Commissioner (emphasis as in original):

> The elders of Lamu and their county council have stood firmly to protect the WELFARE of their YOUTH and Lamu citizens in general from THE MOST HARMFUL EFFECTS OF THE DRUG OF MIRAA. One would have rightly and decently thought that the ADMINISTRATION would also HAVE THE WELFARE OF THE PEOPLE AT HEART and thus support the elders in SUPRESSING MIRAA. But in contrary the ADMINISTRATION clings to the technicality that MIRAA IS NOT BANNED IN KENYA and thus in perspective PROTECT THE MIRAA DEALERS to spread HARMFUL DRUG to the youth and the poverty-stricken Lamu populace.
>
> So the ADMINISTRATION in protecting MIRAA DEALERS, what message is it sending the people of LAMU?
>
> QUESTIONS:
>
> (a) THE GOOD WELFARE OF LAMU islanders is not the first concern to the ADMINISTRATION.
> (b) MIRAA must be allowed to sell in Lamu because it is not banned.
> (c) THE PRINCIPLE OF WANTING GOOD FOR THE CITIZENS OF KENYA is APPLICABLE ONLY TO CERTAIN COMMUNITIES AND NOT TO OTHERS as in this case the GOOD OF MERU PEOPLE IS PARAMOUNT OVER THE GOOD OF LAMU PEOPLE? (THESE QUESTIONS ARE BEING ASKED).

Similarly, in May 2002, the 'Anti-Drug Lobby' wrote to the Minister of Local Government:

> Due to the *miraa* menace, the moral, Cultural and social fabric of the Lamu society is being degraded i.e. losing their traditional values. According to the records in the Kadhi's office and children office, Lamu District, *miraa* is one of the main contributions of divorces, family break-ups and separations. These effects further lead to social crimes such as prostitution, theft and unstable society morally. The high school dropouts of schoolchildren, bad performance and bad discipline among schoolchildren now strongly attributed to *miraa* consumption … All these are signals of community that driving towards doom rather than salvation and prosperity. Hence there is need and very urgent

one to put a stop to *miraa* consumption. In addition the good health of the community is very much at the highest risk e.g. HIV/AIDS etc. Chewing *miraa* is a drug that leads to the consumption of all other drugs and alcoholism, which subsequently lead to crimes and social problems.

The letter also pointed out that Lamu had been a UNESCO World Heritage site since 2001 and that *miraa* use and its effects were putting tourism at risk. A similar approach was taken by the administrators of Lamu Museums, who wrote to the boss of Lamu Police Station in February 2002:

> Increasingly important, the town square is situated at the centre of the town where most of the government offices are situated; it is where most visitors land and get into Lamu town; it is where the National Monument of Kenya in the name of Lamu Fort Environmental museum sited. For that matter their [*miraa* traders] existence to the site is a nuisance, socially and environmentally.
>
> In view of the above reasons we kindly appeal to you to assist in evacuating the *miraa* traders from the site. Notices to that effect have been communicated to them copies to you, the DC and the Clerk to the Council. The *miraa* traders are very stubborn, arrogant and persistently infringing the notice.

This letter appears to have had the desired effect, as in 2004 the wholesale market was operating at the side of the Fort/Museum and not in front of it. While this did not satisfy the campaign leaders, who complained about *miraa* traders paying off the police, it has made the business less prominent.

National Concerns and User Perspectives

The points raised by campaigners in Lamu reproduce widely held views about the detrimental effects of *miraa* use in Kenya. The starting point for popular concern is that khat is dangerous to health, and in particular, threatens sanity. Although some of the international research on khat and its effects have been more nuanced (Kennedy 1987), from colonial times reports on Kenyan *miraa* have linked it with psychosis (Carothers 1945; Dhadphale et al. 1981). More recently, a newspaper article on the effects of khat had the headline 'Price of *miraa*: Your brain or the twig' (*Daily Nation*, 17 May 2001). With Kenya in the midst of the HIV/AIDS plague, health workers routinely link khat use with dis-inhibition and increased sexual risk behaviour. Divorce, increased school dropout rates and family breakdown are often associated with khat consumption. For example, an information leaflet, published by the Nairobi office of the United Nations Office on Drugs and Crime (UNODC) and in circulation in Kenya, expresses a number of concerns about khat use:

Concern has been expressed in a number of khat-consuming countries that, what was traditionally a male activity, is also attracting a growing number of women users. This trend is viewed with alarm, as it is associated with a loosening of moral mores and values. (UNDCP)

Hence, women's khat consumption is viewed as a threat to the moral order. Youth are also considered by the UNODC to be at particular risk: 'Khat consumption by youth may result in serious social and health consequences and impacts negatively on school performance' (UNODC, undated).

Popular arguments concerning the effects of khat appear to be generated from a mixture of research results, hearsay and observation of users and their social milieu. However, *miraa* users also have a wide range of views on the chewing habits and the consequences. Conversations with *miraa* chewers across Kenya in Mombasa, Nairobi, Garissa, Malindi – and in numerous kiosks and tea-huts in small towns and villages – provided insights into users' opinions. Their views on the effects of *miraa* consumption were similar, regardless of ethnicity or social class, and picked up on a number of themes. They talked enthusiastically about '*handas*' or '*nakhwa*', the 'high' from khat chewing that banishes sleep and, makes people by turn garrulous and reflective and causes them to hatch money-making schemes that the next morning turn out to be 'castles in the air'.

There is also a popular perception at the Kenya Coast that heavy consumption of *miraa* mixed with cannabis leads to madness. Yet for most users, most of the time, khat causes pleasurable effects with no great or lasting harm. Popular anecdotes centre on the disorientation that sometimes occurs after chewing for a number of hours and typically describe a chewer roaming around at night. For example, one story from Mombassa describes a late-night chewer who wanted to buy cigarettes and saw a light from a building nearby. Thinking the light was a sign that a shop was open for business he made his way there only to find himself in the Central Police Station.

Many male consumers while in a state of '*handas*' (the *miraa* high) spoke of how *miraa* consumption improved their sex lives and gave them 'power'. Khat certainly appears to increase sexual desire, as reported by both male and female consumers. Yet, women chewers and the retailers listening to tales of khat-induced male potency usually kept silent and or looked contemptuous and sceptical. In one kiosk in Mombasa the woman seller could barely keep the contempt from showing on her face as her customer became more and more crude.[4] Once the effects of chewing have worn off, consumers acknowledge that *miraa* is just as likely to cause impotence as increased 'power', but argue that it depends on the type of khat consumed. Rushby (1998: 28) in his enthusiast's account of khat consumption, also found disagreement among users regarding the effects of chewing on sexuality, and comments that 'it should not surprise anybody that this plant is both good and bad for sex'.

The degree to which khat use leads to physical dependence is a controversial topic. Kennedy's comprehensive study of *qat* consumption in Yemen considered the reported after-effects of chewing and found that

> [t]he mild depressive feelings with lack of energy and experienced powerlessness are probably due to psychological conditions, supporting a notion of psychic dependence; but the general malaise, trembling and bad dreams appear to be purely physiological responses to drug deprivation. These data support the hypothesis that a mild form of physiological dependence does result from extremely heavy use. (Kennedy 1987: 193)

In Kenya, consumers spoke of the ill effects that *miraa* use had had on their lives, in ways that point to both physical and psychological dependence. As Rushby observes, they are among the ranks of khat consumers who can chew while calling for a ban on their drug of choice (Rushby 1998). Across Kenya, we see a similar range of responses, with some consumers complaining of their irritability when daily supplies cannot be secured and others claiming they cannot properly observe Ramadan without khat, while critics of the chewers claim that expenditure on khat has caused misery to households and even contributed to bankruptcy. Other male consumers have been heard to say that khat chewing has led to the breakdown of their marriages, an echo of the complaints of UK-based Somali women who campaign against khat consumption in the UK.[5]

Another problem Mohammed cited was the use of Valium resorted to by many *miraa* chewers in Garissa and north-eastern Kenya to induce sleep. Indeed, NACADA, a Kenyan government body concerned with drug control, has held seminars in Garissa concerning *miraa* and Valium use, and as a result local pharmacies have stopped selling the tranquillizer over the counter. Hence, both government agencies and *miraa* users expressed concerns about the effects of heavy consumption that drew on the same issues that the campaigners in Lamu raised. Nevertheless, some claims – for example that *miraa* causes HIV infection because chewing promotes immorality – appear exaggerated. Although miraa chewing is a recent pastime in Lamu, consumption occurs as recreation with conventions that limit potential abuse. Most consumers conform to these conventions so that rituals of consumption are being developed across Kenya.

Recreation and Ritual

In Ethiopia and Yemen where khat consumption has a long history, chewing is mostly a social event with a well-developed etiquette. In Kenya, although some Meru clans have used *miraa* in marriage broking and peacemaking for centuries, members of other cultural groups have taken up chewing within the last three decades. *Miraa* use has become a popular youth fashion and has spread to all urban areas of Kenya

(Carrier 2005a). However, consumption is most closely associated with Muslim groups, particularly Somalis and, much to the chagrin of Lamu elders, the Swahili.

The Swahili share a common culture and language, but have diverse origins. Yemeni migrants, mostly from Hadramawt, have had a strong influence on religious and cultural expression. Arriving by boat from their homeland, most male migrants from Yemen settled at the coast, while others moved inland setting up businesses in towns across the country (Boxberger 2002). During the twentieth century, they increasingly provided a ready market for miraa from the Nyambene Hills and thus promoted khat consumption throughout Kenya. In Mombasa, from the 1950s to 1980s there was a club that welcomed new migrants from Hadramawt and other parts of Yemen where men sat on mattresses on the floor and chewed together in the style of a Yemeni *mafraj* (Weir 1985). At the Kenya coast, Yemeni migrants married locally and became part of the Swahili community, passing on chewing habits to their children and others they lived among. Yet, *miraa* consumption among the Swahili lacks the social conventions and ritual aspects that a Yemeni chewing session typically exhibits. When in Yemen most chewing takes place in *mafraj*, or reception rooms often dedicated to communal *qat* consumption, much miraa is chewed on street corners at *baraza*, an important feature of Swahili social life for men. The biggest variation between Yemeni and Swahili modes of chewing is probably the adoption of Big G chewing gum. According to Goldsmith (1994), the introduction of Big G in 1975 made bitter-tasting *miraa* palatable to a wider number of people. Most Swahili chewers use Big G, which has become an essential extra, along with soda (soft drinks) or coffee and cigarettes, for consumers to achieve complete chewing pleasure.

As the views of the Lamu elders expressed through their campaign correspondence make abundantly clear, *miraa* chewing is not considered socially respectable and chewers gather together with little regard for considerations of social status, as there is little kudos to be gained from chewing. Yet, the style of *miraa* chewing can enhance status of an individual among his peers if he conforms to the chewers' conventions: starting consumption after lunch, maintaining self-control even when *nahwa* (on a *miraa*-induced high) and not openly indulging in alcohol, cannabis, Valium or heroin to counter the stimulant effects of *miraa*. Many Swahili women chew, although mostly at home. A *miraa* wholesaler in Malindi commented that most of his customers from other cultural groups were men, but among the Swahili women outnumbered men as consumers.[6] *Miraa* consumption is not viewed as status-enhancing for women and the practice lacks respectability. In addition, there is also an association made by men of immorality and a lack of sexual restraint among female chewers. Women khat consumers are thus held to be largely responsible for upholding the morality of the entire community.

While Yemeni migrants played a pioneering role in establishing khat use in Kenya, the strongest association today is between khat and the Somali community, and in particular those working in road haulage as contractors and drivers. Many of these people are descendants of Somalis from British Somaliland who served in the King's African Rifles. Once discharged from the army the men were free to settle in Kenya. Many sent for their families from home. These families are the core of the urban Somali presence. According to Goldsmith (1997: 472), they are 'thoroughly Kenyanized despite the strength of their own culture'. The origins of this group of Somalis lie in former British Somaliland, the area far to the north of Mogadishu that in the 1990s formed the breakaway state of Somaliland. Kenya also has a large population of Somalis living in North Eastern Province. This vast, semi-arid area is the home of Somali pastoralists, but also one of five regions (along with Somalia, Somaliland, Djibouti and Ogaden) claimed by some Somalis as part of the Greater Somali State.[7]

The five-pointed star on the flag of Somalia unites Somalis scattered across east Africa and beyond, but the clan system divides communities. Somali society is made up of clans with rights over certain territory. This system served the needs of rural pastoralist existence, but in recent decades the clan affiliation has been associated more with warfare than with the maintenance of order. Civil war in Somalia led to the collapse of the state in 1991 and the flight of an estimated 800,000 refugees into Kenya. Some found shelter with kin or fellow clan members, while others were housed in refugee camps. Since the early 1990s, Somali refugees have settled in significant numbers in Mombasa Old Town, in Eastleigh, Nairobi and in other towns across the country. Some refugees have prospered and have become wealthy businessmen, but thousands of Somalis remain in refugee camps in the North Eastern Province. Hence, regardless of clan affiliation or current circumstances, khat consumption by Somalis in Kenya has increased in the last decade, causing concern among government officials and development agencies.

Since the war of the early 1990s, sensational media publicity has linked khat consumption to aggression and warfare (Goldsmith 1997; Randall 1993). Yet there is no evidence suggesting that khat chewing makes people aggressive. Somalis throughout Kenya chew at home and in the huts, reed shelters and shops of the retailers. In Eastleigh, Nairobi, which has a predominantly Somali population as well as numerous lodgings catering for Somali visitors, there are more than 300 *miraa* shops/kiosks operating between 12th Street and 14th Street. According to Somali observers, much khat chewing in Eastleigh takes place in lodgings where men bring *miraa* to consume with resident sex workers. Other chewers consume at home, while wealthy consumers send their drivers to Meru suppliers to pick up their orders of high-quality khat.

Consumers in the rural north-east may occasionally find it more difficult to purchase khat on a daily basis. For example, about one hour's drive north from Garissa there are three ethnic Somali Administration Police who have come to a roadside tea stall to purchase *miraa* that has been dropped off from a passing bus earlier that morning.[8] As one enters the straw structure, two Somali women are selling tea and the new supplies of *gisa* and *laare* (or *marduf*) types. The Policemen explain that it was their first chew in three days and they are not planning to wait until after lunch. According to them they suffered a lot of cravings during the past days, and one man describes how he had felt lethargic and as if he could not wake up. In this small roadside village the five women selling *miraa* achieve a combined daily turnover of fifty *kilos*. The customers are local men who come in from their settlements in the bush to purchase khat and other essential commodities. The male chewers said it was '*eib*' (shameful) for women to chew and that this only happened in places like Garissa. In another tea stall a soldier, a Kenyan ethnic Somali, said that it was not correct for women to chew as they were responsible for children's welfare and that if men gave women money they could not spend it on enjoying themselves.

Somali khat chewers, be they in Nairobi or miles from the nearest town in a roadside hut, use certain accompaniments to increase the enjoyment of khat chewing. They drink tea or soda, but scorn the use of Big G to the extent that it is not easily available in North Eastern Kenya. However, some consumers add one or two peanuts with the shell removed to their *miraa* wad to make it softer and to remove the bitterness.

Khat use is also very common in the refugee camps such as Ifo, two hours' drive east of Garissa near the Somali border. Many of the younger residents have lived all or most of their lives here and an air of hopelessness hangs over the place. One popular venue for the youth is a large stick-walled teahouse with local Ethiopian artwork pinned on the flimsy walls. In the teahouse there sit about thirty young men of Ethiopian, Somali and southern Sudanese origin chewing khat. These young men were chewing as they sat on wooden benches lining the walls, and many also were drinking sweet, black tea (Soda, as fizzy drinks are known in Kenya, is too expensive for these refugee chewers). There was no Big G available, but many of them used peanuts which were on sale. One man was seated in the corner selling the cheap khat variety, *marduf*. A couple of young men – a Somali and an Ethiopian – explained how there was nothing to do and how chewing was the main pastime in the camps.[9] They and others in the camps talked about a sense of hopelessness and fading hope of escape. Relatives send remittance money from London and Toronto, and much of this was spent on khat or other substances. It was clear that stimulant use was a major pastime and a form of self-medication: cannabis use was reported to be high; discarded plastic vodka sachets littered the floors of a nearby kiosk; and the market had many pharmacies for those seeking to acquire pills and potions.

The Distribution System: Cooperation and Competition

Kenyan *miraa* reaches consumers all over the country and as far as Europe and North America. The distribution system depends on personal contacts and a high degree of trust between agents, wholesalers and retailers. One of the many paradoxes of the *miraa* trade in Kenya is that although many observers are concerned about ethnic tensions between Meru and Somali khat traders, the industry actually depends on cordial business relationships that transcend ethnicity (Carrier 2003). There have been demonstrations and violence raising tensions between the two groups; however, the smooth running of the distribution system depends on good social relationships, and these are the norm rather than the exception. Consumers in all corners of the country, almost without exception, get fresh supplies of miraa daily. This movement of khat from tree to consumer is effected by men and women from different ethnic and cultural backgrounds, and is usually orderly and peaceful. The efficiency of the distribution system should be the envy of all transporters and business people, and serve as a model for distributing vaccines or medical supplies. Nevertheless, competition is fierce in this largely unregulated, dynamic industry; some of the disputes do take on an ethnic dimension, but this is not an uncommon situation in Kenya.

Meeting Somali Demand: Domestic Markets

As Eastleigh in Nairobi has grown over the past decade into a Somali enclave and a major commercial centre, so has the retail trade in khat developed into a fully fledged industry. More than 300 shops/kiosks selling khat between 12th and 13th Streets in the heart of Eastleigh are supplied via the Majengo wholesale market. The retail outlets are run by Somali and Meru traders and sell many different types of khat from Nyambene, but predominantly *kangeta, gisa* and *allele.* Recently, new competition has sprung up on the pavement in the form of about ten young Embu men selling a rival type of khat, *makokaa.* However, these Embu traders say that most of their customers are non-Somali consumers.[10]

Although the khat trade is highly concentrated and therefore visible in Eastleigh, khat is marketed all over Kenya in very varied settings, both rural and urban. Kenyan khat consumers live in towns and isolated villages, remote islands and refugee camps. Supplies reach these areas on a daily basis with hardly a hitch. Somalis are the most enthusiastic consumers, but all ethnic groups and social classes use khat. This remarkable marketing and distribution system works by linking retailers to wholesaler to agents to producers. Cash changes hand as khat moves throughout Kenya in a marketing system that is based on personal contacts and trust. Meru retailers dominate the trade in many areas, from Lamu to Nairobi, but are far from having a monopoly over distribution. Somalis, who already control the European export market, are vying to be major players in the domestic miraa trade.

Tens of thousands of people live in Ifo camp, with similar numbers occupying two nearby camps. The camp has the character of a town of semi-rural compounds and densely packed market areas. Mainly Somali but also Sudanese and Ethiopian refugees live in Ifo where the only industry appears to be collecting firewood and small-scale livestock keeping. Many people survive on UNHCR allowances and remittance money from relatives who have escaped the harsh and hopeless environment of the camps. Others do manage to travel outside the camps and engage in business. Indeed, the camp markets bustle with consumers buying goods brought in from Somalia, with Dubai being the main source of supplies.

In Ifo and other camps Somali traders enjoy a monopoly in the khat trade. Khat is retailed daily in the busy market of Ifo by between 50 and 100 Somali women and men, refugees of the camp. The *miraa* arrives by bus in Ifo and the other camps, having been repacked in Garissa. The banana-leaf packaging of the Meru farmers has been removed and the *miraa* subdivided into smaller portions (*durba*) for those who cannot afford a full or half *kilo* portion, and repacked into sacks each containing twenty-five *kilos*. In Bosnia, the main market in Ifo, Mishal, a member of the Association of Divorced Women (a self-help group), a Somali woman, sells daily about fifty *kilos* of a cheap variety of *miraa* known as *marduf*, or *laare* after the Nyambene village of Laare where it is grown. Mishal and other members of the Association order *miraa* from a Somali woman in Garissa, the nearest town. Mishal would like direct contact with Meru agents, but this is not easy to arrange as she, like most camp inhabitants, has no Kenyan identity card and is therefore not permitted to enter Kenya.[11]

On its way to Ifo, the bus carrying *miraa* passes through the small market town of Dadaab and offloads supplies. Dadaab is inhabited almost entirely by Somalis, and dominated by the UNHCR camp. The *miraa* arrives on the bus from Garissa during the late morning and is rushed straight to retailers operating from up to 100 huts run by women selling tea and *miraa* in the town centre. Two types of khat are delivered to Dadaab: *gisa*, which retails at about KSh300 (US$4) per *kilo*; and *marduf* much cheaper at KSh100 (US$1.30) a *kilo*. A woman trader explained that she had an agent in Garissa to whom she sent daily orders, but that she had no control over how many *kilos* were sent. She might ask for fifty *kilos* and receive twenty.[12]

When the buses leave for Ifo or other destinations they drop off supplies along the way. In a typical stick-walled hut in a small village on the road from Garissa to Dadaab, women were selling tea and miraa to travellers. Typically woman retailers sell low-grade *marduf* for KSh100 (US$1.30), making a profit of about KSh20 per *kilo*. In one small village on the way to Dadaab, five women were selling about fifty *kilos* of *miraa* per day to men who come to sell livestock and to soldiers manning the local outpost. Miraa selling is associated by Somalis both male and female with women being forced to support themselves in an undesirable way that sometimes overlaps with sex work.

Garissa

The bus supplying Ifo starts its journey in the large town of Garissa. Early in the morning about 300 women wait in central Garissa for the daily *miraa* supply that comes overnight by road from Maua, the main centre of the khat trade in the Nyambene Hills. Two customized Land Cruisers and one pick-up truck arrive amid the waiting crowds. The drivers, paid a premium for speedy delivery, have made the journey fuelled by black coffee and *miraa*. The vehicles are so heavily laden that the sacks tied with rope form precarious heaps. One of the Land Cruisers is owned by a powerful clan-based women's group. Within half an hour about 400 sacks of *miraa* are offloaded into the care of male Somali clerks, who record the volume supplied and supervise distribution to the assembled groups and individuals who had made orders. About half the *miraa* arriving in Garissa is sent on to Ifo and the other refugee camps. The clerks have prepaid the tax to the local municipal council the night before. Meru and Somali agents in Maua direct supply to customers using a simple and effective labelling system. Cash is sent back the next day carried by the drivers of the vehicles transporting the supplies. Unsold stock is sometimes returned, the losses sustained by the supplier. However, stock can only be returned two or three times before the retailer runs into problems with the supplier.

In Garissa, Somali women who constitute about 90 per cent of the retailers dominate the *miraa* trade. These female traders have a little more control over their supplies than their sisters operating in Ifo. Yet, even in Garissa most women *miraa* traders make little profit and are rarely in the business out of choice. Of the hundreds of women who await daily supplies of *miraa*, some have agents in Maua with whom they deal directly. Those who do not have regular suppliers buy supplies from wholesalers on the spot in Garissa. Most women sell about ten *kilos* a day, making a profit of KSh100 (US$1.30). Many of them are in the *miraa* trade because it does not require capital for start-up, as credit is extended for the 24-hour period between receiving the supply and paying for the stock purchased.[13] Most of the *miraa* sold in Garissa is *marduf*, woody, leafy twigs bound by a twig and sold in bunches, not subdivided into *durba*, for KSh50 to KSh100 depending on freshness and the bargaining powers of customers. Typically these women describe themselves as widows, although many are probably divorcees. They also sell tea and coffee, and some may also sell sex. Most of the women said that they would prefer to sell milk or vegetables, and appeared to be effectively trapped in the business, as they were in a cycle of paying for the supplier after selling the *miraa*. While some of the traders are members of women's groups that assist in the wholesale purchase of *miraa*, most of these associations appear small and ineffectual. The women's group controlling the *miraa* transportation is an exception, and poor women spoke of their organization being a closed group for the rich. There are other exceptions: one successful woman trader has been in the business for many years and has a Meru supplier in Nyambene. She sells, mostly by special order, about forty *kilos* a day of expensive high-quality *kangeta* and *gisa* types of *miraa*.[14] In addition to the Somali women traders, there are perhaps thirty Meru men selling *miraa* from kiosks and shops in Garissa. They are supplied with *miraa* by the same vehicles as the Somali traders.

Speeding Northwards: Fly and Drive

Driving north from Garissa, travellers enter the vast, flat arid heartland of North Eastern Province, another of the five areas making up greater Somalia. There are no paved roads in this part of Kenya and little industry apart from animal husbandry. The vast majority of people living here are ethnic Somalis, many of whom have little sense of being Kenyan, so that it is common to refer to people going to or coming from 'Kenya'. *Miraa* arrives daily from Meru by road and by air and is distributed by hundreds of Somali traders and two Meru retailers.

It is early in the morning in the town of Wajir, about eight hour's drive north of Garissa. In the market area, most of the estimated 800 women who retail *miraa* in Wajir wait. At 7.00 am, two laden pick-ups arrive and the waiting women rush forward. The sacks are unloaded into a small stick enclosure in front of a shop. The men inside the enclosure distribute the sacks to the waiting wholesalers and retailers – women mostly. Some of the sacks are opened immediately, while others are loaded onto donkey carts and driven off. Each sack is marked with a name in felt-tip pen. One wholesaler reckons that there are 160 sacks on the first pick-up, each sack containing thirty-two *kilos*. As two pick-ups arrived, it means that about 10,240 *kilos* are delivered to Wajir every morning.

During 2004, tensions among *miraa* traders and the local authorities were running high. Traders asserted that the District Commissioner was in league with a wealthy *miraa* distributor who controlled Bluebird Aviation and wanted to fly *miraa* into Wajir, and thus monopolize supply. Two Hilux pick-ups loaded with *miraa* from Meru had been impounded and the stock destroyed as it was left in the hot sun. Road transportation of *miraa* to Wajir enabled hundreds of people, Somali and Meru alike, to get a slice of the business. However, in more distant Mandera, a trading and administrative centre, which has borders with both Ethiopia and Somalia, khat is flown in daily on charted flights from Wilson Airport in Nairobi without incident or tension.[15]

The Mandera-based Dawa River Women's Group receives *miraa* on Mondays and Fridays, and on the other five days a man from Garissa, of the Somali Ogadeni clan who now lives in Nairobi, monopolizes the male share of the wholesale trade. The Dawa River Women's Group was formed in 1990 and has 240 members. Each pays KSh1,000 membership. There are four Somali clans groups in Mandera: Garre, Dogodira, Morali and Korna, all of which are represented by the female membership of the group. In addition, four Meru men are group members. According to the Chairman and Treasurer of the Dawa River Women's Group in Mandera, 1,250 retailers sell an average of eight to sixteen *kilos* per day. On Mondays and Fridays retailers purchase their stock from the group. Transportation of *miraa* by road from Maua costs KSh120,000 ($923.00) per vehicle, a sum that includes the rent of the car including wages of drivers, insurances and other expenses. The cess tax is paid on the way at Maili Tatu (just outside Maua in the Nyambene Hills), at the tiny village of Garbatula and then at Wajir. The plane costs KSh200,000 for the return flight to Wilson Airport in Nairobi. The plane arrives fully loaded with *miraa*, but returns with twenty passengers, each paying KSh5,000 which goes to the Group. Unlike the majority of poverty-stricken retailers, the Dawa River Women's Group has been very successful and has diversified into retailing, tailoring, shop rental, cattle and textiles.[16]

Flights to Mandera arrive at 9.00 am at the airstrip on the edge of town. Those meeting the flight have their papers and any travel documents checked by Kenyan Army guards and then drive past a dugout manned by soldiers armed with machine-guns. About ten vehicles, about half with Somali licence plates, are parked next to the tarmac. *Miraa* agents and travellers who have booked a flight on the plane that arrives packed with *miraa* and returns with a human cargo wait. The Bluebird plane, resplendent in red and blue livery with 'Allah' in Arabic written on the tail, arrives at 9.45 am. The incoming sacks are offloaded within about ten minutes and put in two piles for collection by members of the Dawa River Women's Group. Each agent receives about sixty sacks, an estimated total of 3,840 *kilos*, and supervises loading into ancient Land Rovers. Five sacks of unsold *miraa* are loaded onto the plane to be sent back to Nairobi and the passengers board the plane without fuss or searches. The Land Rovers pass through the security checkpoints without delay or incident and speed off to the distribution point near the town centre. There the sacks are offloaded into fenced-off areas for immediate distribution to wholesalers and retailers, in a scene similar to that observed in Wajir and earlier in Garissa. This air-freighted *miraa* will be supplemented by about 220 sacks due to arrive by road later in the day. The supply consists of *marduf* retailing at about KSh200 a *kilo* (double the price charged in Garissa).[17] Therefore the total supply arriving in Mandera in a day is an estimated 10,880 *kilos*.

Women such as Yasmin in Eastleigh and the Dawa Women's Group in Mandera have played a significant role in developing the industry. At the other end of the traders' hierarchy, small-scale women rely on the system of remitting money from sales after receipt of the stock. They scrape a living from *miraa*, although many of these women say they would prefer to work in another trade. Meanwhile, many Kenyans, including local leaders such as the elders of Lamu, deplore the spread of *miraa* chewing and point to dire consequences. *Miraa* is blamed for a dizzying array of ills by these detractors: the spread of the HIV virus; divorce and the breakdown of family life; underdevelopment in North Eastern Province; the neglect of children; loose morality among women; alcoholism and the abuse of all other drugs; crime and violence. This is surely gross exaggeration! Although *miraa* consumption does have some negative effects, *miraa* appears to be used as a scapegoat for the social, economic and actual ills of Kenya.

–7–

On the Khat Frontier
Uganda

The distribution of wild khat throughout much of the upland regions of eastern Africa has been well known since early colonial times. Supplies of khat from the Chyulu Hills, from Mount Elgon and Uganda's western highlands, and from the barren northern regions would sometimes be brought to the roadside by enterprising locals hoping to catch the passing trade, or taken speculatively to a town market to make a few extra shillings. Even in the late nineteenth century, wild khat was harvested to supply the porters who carried bundles of trade goods from the eastern African coast to the shores of Lake Victoria, this before the railway was constructed and long before motor transportation was introduced. This scattered, seasonal and opportunistic exploitation of wild khat has seemed unimportant when compared to the large-scale commercial production that later developed in the Nyambene Hills of Kenya: But the relative 'invisibility' of wild khat in the market has disguised its increasing significance as khat consumption has spread to other parts of eastern Africa over the past three decades. This chapter looks at the emergence of newer sites of commercial production and consumption within eastern Africa, to illustrate the ways in which local and regional markets, and not only the global market for khat, have expanded. As with other recent examples of the expansion of khat consumption, migration, mobility and transportation are key elements in this story of khat's new frontiers in eastern Africa.

Uganda's 'New' Producers

It is not only in Kenya and Ethiopia that new production areas have been springing up over recent years. Throughout much of the twentieth century farmers in neighbouring Uganda have been planting and harvesting khat, sometimes in areas where tea and coffee have since the early twentieth century been the dominant cash crops, but also in more remote regions where subsistence farming predominated. However, unlike the Nyambene Hills in Kenya, there is no Ugandan area of production that pre-dates the twentieth century nor ethnic group associated with ritual consumption. In Uganda a new khat market developed initially from the harvesting of wild khat, and with the adoption of domestic production is rapidly becoming an increasingly profitable industry. Ugandan producers supply a growing band of local consumers, and they have also found a small but keen export market to the south in Rwanda, where there is also now a fledgling local production. Not everyone welcomes the apparent success of this new market, however, and Uganda has been influenced by debates elsewhere over the possible prohibition of khat. There are rumours that the government might pass legislation to ban khat production and consumption, although it is not at all clear how this would be brought about in a country where the plant grows wild over many areas. Current global debates about the effects of khat have followed the stimulant even to its new frontiers of expansion.

Interviews with khat producers, distributors and consumers in Uganda, carried out between August 2004 and March 2005 and covering ten different sites where khat is grown, reveal the historical and contemporary role that migrants have played in the expansion of khat. Small-scale migration from Yemen to East Africa has been occurring for centuries (Bennett 1986), while Somali men began to settle in large and small towns across Uganda from the 1920s. It is said that these migrants showed local people how to harvest wild khat, and in some areas they became involved in the cultivation of khat plantations. As Muslims, Yemenis and Somalis appear to have associated primarily with fellow Muslims, often African business or trading associates who had converted to Islam, as well as, in the Yemeni case, local African Muslim families from whom brides were taken. Consequently, there is a very strong association in Uganda between Islam and khat.

But there are contradictions and paradoxes concerning the adoption of khat chewing in Uganda. The centuries-old association of northern Yemenis with khat is well known, as is the popularity of chewing in the bustling city port of Aden. However, most of the Yemeni migrants to Uganda came from the rural Hadramawt region in the south of the country. Here the tradition of khat chewing is far less strong than in the north. Indeed, Boxberger's (2002) study of south Yemen and the history of emigration from the area since the nineteenth century makes no mention whatsoever of khat. It would appear that patterns of consumption have altered in the Yemeni diaspora in eastern Africa, and that all migrants, whether from northern or southern Yemen, have taken to khat chewing.

In every area of eastern Africa beyond the Nyambene Hills, khat chewing is strongly associated with migrant communities, almost becoming itself a mark of identity. Stories of the origins of khat chewing invariably emphasize the 'alien' character of the habit. It seems most likely, for example, that it is the Yemeni diaspora that is responsible for the diffusion of the many 'happy-goat' stories that circulate in the khat consumption areas of eastern Africa, and that are so commonly present as an explanation of how the stimulant effects of khat leaves came to be known (Goldsmith 1994; Varisco 2004). One version of this story tells of a Yemeni boy watching over his herd on a hillside, when he notices that the goats have become very lively. Investigating the cause of the excitement, he discovers that the voracious animals have been nibbling at the leaves of a khat bush. In other versions of this ubiquitous tale, 'happy sheep' replace the goats, and 'Ethiopian herders' (meaning anyone from the far north) play a role in showing local farmers how to use the plant. In Uganda, the Yemeni version now competes with a newer variant that reflects more current patterns of migration. This tale relates the discovery of the properties of khat to Somali herders, who then brought knowledge of the plant with them from their native Somalia as they spread through the region. The idea that Somalis discovered khat chewing and that it is indigenous to their country has almost certainly gained credence in Uganda only since the early 1990s, when increasing numbers of Somalis made there way into the Great Lakes region in the wake of the implosion of the Somali state (Adam and Ford 1997). But although Somalis are a distinctive, visible and highly mobile consumption group within Uganda, and are therefore as easily associated with the plant as were Yemenis in an earlier time, many different ethnic groups in fact have a hand in the production, distribution and consumption of khat in the country. Even if everyone is quick to pay homage to the Yemeni and Somali pioneers who were responsible for bringing khat into their lives, in Uganda the 'flower of paradise' is no longer confined solely to these migrant communities.

Let us consider the example of Robert, a farmer of the Chigga ethnic group living in the remote mountains near the provincial town of Kabale, in south-west Uganda. Robert moved into khat production as a consequence of his dealings with a Yemeni businessman. Back in 1986, Robert used to bring gifts of wild khat leaves, plucked from the hillsides near his home, to an Arab shopkeeper in Kabale whom he had befriended.[1] Until getting to know the shopkeeper, Robert had not understood the properties of khat, although it grows wild throughout this highland district. Glimpsing the possibilities of a little extra cash, Robert began harvesting wild khat on a more regular and systematic basis to supply other consumers in the town of Kabale. In the mid-1990s, following the Rwanda genocide, Kabale enjoyed a boom period, becoming a major centre for the international aid and other commercial assistance flowing south into Rwanda. Workers and temporary migrants from all over eastern Africa came to Kabale, increasing the khat market. Robert recalls that the next stage in the development of his khat business came when a locally based business man of Yemeni heritage, named Ali, asked Robert to supply the seedlings which he might plant to grow khat on a larger scale. This gave Robert the idea to start his own plantation. For the past several years he has managed a plot of around fifty trees. In the excellent growing conditions around Kabale, he can harvest monthly or even weekly, depending upon the season and the rainfall. And he now has a good, steady market for his crop. Not surprisingly, other local farmers have begun to follow his example, and Robert reckons that there are about fifteen people who now harvest from wild khat trees. All of these producers bring the leaves to Kabale, but they have not tried to find other markets. According to Robert, the wild khat fetches the same market price as the cultivated khat and local consumers seem unconcerned by the difference and do not ask for any particular type. In Kabale a large banana leaf-package of about 15 by 15 cm, known as a *fross*, sells for around

USh1,000 – an equivalent to approximately £0.30. Kabale's khat farmers will not make a fortune from this trade, but it brings a significant income for negligible investment and without any risk.

Small plantations such as Robert's are now to be found all over Uganda, from the arid north bordering Sudan to the gorilla country of the forested south-west on the borders of Rwanda and the Democratic Republic of Congo. In some areas, particularly around Fort Portal in the west and near the capital, Kampala, there are larger plantations serving a growing number of domestic consumers. Small-scale exports to Tanzania, Rwanda and DR Congo have even begun in areas close to the most rapid and busiest transport routes (Carrier 2005). Compared with the situation in Ethiopia (Gebissa 2004) and Kenya (Carrier 2003), khat is not yet economically important here, but it has established a secure and steadily growing market – as one discovers during travels to visit Uganda's new khat producers.

Khat has long been known to grow wild in the eastern part of Uganda, especially on the slopes of Mount Elgon. The mountain straddles the Kenya/Uganda border, towering over the small provincial town of Mbale. On the Kenyan side of the mountain wild khat flourishes, but it is on the Ugandan side where local farmers have begun to prosper from the cultivation of the plant. Shaban, a middle-aged Muslim Bukusu man, is typical of the local farmers who have taken up khat production. Shaban sits in the company of a group of traders on the street in Mbale town. The traders were selling bundles of *zakariah*, a locally grown variety of khat harvested wild from the mountain.[2] Shaban has come to town to retail his own khat crop, and once he has sold his stock he travels into the foothills of Mount Elgon and then climbs on foot up a steep hillside path. The appearance of the crops and vegetation in this landscape is similar to that in the Nyambene Hills, and we saw many small homesteads growing coffee and a profusion of food crops. The people passing by appear poor, but well nourished. This is an area where food supplies are relatively secure, and khat represents an easy and low-risk cash crop. According to Shaban, many farmers on this part of Mount Elgon now cultivate up to fifty khat trees on their farms. The plantation owned by Shaban and his brother is substantial, with trees as tall as four metres grouped among other species on the steep hillside close by their homesteads. Shaban explains that the original plants were propagated from local wild trees. Although everyone here acknowledges that Nyambene-grown khat is stronger than the local type and preferable to consumers, no one seems to have thought about bringing seedlings or cuttings from Meru to Elgon. Shaban's trees are regularly sprayed with chemicals to keep the pests down, but he is careful to harvest only after rain washes off the chemicals. In this area all the farmers do the harvesting themselves and take their *zakariah* to town to sell. Shaban explains to us that the name *zakariah* came from the first Elgon farmer who began growing khat commercially. No one seems quite certain whether Zakariah is dead or still alive, but khat has been harvested here and sold in Mbale town for perhaps the past fifty years or so.

But not all farmers on Mount Elgon are making a success of khat cultivation, as a traveller sees while driving to the area of Bubulo close to the Kenya border. Local men are sitting on benches looking at the view and drinking, while the women appear to be doing all the work in the fields nearby. The men with time on their hands are happy to talk to us about khat, leaving the women to their labours. One farmer explains that the Bukusu people here are a mixture of Christian and Muslim. Many are really Kenyans, but they crossed the border into Uganda forty years ago at the time of independence because they thought Ugandan rule might be more beneficial. Here, khat cultivation seems less established: for example one farm has six khat trees, planted only two years before, and other trees that have died in drought or been eaten by pests. The farmers of Bubulo seem not to know how to maintain the trees. They use chicken droppings as fertilizer, but do not spray to keep the pests down. The khat seedlings they have used were bought from the big farmers locally, but the price was low and the quality seems not to have been good. There are three more established and wealthier khat farmers living in this area, and two of them are said to be sons of the Zakariah[3] who first plucked the wild khat and brought it to Mbale market. Times have changed here now, and men come up from Mbale to harvest the crop, paying the farmers a fee. The payment varies according to the quality of the trees and the bargaining powers of the parties involved: Last time the harvesters paid only USh500 for the whole crop on one farm – approximately £0.18. With *zakariah* fetching USh500 a handful in Mbale town, it seems perverse that these farmers should accept so low a value for their crop. They explain that the men who harvest their crop have issued threats to prevent them selling their crop directly to the retailers in town. Even when the sums of money are so small, vested interest still pervades the khat market.

Despite the abundance of wild khat here, there is no tradition of cultivation or consumption on this part of Mount Elgon. But in recent years local consumption has begun, and some now estimate that one in ten men here is a khat chewer.[4] The habit has not been taken up by women, though, nor by youths, and there is no sense that khat is likely to be a vehicle for agrarian change in these parts. The farmers of Bubulo were prouder of their carrot crop, and keen to explain that they are enthusiastic members of a Christian NGO dealing with agricultural extension. It seems that on this part of the mountain, carrots, not khat, are the future.

Driving north from Mbale, the traveller enters very different terrain. Dramatic mountains appear, the vegetation changes to grassland and savannah and very few people are to be seen. Along the dirt road government army posts appear at regular intervals. The soldiers patrol the area to guard against the activities of bandits, local armed pastoralist raiders and the remnant troops of the war continuing in northern Uganda (Hansen and Twaddle 1988; Keitetsi 2004). In this harsh environment, wild khat thrives on the mountainsides. Several varieties of khat are known to the local inhabitants, each with its own distinctive quality and taste. Informants in the town of Moroto[5] listed the types of khat sold there: *Nakapiripirit*, from Nakapiripirit

Mountain; *Namalu*, from Namalu Mountain; *Lotunuk* khat, from the Amudat/ Komaret area; *Chakdum Massawa* khat, from the Sudanese borderlands; *Tima*, from Morugole mountain in northern Karamajong; and *Hirihiri* khat, from the Hirihiri Mountain, to the west of Moroto on the road to Soroti.

These areas are all inaccessible, and sometimes dangerous to visitors and potential khat traders alike. Mahmoud Abdi Jama, a local Somali khat agent, who has lived in Moroto all his life,[6] told us about *Lotunuk* khat from Amudat, along the Kenya border. He explained that the Pokot people living at the bottom of the mountain do not grow or consume khat, but that the Kadama people who live at the top of the mountain are keen cultivators, growing quantities of tobacco as well as khat on their farms. The Kadama farmers are avid chewers of khat, selling only some of the crop to traders such as Mahmoud. Not all khat production from this region is intended for the market, making it difficult to assess the full extent of consumption.

Mahmoud guides us to a safer and more accessible area, Nakapiripirit, about two hours south from Moroto. Along the dirt road, through largely unpopulated savannah scrub, Mahmoud nervously points out the army posts that guard the road every 30 km, and shows the sites where missionaries had been killed by local Karamajong raiders. There is a government campaign to disarm the Karamajong and prevent them from raiding the cattle of their enemies, mostly the Pokot across the border in Kenya (Knighton 2003). Insecurity makes this area difficult for traders such as Mahmoud and acts as a brake on the development of the khat market. Nakapiripirit is a small trading post and government centre, where itinerant traders gather at the Bamburi Hotel, a café run by a Kenyan of Oromo and Somali descent who had studied at the Riyadha Mosque in Lamu.[7] Khat is brought down from the nearby mountains and sold to Mahmoud and other traders outside the café. According to Mahmoud, the market in these areas is supplied by maybe 500 khat growers and harvesters, but there is little evidence of a vibrant economy: There is no khat for sale at the Bamburi Hotel, although we soon encounter a man and a boy carrying khat fresh from the Nakapiripirit mountain. The man, Lobalu, is an elderly Sudanese and his companion, Kosike, a young Karamajong. Before descending from the mountain, Lobalu and Kosike had tied the freshly harvested khat into small bundles (*durba*) and wrapped them with grass. Mahmoud bargains briefly and buys their stock for USh1,000 per bundle, the dry-season In the rainy season, when supply greatly increases, the price here falls to USh500 per bundle.

At Namalu, thirty minutes to the south, it is market day and the atmosphere is quite different. Hundreds of Karamajong by the roadside trade livestock, clothes, food, even vehicles. Mahmoud describes Namalu as a 'khat factory' in the rainy season, but there was no sign of khat trading in Namalu on this market day, although we eventually came across one farmer with a stock of leaves for sale. This khat, like virtually all the produce coming from the Namalu area, was harvested wild, although even here a few farmers have begun to cultivate commercially. One farmer, named Lopilipili, cultivated about thirty khat bushes from seedlings taken from the mountain and planted five years ago.[8] Lopilipili was enthusiastic about his plantation, but he did not use fertilizers or pesticides and he was keen for advice about the mould that was apparent on the leaves of his khat bushes.

In the remote regions of Mount Elgon and the north-east it is evident that the khat market is fragile. Hindered by insecurity and underdeveloped infrastructure, traders can negotiate advantageous prices, and so the benefits to farmers vary considerably from place to place and over the seasons. Nearer to Uganda's larger centres of population, where there are many more accessible consumers, the growth of the khat economy has had a more obviously dramatic impact. Around Kampala, Uganda's capital city, production has been expanding since the 1970s and has really boomed more recently. Kasenge, about half an hour's drive from the city centre, is one of the centres of khat production. This fertile area is characterized by rolling green hills covered with banana stands. The local Baganda farmers here, a mixture of Muslims and Christians, estimate that there are about 500 farms producing *kasenge* khat.[9] The conditions are so good for growing khat here that it takes only two years from planting the seedlings to harvesting the leaves. Typically, farmers in Kasenge can afford to use pesticides and then wait two weeks, or for the first heavy rainfall, before harvesting. Kasenge is a major growing area, sending supplies to the khat markets of Kampala.

Farmers in Kasenge obtained their khat seedlings from Sheikh Semakula of Kabasanda in Mpigi District, a forested area about 50 km to the south-west of Kampala that has recently become wealthy through khat production. Sheikh Semakula's prosperous home is reached down a narrow winding lane that leads off the main dirt road. The houses making up the homestead are substantial, surrounded by mature khat trees extending for many acres. There is a mixture of mature trees and recently planted stock, all well kept and closely cropped. This is clearly a well established and carefully managed business. In the rainy season, Sheikh Semakula sells thirty small banana-leaf packages (*fross*) daily, and even in the dry season he harvests four times a week.[10] At this time Semakula has to drive away customers because there is always a shortage of khat in the dry season and supplies are in high demand. It is not surprising, therefore, that his neighbours have followed Semakula's lead over recent years, and khat farms are springing up all over the area. With increasing supply, *Kabasanda* is now a recognized brand name in the Kampala khat market.

The seedlings from Sheikh Semakula and Kabasanda have travelled another 100 km or so further west to the area of Kiti, near the town of Masaka. Here Semakula's son, Sheikh Yusuf, has pioneered the cultivation of high-quality khat. The area is flat farmland, and although the Baganda farmers here are a mixture of Christian and Muslim, it is notable that all the khat farmers are Muslim and were described by people in the area as 'sheikhs'.[11] Yusuf had been farming khat here for perhaps thirty years, and it was clear that all of the family were involved in the cultivation and marketing of the crop. Some 1,000 khat trees stand on Yusuf's land, being regularly sprayed and generally well cared for.[12] Although the original seedlings for this plantation came from Sheikh Semakula in Kabasanda, the Kiti khat trees look completely different, being tall and thin and very dry in appearance. They produce small, very tender leaves that also command high prices in the Kampala market.

To the other side of Kampala city, in the east toward the industrial town of Jinja, khat seedlings are also being cultivated in numerous farms within the Mabira Forest. This area consists of dense forest with homesteads carved out of the undergrowth. According to Umaru Sendi,[13] a young khat agent who inherited a khat plantation here from his father, these farmers were granted rights to live in the forest in 1954, though they did not begin to cultivate khat until the 1970s. Umaru reckons that there are perhaps 100 khat farms in the area, all with hundreds of trees. Khat in Mabira is harvested by the farmers themselves, packed on the farms and then sent by public transport to Jinja, the nearest large town. Umaru's uncle Kizito[14] claims to be the descendant of the first person in the forest to cultivate khat. Kizito explained how his father, a Muslim who spoke good Swahili, became friendly with people of Yemeni origin who introduced him to the idea of khat cultivation in 1975. From small beginnings, the farm is now devoted to the commercial farming of khat. The trees here are pruned to prevent them becoming too tall to harvest easily, and chemicals are used to keep down pests. This farm produces two types of khat, *mabira* and *kasenge*, the latter reputedly being of a higher grade, although it is not easy to discern one type from the other. This is a successful and very stable business, benefiting from the economic recovery of Jinja and its expanding population.

In the western parts of Uganda, too, khat production has become an important element in the rural cash economy. The Toro kingdom, with its capital Fort Portal, lies toward the border with the Democratic Republic of Congo. Tea and sugarcane are the main cash crops here, but khat cultivation has a long history and is now spreading. The first farmer to grow khat around Fort Portal was a Muslim Mtoro called Byarufu.[15] A local policeman, and then District Khadi (the equivalent of a magistrate in the local Muslim court), Byarufu spent his working life among the Muslim migrants employed by the colonial government in this district, many of whom are likely to have been khat chewers, and started his plantation in the 1930s. Since 1990, following Byarufu's death, his son has run the farm. Some four acres of khat grows here, pruned and maintained like tea bushes. Specialized pickers are engaged to harvest the crop on all the farms in this area, being paid directly by the farmer for their labour. There are about 300 khat farms around Fort Portal, most being smallholdings on which khat provides an important source of cash income. The trade here is brisk and busy. Agents travel daily to the farms where khat is bought at small roadside depots. Four types of khat are produced on these farms: *Bysangu*, *bode*, *kamtebe* and top-quality *byarufu* – named for the founding-father of Fort Portal's khat growers. Some of the supplies are then retailed nearby in Fort Portal and Kasese, but the agents who visit the farmers also dispatch khat by minibus and public taxis to towns all over western Uganda, the eastern DR Congo and north-western Tanzania. The trade is clearly lucrative, and the bigger khat farmers here are prosperous. Informants relate how Byarufu and several other farmers visited President Museveni in 1989, to request that khat not be made illegal.[16] Museveni is said to have agreed to this, but only on condition that Byarufu and other large-scale khat farmers share the seedlings so that many others could benefit from production of the cash crop. The story may be apocryphal, but it reflects the importance attached to the crop by its leading farmers and the extent of their anxieties about a possible ban.

Aside from these centres of khat production, where individual landholders have planted stands of 100 or more trees to supply established urban markets, throughout Uganda farmers are experimenting with khat production on their smallholdings. The scale of this production is of course small, and its longer-term impact is difficult to judge, yet the number of farmers prepared to try out the plant suggests that khat growing in Uganda is far from its peak.

Much of this isolated, small-scale production follows the transport routes that flow across Uganda, linking it to Congo in the west and Rwanda in the south-west. These busy arteries carry the trucks that traverse the African continent, bringing goods to remote towns and villages. In this region many are driven by khat-chewing Somalis, Ethiopians and Swahili-speakers from the eastern African coast. These men provide a market for khat. An example of a very small producer who has capitalized upon the opportunities this presents is Bright, a farmer from Kegezi village, just outside the town of Kisoro on the border with DR Congo and Rwanda.[17] Bright is an active member of a local micro-credit group, and is enthusiastic to find ways to make his farming more profitable. He has a khat plantation of about forty trees, located on the steep mountainside above his home. Bright explains that his relative, Richard, a policeman, taught him that he could do good business by cultivating *enebwe*, as khat is know around Kisoro. He uses insecticide on the trees, harvesting every second or third day. But it is apparent that Bright simply tears the leaves from the trees, and is unaware of the best methods of harvesting and pruning that would greatly improve yields. Nevertheless, he still makes a handsome profit from his khat: Kisoro sits astride the main route into the Congo, and Bright finds a ready market for his khat in the town or even at the roadside as the Somali drivers roll by in their heavy trucks. For Bright, this involves no dealings with middlemen or other traders: Khat means easy money.

Hidden Retailing

The distribution of khat throughout Uganda operates on the basis of personal contacts and trust. A well-organized and highly adaptive marketing and distribution system brings supplies from local farms and mountainsides to the main retail centres of Kampala, Jinja, and the towns of the west. For the most part, this distribution network is efficient but fragmented. While a few bigger harvesters, traders and retailers undoubtedly make a very good living from the crop, for the majority of those involved the profits are relatively small. Khat is not a crop easily associated with huge wealth, then, and its traders and retailers must also operate in the face of opposition to khat consumption by many local authorities. This factor significantly shapes the way that khat is marketed in Uganda,. The illegality of khat in Tanzania is well known, as are international concerns prompted by the American banning of khat imports. Rumours of an imminent ban of khat exports to Europe from neighbouring Kenya over the past three years have made Uganda's major producers edgy about the future. Although the stimulant remains a legal commodity, a new law has been proposed that would restrict production and trade. This bill has not been ratified by the Ugandan parliament, but the continuing uncertainty causes anxiety to those involved in the khat industry and has provided opportunities for some unscrupulous policemen to exploit the vulnerability of those involved in the khat business by harassing them – principally to extort bribes or to gain favours of other kinds from traders and retailers. However, in this atmosphere of uncertainty some local government officials are genuinely concerned about the possible effects of chewing khat on the local youth. Using their local powers, they have taken measures to try to reduce or stop khat consumption in their municipal domains. For all these reasons, the retailing of khat in Uganda is cloaked in a veil of secrecy, retailers being willing to sell the commodity but seldom prepared to display it openly.

Visitors to Uganda may easily be completely unaware that khat is on sale in almost every town. Unlike in Ethiopia and Kenya (Carrier 2003), where a banana-leaf 'flag' is hung from the entrance of a retailing establishment to advertise the availability of khat, in Uganda the banana-leaf insignia indicates only local beer for sale. Khat consumers here must ask around to find what they want, although at any truck stop, bus station or market it seldom takes long to locate the right retailers. Uganda's khat-sellers operate from every conceivable type of outlet – pavement stalls, kiosks, roadside shacks, the forecourts of petrol stations and bus depots, shops in more prestigious areas of town, and even from the porches of private homes. Even in those towns where the local municipal council has sought to outlaw the retailing of khat, there is still a good supply of khat varieties. Let us take the example of Kabale, a town in south-west Uganda.

A Chigga farmer named Robert planted khat and supplies Kabale retailers with his crop. Robert explained that the Kabale Town Council had turned against khat in 2003, claiming that it had bad effects on local youths. In the past consumption had been confined to 'respectable businessmen', said Robert, but young men have more recently taken to chewing and they have given a bad reputation to khat. A prominent Kabale politician of Yemeni descent shed further light on the municipal politics of khat.[18] A successful entrepreneur, with many business interests in the area, Ali has some khat trees on his own land and gives regular supplies to young men in Kabale who are his political supporters. According to Ali, the trouble with Kabale's youth is that they often mix khat with cannabis and alcohol. When this makes them boisterous and rowdy, people blame the resultant behaviour on the khat. In Kabale, it seems that khat is viewed as being 'worse' than cannabis, the consumption of which has long been very widespread in this area. As in Kenya and Ethiopia, local Ugandan discourses on drugs do not treat khat in a uniform or coherent way (Beckerleg 2006).

Despite the official concerns about khat consumption in Kabale, the commodity is still being sold in the town market by two retailers. Fred's stall was in the main vegetable market, but he kept the khat in a cupboard under a counter displaying large cabbages. He has traded in khat in this market for more than five years, and before that the trade had been run by a woman vendor.[19] Though he sees nothing wrong in the trade, Fred does not like the effects of khat and is not a chewer. He receives his supplies from four agents, who variously bring locally harvested wild khat, cultivated varieties from nearby plantations, including Robert's farm, and khat brought by bus from Fort Portal. Kabale's second khat retailer, Moses, whose vegetable stall is on the edge of town, began selling as a mobile hawker a few years ago.[20] His supplies now come from Kasenge, near Kampala. Moses has fifteen regular customers who buy *kasenge* each day. When the weather is dry and the price rises he sells a little more, because cheaper local supplies are not available and more chewers switch to imported *kasenge*. The price of all wholesale supplies fluctuates depending on rainfall and supply. Fred boasts a larger base of around 100 customers, the majority of whom are Muslim and male, including the Somali and Ethiopian drivers, trucking en route to Rwanda and DR Congo, who are among his very best customers. According to Fred, the government has decided that 'khat is bad'. He has been harassed by Kabale's police, and it is because of this that he keeps his stock under cover. On one occasion the local police arrested Fred, and his customers paid the money that was needed to extricate him from the cells. Fred seemed to accept that this harassment was a necessary corollary of trading in khat.

It is not only in Kabale that khat is sold under cover of foodstuffs. In the small town of Rukungiri, north of Kabale, khat from Kasenge was on sale in a butchery. Meat and offal was displayed prominently on the counter, behind which was a large black plastic bag full of *kasenge* khat from Kampala. Five men – the butcher, the khat seller and three others – sat at the back of the butchery enjoying bunches of the *kasenge*. To the south-west, in Kisoro, the main khat retailer is named Salim, a second-generation Yemeni who was born in the town.[21] Salim runs a video shop and general store, selling khat that comes in by bus from Kampala. His wife Fatuma, also Yemeni by descent, works in the shop with him. On the Sunday afternoon, a video shop is packed with male youth watching African pop videos and waiting for the main feature to begin. Salim says that he usually receives ten to fifteen bundles of *kasenge* from Kampala daily, and remits the money the second day, following the procedures that are common across Uganda and Kenya (Carrier 2003). Sometimes he receives less than he asked for. Demand here seems pretty steady. He has about twenty regular customers who are all local people. In addition to supplies from Kampala, locals bring him wild-harvested khat and the one man, Bright, who has started farming khat locally also sometimes brings him bundles of leaves. Bright and other local harvesters also sell khat privately in the town. As in Kabale, there is a fashion here among youths for mixing khat with alcohol and cannabis and, according to Salim, this has raised opposition to his business. The municipal authorities here have told Salim not to sell khat after 9.30 pm, in an effort to reduce the negative impact upon the town's youngsters.

Travelling east from Kisoro, heading toward Kampala, the traveller comes to the large town of Mbarara. *Kasenge* is retailed here at the bus station, from a cardboard box on the verandah of a parade of small shops, but most of the khat available in Mbarara is of the *byarufu* type that grows near Fort Portal. *Byarufu* is wholesaled in the courtyard of a private house in the middle of town, from where several local retailers collect their supplies each afternoon. *Byarufu* sells here for USh3,000 (just under £1) a banana-leaf *fross* (package), but *kasenge* is cheaper. According to one veteran Mbarara retailer,[22] concern about khat consumption began under the Museveni government in the late 1980s, heralding the start of police harassment of khat retailers. By 'squeezing' khat dealers and consumers, the police have greatly reduced the profitability of the Mbarara trade. Things are quite different in Masaka, the next big town as one heads east on the road to Kampala. Khat is sold openly on a street corner in the central business district here, and young men were to be seen selling khat in a shop doorway, and others in the shade of a tree on a traffic island. The khat sold here included a range of varieties from the vicinity of Kampala – *shikio, kasenge* and *kiboko*. Further out of town, *kiti* khat was on sale outside a row of shops on a busy highway frequented by truckers. In contrast with Mbarara, the khat trade in Masaka is conducted openly and without fear of police harassment.

In the east of the country, khat retailing centres on Mbale. Khat reaching Mbale from the remote farms of north-eastern Uganda arrives by bus via the market at Moroto. Mahmoud Abdi Jamaa, the Somali encountered earlier in this chapter, is typical of the khat agents operating in the north-east production areas from Moroto. Mahmoud travels around this district buying khat directly from the farmers or the harvesters. Prices are generally low, and quality is variable. Mahmoud and other agents buy the lower-quality varieties at around USh300 a bundle in the dry season. This khat, much of it *namala*, has variations in length and colour, and there does not appear to be any uniform size of the packages, but it is all sold on to the wholesalers in Mbale at USh500 (approx. £0.20) per *durba*. Better-quality *Hirihiri* khat reaches the retail market at double this price in the dry season.[23] In the wet season, when supply increases, the prices fall by around 50 per cent. Traders such as Mahmoud buy cheaply, but must work hard for their profit when sending supplies on to Mbale.

Harassment of the khat trade is also evident on the eastern side of the country. In Mbale, khat retailing is concentrated along one side of a main street and outside the Taufiq Hotel, an old Yemeni-owned establishment. When supplies are abundant, as many as 40 retailers gather here, but in the dry season there might be a few as four or five. Weekends and afternoons are the busiest period. Sales are from boxes and plastic bags on the pavement. Most traders also sell the 'paraphernalia' that so often accompanies khat consumption: cigarettes, Big G chewing gum, peanuts and the white root used as a chewing stick, *mrondo*. Most of the retailers are male Bukusu, and many are Muslim. However, the biggest khat retailer among them is a Muslim woman of Baluchi (South Asian) descent. Known locally as Mama Mbale, this trader has been in the business about six years, selling a wide range of khat varieties on the pavement outside the Taufiq Hotel. Her product range provides an excellent sample of the types of khat grown and sold within southern and eastern Uganda: *Mbira*, from near Jinja; *Kabasanda* or *utambala*, *Kasenge*, and *Shiko*, all from the vicinity of Kampala; *Namala* and *Hirihiri*, brought from Moroto market; and the local Mbale varieties of *Zakariah* and *Mrita*. *Kasenge* is of course the most expensive variety on sale here, and the poor-quality *Namala* is the cheapest.[24] At the time of our visit, in late August 2004, Mama Mbale's trade was a little slow. Young male customers purchase the bunches of leaves of the cheaper variety for UShs500 (£0.20) a handful, many also buying Big G chewing gum imported from Kenya and retailing at USh50. Mama Mbale buys her supplies from four different agents, paying up front for all varieties (apart from *kasenge*, which is paid the following day). The khat arrives in public transport minibuses. Aside from the bribes that must be occasionally paid to the police, the khat business in Mbale appears to be doing very well.

Uganda's largest retail khat market is in Kampala. Chewers can buy from pavement stalls and kiosks in Kisenyi, Mengo, Arua Park and a host of other discreet outlets scattered across the capital. In Kisenyi, the sprawling slum area in downtown Kampala where the metal recyclers are concentrated, khat consumption and trade is centred on some scruffy shops and cafés opposite the Nakivubo Stadium. From mid-morning each day scores of retailers do a flourishing trade in *kasenge* and *kabasanda*, both produced close to the city. Around half the retailers are women, and the vast majority Muslim, although they represent a wide range of ethnic groups. Up the road in Mengo, a predominantly Somali area, the same Ugandan varieties are offered alongside imported *kangeta* from Meru. The premium regional brand, *kangeta* retails at several times the price of local supplies but demand is nonetheless strong. At Arua Park, a group of fewer than a dozen traders sell from plots around the lorry park and bus station. The chewers here are predominantly urban manual workers and travellers about to board buses for the north. They tend to buy the cheaper varieties here, but in other parts of the city premium brands have found a niche market among wealthier consumers. One, called *kasuja*, is grown and marketed by a single farmer, who harvests a small section of his plantation each day, ensuring a regular but limited supply. The *kasuja* leaves are wrapped in neat banana-leaf packages which the farmer then signs, effectively creating a unique and much prized brand. There are said to be four other suppliers selling 'branded' khat to the Kampala market in this way. In August 2004, a small package of *kasuja* was retailed at USh1,000 (approximately £0.30), a mark-up of about 100 per cent compared with that for the cheaper *kasenge* or *kabasanda* varieties.

Uganda's khat industry as yet lacks the infrastructure of its Kenyan and Ethiopian counterparts (Carrier 2005b; Gebissa 2004), and although some wholesalers move the crop from the farm to market themselves, the majority of dealers depend upon an elaborate system of public buses and minicabs to get their daily supplies to consumers. The proximity of some key growing areas to Kampala eases the transport problems, but there is still a scramble among buyers each day to secure the best supplies. The furthest that Kampala's wholesalers travel in search of supplies is Kiti, near the town of Masaka. Here they can purchase Uganda's premium brand, the high quality *kiti* khat, but relatively small quantities are brought into the city. Kabasanda, some 50 km to the west of the city, is a more significant area in terms of the quantity of khat reaching Kampala. Buyers come from the city in minibuses and travel around the farms buying khat here by the *fross*, but there is no centralized system here for bulking the supply. Kasenge, only 30 minutes' drive from Kampala, sends supplies into the city every morning, and here the trade is both more intense and more highly organized. The *fross* are first taken to roadside bulking areas to await collection by local buyers. Arriving on foot and by moped at these muddy roadside stops, these buyers deal directly with the farmers, bargaining over the price of each *fross*. Having made a purchase, some of the buyers head straight back to Kampala, by moped or by public transport; but most go to the central wholesale depot on the main road to Kampala. At the depot the local buyers sell on the khat to wholesalers. As many as 500 buyers use the Kasenge depot each day. From here, khat is dispatched on public transport not only to Kampala, but also to other Ugandan towns and even into Rwanda.[25]

Outside Kampala itself, Jinja is the home of Uganda's most highly organized khat market. Jinja is a charming town of slightly faded colonial grandeur, perched on the banks of the Nile close to the river's source at its estuary with the great lake. Once the industrial capital of East Africa, Jinja's predominantly art-deco centre of colonial bungalows and municipal buildings has undergone a renaissance since the early 1990s. Many Asians, expelled in the early 1970s under Idi Amin's tyranny, have returned to contribute to the urban rejuvenation. Jinja's discreet but busy khat market is located close to the main bus station. Opposite a petrol station, a Somali-owned depot, known locally as Master Coffee, is the hub of khat distribution and retailing for Jinja and the surrounding districts. From mid-morning each day the large black plastic bags (*fross*) filled with khat begin to arrive at Master Coffee from the farms of the Mabira Forest. Prices are strong here, with a wholesale *fross* costing USh10,000 (approximately £3.20), this being divided into units of USh1,000 value and sold in small clear-plastic bags or wrapped in banana leaves.[26] Some *mabira* goes to the east to Mbale and small towns along the way, but never westward to Kampala, while *zakariah* khat from Mbale seems never to reach Jinja. The two main types of khat on sale in Jinja are *mabira* and the superior *kasenge*. Chewers often sit at the stalls consuming their khat at the point of sale, within easy reach of Big G, cigarettes and coffee that are also sold by the retailers. Most of the customers are young Ugandan African men, with a smattering of 'Arabs' and ethnic Somalis.

The khat traders in Jinja have formed a trade association to represent their interests. Only members are allowed a pitch at the market around the bus station. Membership costs USh15,000 (approximately £5), but in addition payments of USh10,000 a month are made to a welfare fund, which acts as a revolving credit fund as well as providing money for members' funeral and hospital expenses. The formidable Mama Fatouma is the association Chairman. The widow of Kenyan Somali origin from the Garre clan near El Waq in north-eastern Kenya, Mama Fatouma has lived in Uganda for 30 years and has long been a prominent khat trader. Although most farmers from Mabira bring khat directly to Master Coffee, Mama Fatouma was responsible for the introduction of an innovation: she rents the khat crop from the farmer for a fixed period of one month per contract, and arranges for its regular harvest.[27] Among the Jinja traders, some are keen to explore the possibilities of developing an export trade to Europe, following the example of khat traders in Kenya and Ethiopia.

Uganda's present export markets are only regional, and small-scale. Smuggled khat finds its way into Tanzania, and since the mid-1990s there has been legal trade into both Congo and Rwanda. There is no legislation concerning khat in Rwanda. Supplies of *kasenge* are taken across the border each day bound for consumers in Kigali. These goods may be subject to customs duty, but the decision is only made upon the whim of the Rwandan Customs officials. They are of course aware of the ambiguity surrounding khat in Uganda, and this makes the traders both nervous and vulnerable. The leading cross-border trader, a prosperous Ugandan woman named Salima, told us that the officials of the Rwandan Revenue Authority regularly seize her supplies.[28] Salima deals in bundles of *Kasenge* khat purchased in Uganda for around USh1,000 (approximately £0.30). For the Rwanda trade, these are packed in plastic bags (*kavera*), 100 being moved in each consignment, taken across the border by couriers using public buses. In Rwanda, each *kavera* sells for Rwanda Francs 270, representing a mark-up of nearly three times.

With a small but strong local market around Kigali, it is not surprising that cultivation of the crop has also begun in Rwanda. Although production is still very limited, it is likely to increase in scale fairly rapidly. As well as supplying local chewers, some khat growers here have been motivated by the incentive to smuggle the crop across the border into neighbouring Tanzania, where the stimulant has been banned by the government. At Rohanga, on the Tanzanian border some two hours' drive east of Kigali, there are half a dozen large plantations serving the illegal Tanzanian market. One of the farmers here, a Muslim named Rajab,[29] showed us a farm of up to 400 low bushes scattered across a steep hillside and intercropped with banana plants and other food crops. The trees appeared to be no more than 10 years old. Only the day before our visit these bushes had been harvested and the produce smuggled into Tanzania, in heavily loaded pick-up trucks rushing along the back roads to avoid border checks and Customs officers. Rwanda's khat economy is as yet embryonic, but with local consumers, a flourishing itinerant market, and the incentive of a regional black market to supply, the signs are that it will soon grow. Khat is finding even newer frontiers in East Africa.

Surveying Consumption

Who chews khat in Uganda? The public perception of consumers identifies khat with poorer, lower-class people, and the long-distance drivers, a labour group especially associated with the spread of khat chewing around the country. But how accurate is this public perception? Direct observation of chewers in urban Kampala immediately suggests a wider and more varied consumer base. The groups of men and women who gather to chew together in the shops and alleyways of Kisenyi include prosperous businessmen, struggling young male wage labourers, and female sex workers. These diverse citizens rest companionably on makeshift benches, chewing khat while sipping sodas, smoking or drinking coffee. They tell each other tales, discuss politics or the events of the moment, or sit in quiet contemplation. A range of khat is available to them, mostly *kasenge* and *kabasanda*, but also the premium brands, including the prized *kasuja*. The usual accompaniments that make consumption more enjoyable are all readily available to them – bottled water, soda, cigarettes, coffee, Big G chewing gum. There is a rhythm to these and all chewing sessions that is dictated by the effects of the khat (Kennedy 1987). In Kisenyi, chewers use the same accompaniments as are common among Kenyan consumers and, as in Kenya, the ritual aspects of consumption here lack the depth that they have acquired in Ethiopia and Yemen (Gebissa 2004; Varisco 2004). These Kampala chewers have developed a sense of identity as khat consumers and refer to themselves as *magatna*. However, their language also points to connections with older cultures of khat consumption. The usual verb used in Kampala, and across Uganda, to refer to chewing points to the Yemeni connection: the word *khazan* means literally 'to store', and is the usual term for khat chewing in Yemen.

Khat is sold and consumed openly in Kisenyi and in other districts of Kampala. Periodic debates in newspapers and among politicians and policy-makers about the possible prohibition of khat causes them little apparent concern. Since 1994, *The New Vision*, a pro-government newspaper, has run several features that portray khat as a harmful narcotic and have highlighted the ambiguous nature of international legislation concerning the production, sale and consumption of khat. Khat is not under the control of the Uganda Drugs Authority, but is classified under the International Control Section of the 1993 Amendment of the relevant Ugandan statute.[30] While there is no Ugandan statute dealing directly with khat as a domestic product, the uncertainty about the international status of the plant is real enough. The theme has been taken up by local academics, writing a report about khat consumption in three

Ugandan towns. These authors directed attention to the contradictory reports in the Ugandan press:

> At present there appears to be no clear indication of the legal status of khat in Uganda. According to Mutali [*The Monitor*, 3 August 2001], khat usage is illegal in Uganda while Kimani [*The East African*, 15–21 April 2002] reported that it is legal in both Kenya and Uganda. Uncertainty was experienced in the course of data collection as an air of apprehension was visible during the request for consent from respondents. (Ihunwo et al., 2004: 472)

This ambiguity has caused a good deal of public confusion: some chewers and sellers across the country believe that khat is illegal because their local municipal authorities treat it as if it were, while public anxieties associate khat's youthful chewers with images of criminality and social disorder. These concerns make it more difficult to obtain a clear picture of who consumes khat in Uganda.

If we first try to trace the emerging pattern of consumption over time, it seems clear enough that while khat seems to be gaining in popularity it is by no means an entirely new phenomenon in Uganda. The British colonial authorities produced a comprehensive inventory of *The Indigenous Trees of the Uganda Protectorate* (Eggeling 1951), which states that *Catha edulis* was known to grow wild in Uganda and that its timber was good for cabinetmaking. Among the list of local names provided for *Catha edulis* is 'Somali tea' (ibid.: 78), but despite this clue the author writes only that 'The leaves are chewed as a stimulant by the natives of some African countries (but not apparently in Uganda). Too much has an intoxicating effect, finally causing coma and death' (ibid.: 79). Hence, only fifty years ago local consumption of khat in Uganda remained unrecognized and the reported effects were being confused with those of a central-nervous-system depressant. Colonial knowledge of khat was sparse, to say the least.

Discussions with elderly Somalis and Yemenis resident in Uganda make it clear that these migrant groups introduced domestic production across Uganda during the earlier part of the twentieth century, and that consumption had already started to spread by the time the British were cataloguing Ugandan khat as 'Somali tea'. Khat consumption is of course an important expression of the national and ethnic identities among Yemeni and Somali communities in Uganda. For Yemenis in particular, khat consumption has been an important part of daily life for hundreds of years and its use follows set rituals of consumption (Varisco 2004; Weir 1985). Emigration from Hadhramawt and north Yemen to eastern Africa has been occurring for centuries, and was particularly widespread in the first half of the twentieth century. Men typically came alone, succeeded in setting up small retail businesses and married local women (Boxberger 2002). The Somali case is somewhat different. The first Somali settlers in Uganda came from Somaliland – a historic centre of khat consumption – during the period it was under British rule. Many of these early Somali settlers were former colonial militia, having served in the King's African Rifles or in the police. Upon discharge from service, these men were free to settle anywhere in British East Africa. Many selected Uganda, then bringing their wives and setting up businesses in the transport and catering sectors.

Due to these numbers of Yemeni and Somali migrants, khat production was evident in Uganda by the 1930s. Production and consumption both increased in the 1970s, when chewing first began to spread well beyond the original Yemeni and Somali consumers and into non-Muslim groups. Numerous elderly informants confirm that at this time the vast majority of consumers were respectable businessmen, but the most recent surge in the popularity of chewing has seen the habit being taken up by younger consumers. Khat has become something of a youth fashion in Uganda, and as a consequence it is no longer perceived as respectable. A similar process has occurred in Kenya, and has been documented by Carrier (2005), where khat's associations with poverty and disorder are especially strong (Anderson and Carrier, 2006). In Kampala and the larger towns of Uganda, video shows, where most young people pay a small fee to view action movies on TV screens in makeshift cinemas, are a favourite venue for youthful chewers. It is common to find khat being retailed from premises adjacent to the video stores, as is the case in the town of Mubende in central Uganda.[31] Having been directed to a hut just off the main road in Mubende, several young men were chewing *shikio* khat from clear-plastic bags, with Big G as an accompaniment. A teenager attending the video show, the son of a local khat farmer, had brought the *shikio* to town in a cardboard box for the night's entertainment. He was selling measures at USh500 and USh1,000. The film on show was a popular kung-fu classic.

The youthful character of khat consumption in Uganda is to be seen everywhere. In Bugemebe, a suburb of Jinja town, a pool hall is frequented by male youths.[32] Squeezed into a tiny kiosk selling sweets and khat, and with pungent incense burning, we found a retailer and two of his customers, both workers on public-transport taxis, who were sitting on the floor chewing the khat they had recently purchased. One of these young men, named Ronald, had been chewing for about ten years, having been introduced to khat by his brother. In turn, Ronald had introduced his fellow chewer to the habit about four years ago. Like many others in the pool hall, they now chew daily after work.

Besides the video show and the poolroom, entrepreneurial youth are developing other settings for chewing that are similar to the *mafrish* of London. In Mpugwe, just outside the town of Masaka, local youthful chewers meet in a backroom in a modest residential home, where fresh *kiti* wrapped in banana leaves was available.[33] The room was a sort of clubhouse for chewers, equipped with easy chairs, soda, Big G and thermos flasks. Most customers here, including a few girls, bought the *kiti* for use on the premises and also purchased various accompaniments. In Uganda, as elsewhere, khat chewers have evolved their own distinctive cultures of consumption.

Despite the spreading of consumption to urban youth of all religions and ethnicities, Uganda khat chewers are still thought to be predominantly Muslim and it is certainly the case that a majority of producers are Islamic. Though Muslim producers are happy enough to sell khat, they often express considerable doubts as to the benefits of consumption, and will freely discuss the religious ambiguities surrounding consumption. One of the pioneering growers of *kiti* khat is Sheikh Yusuf, a former Chief Mufti of Uganda. According to Yusuf Kator,[34] Uganda's Muslim Council has never issued a decree on khat consumption. His personal opinion is that khat is *makaruu* – neither *halal* (permitted) nor fully *haram* (forbidden). While Sheikh Yusuf discussed with us the status of khat within Islam, his young male relatives chewed as they listened to our conversation. Another local Muslim scholar explained *makaruu* as something that is not particularly bad in moderation, but if used in excess becomes *haram*. This view was reflected by several other Muslim scholars encountered in different parts of Uganda, all gently disapproving of khat consumption, but stopping short of condemning it outright. They have a more benign attitude than the Muslim leaders of Lamu in Kenya (Beckerleg 2006), who have forcefully declared khat *haram* and a modern scourge. In East Africa, as in Yemen, where the debate has been conducted over many centuries, there is no unequivocal verdict on the permissibility of chewing within Islam (Kennedy 1987; Varisco 2004).

In researching patterns of khat consumption in Uganda we have located only one previous consumer survey, a study of a sample of 181 university students, law-enforcement officers and road transporters carried out by a team from Mbarara University of Science and Technology in south-western Uganda. Some 20.4% of this sample admitted to being current khat users (Ihunwo et al. 2004: 468). These current chewers were concentrated among the law-enforcement officers, 96.8% of whom reported using khat at the time of interview (ibid.: 470). While the popularity of khat chewing among the police reported in this study is striking, a larger survey carried out as part of the research for this book has revealed a much wider spread of occupations among Uganda's khat consumers.

Our study, conducted between October and December 2004, surveyed a sample of 300 khat consumers. The results provide valuable additional data on the type of people who chew in Uganda, their chewing behaviour and their attitudes toward khat. Interviewers[35] were trained to administer a brief questionnaire to khat users as they chewed in meeting places, homes and businesses around Kampala and other major towns (primarily Kasese and Fort Portal) in the extreme west of Uganda.[36]

Of the sample, 166 respondents came from Kampala and 134 respondents from the west. Although convenience sampling was employed and the results are not therefore in statistical terms a fully representative sample, the demographic profile of the respondents points to khat consumption being an activity pursued by a wide range of people across Uganda. Hence, the respondents were almost equally divided in terms of religion: 52% of respondents were Muslim and 43% were Christian, while the remainder reported that they had no religion or were pagan. Of the respondents, 50% were aged 18–29 while (apart from one 74-year-old) the remaining 50% were aged between 30 and 50 years. The respondents also included both relatively recent as well as long-term chewers: 47% of respondents reported chewing for between one and seven years, while 53% said they had chewed for the past eight to thirty years. These figures alone clearly indicate that Ugandan khat consumption is not merely a recent activity taken up by male youth. Indeed, about three quarters of the respondents were women, and just over half of both male and female respondents were married (see Tables 7.1 and 7.2).

The respondents had a wide range of occupations and were drawn from many varied sectors of society. However, hawkers and transport workers account for about one-third of the consumers interviewed. In research conducted in neighbouring Kenya, Carrier (2005) found that, in addition to long-distance drivers, '*matatu*' transport workers, who run vehicles on the commuter routes into Nairobi, were enthusiastic khat users. Khat chewing is an activity that could provide useful stimulation for those who are walking long distances selling their wares, as well as for drivers. It is also notable that teachers and civil servants make up 5.4% of the khat chewers in the sample (see Table 7.3).

Table 7.1 Gender of Survey Respondents

Gender	Frequency	Percentage
Male	227	75.7
Female	72	24.0
No data	1	0.3
Total	300	100.0

Source: Uganda khat consumers survey, October–December 2004.

Table 7.2 Marital Status of Male and Female Survey Respondents

Marital Status	Sex		Total
	Male	Female	
Widowed	8	3	11
Divorced	15	6	21
Married	114	40	154
Single	90	22	112
Total	227	71	298

Source: Uganda khat consumers survey, October–December 2004.

Table 7.3 Reported Occupation of Survey Respondents

Occupation	Number	Percentage
Hawker	59	19.7
Transport	47	15.7
Trade/repair	34	11.3
Retailer	32	10.7
None	18	6.0
Driver	18	6.0
Teacher	14	4.7
Farmer	11	3.7
House wife	6	2.0
Cleaner/service	6	2.0
Schooling	5	1.7
Watchman	5	1.7
Sex worker	5	1.7
Labourer	5	1.7
Porter	4	1.3
Conman/smuggler	4	1.3
Bar worker	4	1.3
Car washer	4	1.3
Self employed	3	1.0
Musician/DJ/video	3	1.0
Fisherman	3	1.0
Pimp	2	0.7
Civil servant	2	0.7
Gardener	2	0.7
Vacation	1	0.3
Army	1	0.3
Engineer	1	0.3
Trade	1	0.3
Total	300	100.0

Source: Uganda khat consumers survey, October–December 2004.

As well as being a varied group in terms of occupation, the respondents were even more diverse in terms of their ethnic and national affiliations. A total of 288 respondents reported their ethnic group or nationality. The foreigners sampled included nine citizens of the Democratic Republic of Congo, a Tanzanian, a Burundian and a German national. The six Rwandese respondents may very well be Ugandan citizens long settled in the country (Keitetsi 2004; Taylor 1999), and the Rwandans are anyway counted as an ethnic group in Uganda. However, the data on ethnic group show that the biggest groups of chewers are the peoples for whom Kampala and the west are their home areas. Kampala is the capital of the Buganda kingdom (Fallers 1964) and, although a multi-ethnic city, has a high concentration

Table 7.4 Ethnic Group/Nationality of Respondents

Ethnic Group/Nationality	Frequency	Percentage	Cumulative Percentage
Mganda	59	19.7	19.7
Toro	39	13.0	32.7
Konjo	30	10.0	42.7
Arab	25	8.3	51.0
Ankole	17	5.7	56.7
Somali	15	5.0	61.7
Nubi	14	4.7	66.3
Musoga	13	4.3	70.7
No response	12	4.0	74.6
Congo	9	3.0	77.6
Lugbara	8	2.7	80.3
Mchiga	8	2.7	83.0
Aringa	7	2.3	85.3
Rwandese	6	2.0	87.3
Munyoro	5	1.7	89.0
Mixed race	4	1.3	90.3
Mugisu	4	1.3	91.6
Munyalunguru	3	1.0	92.6
Acholi	2	0.7	93.3
Masai	2	0.7	94.0
Madi	2	0.7	94.6
Musongora	2	0.7	95.3
German	1	0.3	95.6
Kikayo	1	0.3	96.0
Aluru	1	0.3	96.3
Lugwala	1	0.3	96.6
Teso	1	0.3	97.0
Tanzanian	1	0.3	97.3
Swahili	1	0.3	97.6
Singapore origin	1	0.3	98.0
Nyawenda	1	0.3	98.3
Musharahisu	1	0.3	98.6
Murundi	1	0.3	99.0
Mugweri	1	0.3	99.3
Mokuga	1	0.3	99.7
Mugano	1	0.3	100.0
Total	300	100.0	

Source: Uganda khat consumers survey, October–December 2004.

of Baganda people. In the west, the Bakonjo are concentrated around Kasese, while Fort Portal is the capital of the Toro kingdom (Stacey, 2003) (see Table 7.4).

The survey results reveal differences between patterns of consumption. In Kampala, there are a larger number of weekend chewers, while in the west a larger proportion of respondents reported chewing daily. However, bigger spenders are more likely to live in Kampala (see Figures 7.1 and 7.2).

When khat expenditure is analysed in relation to gender, the data show that women spend less on khat than men do. For men, expenditure of USh3,000 (approx. £1) is the most common outlay, while for women expenditure of only USh1,000 is more common (see Figure 7.3).

Consumers were also found to spend significant amounts of money on the accompaniments to khat chewing, such as cigarettes, sodas, coffee, bottled water, Big G chewing gum and peanuts. This pattern is familiar from other locations, including Kenya (Beckerleg and Sheekh 2005), Yemen (Meneley 1996), Ethiopia (Gebissa 2004) and London (Carrier 2005). The Uganda data show that women spend significantly less on extras when compared to male chewers. This is probably a simple function of relative spending power, rather than indicating preference or taste (see Figure 7.4).

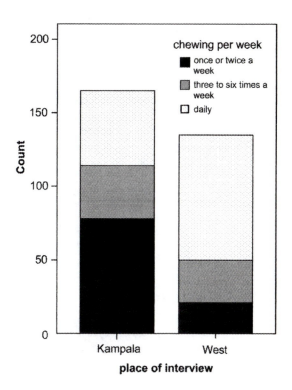

Figure 7.1 Frequency of khat chewing in the last week as reported by residence. *Source*: Uganda khat consumers survey, October–December 2004.

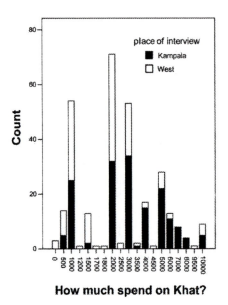

Figure 7.2 Amount spent on khat on day of interview according to area of residence. *Source*: Uganda khat consumers survey, October–December 2004.

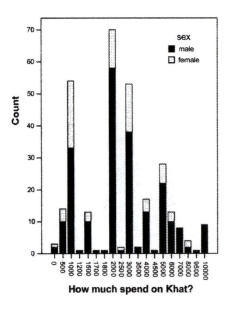

Figure 7.3 Amount spent on khat on day of interview according to gender. *Source*: Uganda khat consumers survey, October–December 2004.

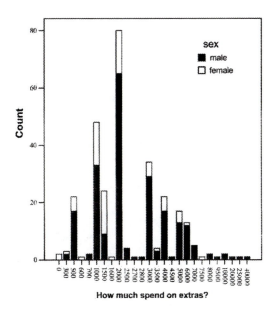

Figure 7.4 Amount spent on extras on day of interview according to gender. *Source*: Uganda khat consumers survey, October–December 2004.

In addition to questions concerning expenditure and frequency of chewing, respondents were asked what they did while they were chewing. This open-ended question elicited a wide range of responses (set out in Table 7.5). Many chewers reported carrying on with work whilst chewing, but the majority pursued a range of leisure activities, from 'nothing' to watching TV and reading.

There was an even wider range of responses to the question 'What do you do after chewing?' These have been grouped together to reveal patterns of work and leisure activity during the post-chewing period. Although some respondents mentioned going to a nightclub and drinking beer, and others said they drank alone at home, all responses including mention of alcoholic consumption have been included in the category, 'drink alcohol' in order to highlight the link between khat chewing and alcohol consumption. As there was no specific question concerning the use of other substances, the number of respondents drinking alcohol may be considerably higher (see Table 7.6).

Respondents were asked a number of questions about what they thought about the effects of khat chewing. The results show the responses of male and female chewers, although there is no great gender-based difference in attitude to chewing. As with nearly every aspect of khat consumption, the responses illustrate uncertainty and doubt concerning the activity in which they were engaged at the time of being questioned. Hence, while many respondents refuted the assertion that 'khat is bad

Table 7.5 Reported Activity of Respondents while Chewing Khat

Activity while Chewing	Number	Percentage	Cumulative Percentage
Work	52	17.3	17.3
TV video	50	16.7	34.0
Business	45	15.0	49.0
Nothing	20	6.7	55.7
Reading	19	6.3	62.0
Chatting with friends	18	6.0	68.0
Doing accounts	14	4.7	72.7
Doing revision	13	4.3	77.0
Driving	12	4.0	81.0
Listening to music/radio	9	3.0	84.0
Playing cards/games	9	3.0	87.0
Gambling	6	2.0	89.0
No data	5	1.7	90.7
Relaxing	4	1.3	92.0
Bicycle riding	4	1.3	93.3
Housework	4	1.3	94.7
Drinking alcohol	3	1.0	95.7
Playing pool	3	1.0	96.7
Cooking	2	0.7	97.3
Walking about town	1	0.3	97.7
Politicking and doing business strategies	1	0.3	98.0
Jogging	1	0.3	98.3
Braiding hair	1	0.3	98.7
Reciting the holy Koran	1	0.3	99.0
Travelling	1	0.3	99.3
Writing novels	1	0.3	99.7
Doing preparation	1	0.3	100.0
Total	300	100.0	

Source: Uganda khat consumers survey, October–December 2004.

for health', more were uncertain about the effect of health on chewers. The majority of respondents, however, did not agree with the statement 'khat should be banned' (see Figures 7.5 and 7.6).

As khat production across Uganda expands to keep pace with growing consumer demand, doubts and controversies abound. Some consumers are not sure if khat is a legal substance or not and some even report that it should be banned. In the west of the country the police harass the industry, pushing traders and consumers underground. Rumours of a possible government ban add to the uncertainties, while municipal controls on khat sales in some towns further confuses the picture. Yet there is little

Table 7.6 Reported Activities of Respondents after Chewing Khat

Activity after Chewing	Number	Percentage	Cumulative Percentage
Drinking alcohol	67	22.3	22.3
Doing accounts	34	11.3	33.7
Working	19	6.3	40.0
Clubbing	18	6.0	46.0
Preparing for today and tomorrow	17	5.7	51.7
Relax/rest/leisure/home	17	5.7	57.3
Listening to music/radio	15	5.0	62.3
TV video	15	5.0	67.3
Nothing	15	5.0	72.3
Sleeping	9	3.0	75.3
No data	8	2.7	78.0
Eating and sleeping	8	2.7	80.7
Bathe and sleeping	8	2.7	83.3
Reading novels	7	2.3	85.7
Cleaning and housework	6	2.0	87.7
Islamic observance/Prayers	5	1.7	89.3
Jogging/exercise	5	1.7	91.0
Cannabis	5	1.7	92.7
Sex	5	1.7	94.3
Smoke cannabis	5	1.7	96.0
Playing pool	2	0.7	96.7
I look after my vehicle	1	0.3	97.0
Milk and bed	1	0.3	97.3
Con people	1	0.3	97.7
Supervise farm	1	0.3	98.0
Art	1	0.3	98.3
Eat	1	0.3	98.7
Milk and food	1	0.3	99.0
Looking at money	1	0.3	99.3
Cannabis and alcohol	1	0.3	99.7
Gambling	1	0.3	100.0
Total	300	100.0	

Source: Uganda khat consumers survey, October–December 2004.

doubt that khat has a secure base of consumers and that their numbers are growing. As our survey of consumers revealed, chewers include people of all ages, religions, ethnicities and occupational groups. However, production and distribution networks are heavily concentrated in Muslim hands, an association that is strongly linked to the historical role of Yemeni and Somali migrants in popularizing khat in Uganda. Muslim religious authorities in the country remain ambivalent about the status of

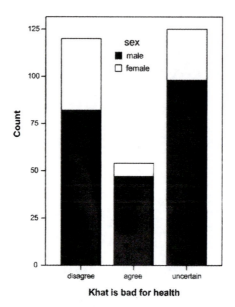

Figure 7.5 Responses to statement that khat is bad for health, by gender. *Source*: Uganda khat consumers survey, October–December 2004.

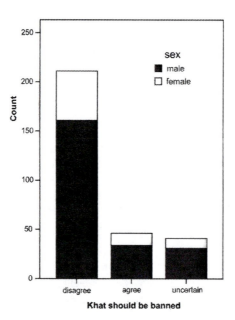

Figure 7.6 Responses to statement that khat should be banned, by gender. *Source*: Uganda khat consumers survey, October–December 2004.

khat chewing within Islam, while the Christian Churches as well have mostly kept silent on the topic. Yet, amid the ambiguity and doubt, Ugandan khat production is steadily expanding and the commodity is reaching new consumer groups. And, as this khat economy is consolidated, the most enterprising traders look toward the new frontiers of production and consumption beyond Uganda's borders, as khat follows the truckers and migrants into Rwanda and the Congo. Khat's expansion in eastern Africa has some way to go yet.

Part III
Khat in the Diaspora

–8–

The Ambivalent Amphetamine

On a November afternoon in Streatham, South London, a squad of law-enforcement officers swoop down on an old Nissan parked in a residential street. As they approach, the knot of men of African origin breaks up in confusion. While some manage to sprint away from the scene, three are caught with drugs in their possession. More drugs in the boot of the car, wrapped in bundles ready for sale, and neatly arranged in cardboard. There is no struggle, no physical violence, but shouting and wild gesticulation by one of the arrestees attracts a crowd of onlookers from the neighbourhood and nearby cafés.

It would seem like just another afternoon in Lambeth, famous for a series of riots during the 1980s, motivated in part at least by racial tensions. Since then at least the area has developed a reputation for drug dealing, in which Afro-Caribbeans play a prominent role. Yet the officers at the scene of the incident appear passive, making little effort to process the three suspects. The main role in this piece of street theatre is played not by the police, but by a civilian bureaucrat. He is the trading-standards officer of the local council. He records the details of the persons present, and confiscates their goods and their vehicles for 'unlicensed retailing in a public place'. Three suspects supply their names and addresses before being allowed to move on. As for the drugs in question, khat is a perfectly licit substance in London, imported regularly into Heathrow as a 'vegetable'. The police constables appeared on the scene only to prevent a breach of the peace, not to effect an arrest. Neither unlicensed trading nor illegal parking is a high priority for the hard-pressed police of Lambeth borough. The reasons why the Streatham community partnership expends resources and considerable energy in launching raids against the roadside khat sellers is to be found not in any 'crackdown on serious crime', but in local politics and community relations.

Strains and Tensions

Streatham is one part of Lambeth that has failed as yet to benefit from the regeneration of the wider borough. Dense traffic along Streatham High Street, one of the main traffic arteries into Central London, is placing a heavy environmental burden on the neighbourhood. As a shopping centre the High Street has still to recover from the closure of Pratt's Department Store in the 1980s. The influx of national retail and service-industry outlets such as Iceland and Blockbusters Video Rentals at the upper end of the stretch has lent the area some of the uniformity of any national shopping high street. In between the brand names a few local businesses are hanging on.

At the lower end, an area known as the 'Dip', small shops and restaurants cater to the needs and fancies of a highly diverse community. Halal butcher shops and Moroccan tea rooms are interspersed with Nigerian, Chinese and Thai restaurants. Only at the junction of Gleneagle Road does a cluster of Somali establishments break the pattern of heterogeneity. In a concentrated space along the 100-metre stretch of commercial premises on either side of Gleneagle Road there are eight Somali-owned businesses, including two long-distance telephone shops, of which one at least provides *hawala*[1] money transfers, one barber shop, a food store and three cafés. They cater almost exclusively to Somali customers many of whom come from outside the borough to use the amenities and to socialize. The nearby Waaberri community centre provides advisory services, computer training and youth activities, while the South London Islamic Centre on Mitcham Lane tends to the spiritual needs.

The first Somali business opened in 1999 when most of the shops were closed and in disrepair, with rents as low as £5,000 per annum. Residents were applauding the entrepreneurial spirit of the newcomers and glad for the investment of energy and effort. Other businesses followed and within a few years the commercial end of Gleneagle was once again thriving with activity, and rents climbed up to £15,000 in 2004. Commercial success, however, came at a price. Over the years much of the erstwhile support by the local community turned into outright hostility on the part of some. A number of residents resenting the Somali presence organized themselves into the Gleneagles Residents' Association, and approached the Council in 2001. They complained about a range of issues, including rude behaviour and verbal aggression by some of the incoming Somalis against pedestrians, exclusion from the cafés operated by the Somalis, double parking and the repair of cars outside the homes of residents, the loud, noisy and intimidating presence of large groups of men on the pavements outside the shops, and in particular about the open sale and widespread use of khat.

The 'arrival' of khat caused a stir in sections of the residential community. The rumour went out that the Somalis were coming down to take drugs. Local newspapers fanned the flames of public alarm with irresponsible and ill-informed stories on the 'roadside drug trade',[2] even describing khat as 'a legal form of crack cocaine', and as a consequence the national tabloid press picked up on the issue. Disturbed by the prospect of large numbers of African men scoring drugs in the midst of their community, Lambeth residents' group mounted a campaign, exerting concerted pressure on local authority bureaucrats, the police, local councillors and the MP for the area to 'do something' about this new 'drugs scare'. Local lobbyists expressed the problem in vividly emotive terms: 'Sometimes we have large gatherings on the weekend. Imagine 150 men high as kites hanging around on your doorstep?' With tensions in the community running high, efforts were made to bring representatives of the local Somali community to a meeting with the residents group at the Streatham Town Centre Office, part of Lambeth Council. As a result of this initiative, the 'Dip Working Group' was founded in 2003 to look at the area's problems in greater depth, and this working group then invited a Drug Action Team into the Gleneagle Road area to gain better understanding of the issue of khat.

Khat use, it soon became evident, was not the only complaint. Some residents resented the rundown appearance of the Somali-owned establishments in the Dip, and the double standards that the local authority appeared to apply to breaches of licensing laws. One letting agent explained how his firm was fined for fixing a satellite dish to the wall of a property without permission, while at the same time he claimed that Somali cafés had been operating without licence out of marked retail premises for many years without any official sanction. Other residents harboured grievances about the 'large number of foreign men' appearing in their neighbourhood. Many residents thought these immigrants to be acting strangely, felt threatened by their presence, and claimed that at times the men were abusive. It was also apparent that few of the Somalis to be seen on the streets here actually lived in the neighbourhood; so where did they come from, and what brought them here other than the chance to buy khat? The suggestion that their neighbourhood was being turned into a drug market was particularly explosive in the London Borough of Lambeth, conjuring associations of turf wars, crazed addicts and waves of acquisition crime then being reported in others parts of the country.

Political opportunists looking to turn the situation to their advantage arrived in 2002, when the fascist and racist British National Party identified Gleneagle Road as a battleground. For several months the party website featured the report of a driver caught in a traffic jam and threatened by khat-using Somali men. The story of the innocent motorist becoming a stranger in his own country and a victim of drug-fuelled violence found resonance with some residents, even if the political association was rejected.[3] Several members of the residents' association sought to distance themselves from the BNP, emphasizing that they themselves were not racist, but merely worried about public safety. Others were mainly concerned over the potentially adverse impact of open drug markets on property prices.

With a well-organized and articulate residents' lobby calling for action at local and national level, the local council now felt that it had to be seen to act. The first move was to install fencing on the wall outside an empty property to prevent people from gathering there and sitting on the wall. Traffic wardens then began patrolling Gleneagle Road with greater regularity, mounting a major clampdown on illegal parking. To tidy up the neighbourhood, the council also improved the street-care services, increasing the number of road sweeps and the regularity of rubbish collections. Finally, and at the dramatic end of the campaign scale, came the inter-agency raids against the 'mobile khat traders' on Gleneagle Road. During 2004, the street witnessed four such raids, and on each occasion the vehicles of the traders were seized.

After this show of strength some of the residents conceded that progress had been made, while others continued to dismiss the Council's efforts as a talking shop. These dissatisfied residents formed a local pressure group, alarmingly named SOS – Save Our Streatham.[4] This group has taken a hard-line view of the problem, and is pressing for a general prohibition against khat. In this dramatic aim they now enjoy support from some unexpected quarters, including the imam from the local mosque and the Waaberri Community Association, a Somali organization. For its part, Lambeth Council has maintained the policy of merely seeking to get the khat trade off the street, and this has also gained the backing of numerous members of the Somali community, including – very significantly – the owners of two khat-retail outlets in the neighbourhood, known as *mafrish*.

Khat's presence on the streets of Streatham, then, has spawned quarrels that first pitted local residents' associations against immigrant communities, but has now also divided those immigrant communities among themselves. The debate has not succeeded in clarifying the position of khat in the problems faced by the neighbourhood, instead becoming a classic 'moral panic' in which the anxieties fanned by moral entrepreneurs, soliciting public support and political influence for their own programmes and policies, have become more important than a better understanding of the issues themselves. At the same time, events in Streatham have been part of a wider upsurge of concern about khat use in the UK, and it is pertinent to trace just how this delicate African psycho-stimulant has moved from relative obscurity to the centre of a political debate.

A *Mafrish* in the Neighbourhood

Khat is intertwined with the history of Somalis and Yemeni immigration to the UK. The oldest immigrant communities from the Red Sea region are to be found in the port cities of Cardiff, Liverpool and London. Although there is some evidence of earlier migration, the origin of these communities dates back to the late nineteenth century, when Aden was the bunkering depot for Welsh coal used by steamers on the route to India and the Far East. Seamen, known as Lascars, were recruited in Aden and some came to settle in British ports, often intermarrying with local women. Many were Yemeni, but they also included many Somalis and some Ethiopians. Before the arrival of air cargo, and the technology to transport fresh khat speedily around the globe, these early migrants left merely a faint 'footprint'[5] of khat use. The next wave of migrants, in the 1950s, marked the real beginnings of khat consumption in the UK. At this time, small numbers of Yemenis and Somalis arrived to work as industrial workers in Sheffield, Birmingham and Manchester. Unlike the Lascars, these migrants were accompanied by wives, and they soon formed families and began to build communities in the industrial cities of northern England. They were then joined from the 1980s onward by a different type of arrival – refugees fleeing the wars of the Horn and the Red Sea littoral, and especially the violence embroiling the collapse of the Somali state.

The presence of these migrants fomented the gradual creation of a market for khat. Supplies into the UK were first arranged by individual migrant workers returning from the booming oil economies of the Persian Gulf, via Yemen or Ethiopia.[6] Coming back with gifts and money, these men presented a prestigious advertisement for khat, which then enjoyed family endorsement and still had a strong cachet of respectability (especially so in the Yemeni tradition). One informant remembered her father coming back with several bundles to share with friends in the living room of their Sheffield home. The men were all dressed in clean white robes, the room was aired and tidy, and the atmosphere was one of cultural refinement and communal well-being. The first commercial cargos to be brought into London were organized by Yemeni importers, who distributed via a small network of outlets which included Somali women who retailed the khat from their own homes. In those early days, khat consumption was very much part of domestic life, not something done in a public place or in a club designed for the purpose. It is interesting also that the pattern prevailing in Kenya, where women are the main sellers of khat, prevailed in the early khat market in the UK.

According to another informant, selling and using khat at this time was seen as symbolic of a cultural revival among the communities from the Red Sea region, who were then taking a renewed pride in their culture of origin. This view is very much endorsed by the testimony of the owner of one of the oldest running khat cafés – *mafrish*[7] – in Tower Hamlets. Now known locally as the Almati, this man recalled encountering a group of young Somali customers who had taken to drinking alcohol. To save them from dissolution and apostasy, and to restore their sense of cultural identity, he introduced them to the chewing of khat. Conducting himself with the quiet dignity of a pillar of the community and a defender of the faith, he is still providing a service in his khat café to a mixed clientele of people of African and Arab origin. From the earliest incidence of use, then, khat chewing was about more than the simple pursuit of pleasure. It was a manifestation of identity, a celebration of culture and self, and even a way of preserving Islamic purity. All of this meant nothing to others in Britain, for whom there was no interest whatsoever in khat.[8]

From the mid-1980s this began to change. Concerns were first raised in newspaper articles linking khat consumption with crime. In October 1987, The *Observer* (18/10/1987) related the tragic death of a Somali refugee and his baby nephew to the intense use of khat. Two years earlier, in one of the first reports on khat consumption, *The Sunday Times* worried about the spread of the habit to other population groups (10/01/1985). The authorities, however, took little interest in the spread of khat use among quiet ethnic minorities, and there was no sign that consumption was destined to extend beyond the small immigrant groups. Initial policy approaches, in the UK at least, were to leave the communities concerned to handle these issues themselves, and to maintain a watching brief in case of transmission.

And the 'watching brief' was real enough. In the autumn of 1990, the Central Drugs and Illegal Immigration Intelligence Unit issued a Confidential Intelligence Bulletin on khat, reporting the sale of 75–100-gram bundles in the UK for £3–4 each. The customers were a mixture of Somali and Yemeni residents and Saudi tourists. Though the report reflected upon the potential danger of a new drugs trade breaking into the country, the report's author listed two arguments against prohibiting khat: 'Europe has little to fear from khat owing to its unattractive mode of administration, its relative low potency, as well as the difficulty in extracting cathinone ...'. 'There is also concern that any form of restriction', he continued, 'would result in users abusing controlled drugs or alcohol' (NDIU 1990). In other words, British kids had easier ways of getting a hit and were unlikely to consider khat cool and, looking at the wider picture, there were worse things in the legal marketplace than khat.

Such a laissez-faire approach, in line with a model of immigration celebrating a diversity of cultural practice, has subsequently come under attack from different camps. On the one hand, there is growing pressure for adaptation and acculturation of immigrants. Cultural difference is giving way to an idea of black Britishness, of an identity around core values and other markers. On the other hand, should such cultural relativism be tolerated? As one Somali women activist expressed it, albeit in strident terms: 'Khat is allowed in this country because it is used by Somali men. It is part of a deliberate plot to weaken and destroy our people.'[9] To put the point another way, her question asks whether the British authorities would be so sanguine about khat if it were being consumed by British youth rather than by immigrants.

The argument masks a significant shift in the constitution of the UK Somali community and its relationship with the state. The immigrants of the 1950s and 1960s were workers with aspirations of social mobility and a pride in self-reliance. Over the course of their working lives they became property-owners, some formed small businesses, and through their communities they were proud to maintain a constructive relationship with the authorities. Somali as well as Yemeni community associations were centred on Islam, and made efforts to pass on language and traditions to the next generation born and raised in the UK. The next wave of Somalis, by contrast, arrived as asylum seekers. The civil war beginning in the early 1980s, and leading eventually to the collapse of the Somali state, drove an estimated 2 million Somalis into exile in Africa, Europe and North America.[10] Most families were fragmented, mothers arriving with their children first, before being joined by their men, often years later. The constitution of the UK Somali community, then, changed from one of single or intermarrying seamen complemented by family units in industrial towns to a refugee population, with at least as many women and a high proportion of children (see Table 8.1) (Harris 2004: 23). From the outset, dependent on benefits and with poor employment records, they have had a very different relationship with the authorities. For this latest wave, personal advancement is achieved by accessing the different government agencies and by manipulating the welter of welfare entitlements administered by the state.

Table 8.1 Estimates of Somali Immigrant Population in the UK

Year to which Estimate Refers	Estimated Numbers of Somalis Living in the UK	Source
1994	25,000	McGowan, R. M. (1999), *Muslims in the Diaspora: the Somali Communities of London and Toronto*, Toronto: University of Toronto Press, p. 240
2001	43,691	2001 census (England and Wales, Scotland and Northern Ireland)[1]
2002	250,000	Estimate by Ion Lewis, Liberation meeting. London 26.11.02
2003	95,000	Holman, Christine and Holman, Naomi (2003), *First Steps in a New Country: Baseline Indicators for the Somali Community in LB Hackney*, London: Sahil Housing Associations, p. 6

Source: From Harris 2004.
[1]http//neighbourhood.statistics.gov.uk.

Coinciding with the shift in the Somali migration from migrant workers to refugees was the mass importation of khat to feed the growing market in both the UK and other countries where the diaspora had settled. In the late 1990s, HM Customs and Excise estimated that London imported 7–10 tons of khat per week, or a maximum of 500 tons per annum. By 2005, the estimated annual inflow had risen to well over 10,000 tons. And whereas in the 1980s khat users would chew khat in the domestic settings that had always characterized consumption in the diaspora, by the end of the 1990s the typical venue for khat chewing had become the *mafrish*. The evolution of the *mafrish* as a social institution is of significance in the emergence of the Somalis as a community, but it also reflects on the changes within that community. Most Somalis in the UK up till the 1980s were living in family units, were in employment and owned or rented their own houses. They would chew on occasion, to celebrate, to assert self and culture, and within a domestic setting. Over the next two decades, khat slipped downmarket and was displaced from the living room to the public café. In the domestic context, khat was no longer an item of conspicuous consumption but the spark of controversy and domestic dispute. The impact of this was dramatic.

The Nura café, on Gleneagle Road in Streatham, looks like an ordinary 'transport café' from the outside, with plastic chairs around small tables where customers sip their hot drinks. To the back of the café is a pool table. But the clientele here is exclusively Somali, and in the basement there is a *mafrish*. In this small room, without any windows to the world outside, up to a dozen men will gather together. Each has his own bundle of khat, usually a packet of cigarettes, and a ready supply of sweet drinks – the things they need to engage in a chewing session. The Nura café is typical of the many *mafrishes* that have sprung up all in towns and cities all over the UK over the last decade.

Research into the establishments is hampered by a deep-seated suspicion against 'journalists', and the fear, widespread among khat-using Somalis, that the British government will close down the *mafrishes* if it finds out about them.[11] This does not mean that individual visitors are not treated politely, but filming, photography and even note taking are ill-advised activities in such places. As a consequence of the prevailing suspicion and secrecy, information about the actual number of *mafrishes* is necessarily speculative, and while the information derived from field visits and key informants gives us a clear enough picture of behaviour in these establishments, we do not know how many *mafrishes* are operating or what their cumulative turn-over might be. Their significance in terms of the khat trade and in the social lives to the Somalis is accordingly difficult to enumerate. But the absence of hard facts about the *mafrishes* does not prevent many Somalis in the UK, khat users and non-users alike, from asserting confidently that the *mafrish* 'is part of our tradition'.

Indeed, both the furnishings and the menu of consumables at Nura diverge sharply from those of the conventional British café. For a start, customers are lying on a carpeted floor, leaning against cushions with their back to the wall. Their drinks and other personal items are arranged on small tables in front of or beside them, these often being improvised from boxes or cushions. These seating arrangements can be elaborate and very beautiful, with cushions and pillows imported from Yemen where they are called *divani*. But in most cases the look is far from elegant; these are tired-looking, dingy places, struggling – and sometimes failing – to maintain an air of respectability, where threadbare carpets, dirty cushions strewn along unadorned concrete walls and heavy smoke-filled air are the norm. Amid the faded squalor, there is a conspicuous absence of alcohol: this is not allowed. Loud Somali and Arabic music often plays, or televisions blare out, usually transmitting the Al Jazeera channel. At the heart of the *mafrish* are the small bundles of green foliage that each customer unwraps from the encasing banana leaves and lovingly begins to chew, plucking off small leaves and shoots at a time to gather into a wad that is stored in one cheek for the remainder of the session. The vegetable matter is masticated over hours, with a session lasting between 2 and 6 hours, and considerably longer in the case of some heavy users. Leaves are slowly reduced, and eventually swallowed or spat out. The process can go on continuously, each man chewing at his own pace, until the end of his bundle or bundles. In the main, chewers report consuming one or two bundles at a session, but can go up to six.

Because of the length of time required for each session, most customers arrive and leave in their own time. They may meet up with friends and acquaintances even at arranged times, but people rarely move in groups. Moreover, it is uncommon to leave one *mafrish* to go on to another, even though chewers may leave to buy additional bundles elsewhere. As a result many *mafrishes* have a wide range of customers, many of whom are strangers to one another, and who come and go. Interestingly, this social mix comes in for criticism. One informant in Tower Hamlets, for example, said that the problem with the local *mafrish* was that you never knew who would end up sitting next to you. With a bit of bad luck you could get stuck next to someone who was both uneducated and boring and have to listen to him for the next four hours. Another complains that 'in khat sessions, there is no peer group, as such, the young and the old mingle in the *mafrish*'. Diversity is levelled and, moreover, social distance collapses on the *divani*, and the traditional Somali values such as respect for elders and their wisdom are forgotten. Accordingly, conversation too often degenerates into argument, fuelled by the cycles of cathine and cathinone.

Even when arguments flare, chewers usually step carefully around the explosive subject of identity and politics. After two decades of a civil war in which political affiliation often overlapped with clan membership, the collapse of the state and the breakaway of northern Somaliland, most Somalis are highly aware of the potential destruction of identity politics and tend to avoid it. *Mafrishes* therefore tend to cater for specific clans, even though they are not openly exclusionary.

Most Somalis will claim that the *Mafrish* is a part of their cultural heritage. It is difficult to find evidence for that claim in the literature on khat use, or in the wider literature on Somali history. Khat, first of all, was only cultivated, traded and consumed in the northern part of the country, roughly coterminous with the former British colony and today's aspiring independent state of Somaliland. The first recordings of khat consumption outside the traditional festive use located it in the social clubs and welfare associations of the 1940s (Cassanelli 1986). Southern Somalia had to wait for the construction of motor roads and the migration of labourers to the oil fields of the Middle East in the 1970s before it began to enter the world of khat consumption on any significant scale. Migrant labour to the oil industry played a huge role in the expansion of consumption, involving an estimated 250,000 Somalis at its height (Miller 1981). Their remittances quickly displaced livestock exports as the major source of foreign-exchange earnings for the national economy at that time. At an individual level, migrants were deeply affected by the experience of relative personal wealth and exposure to the thriving bazaar economy of the Gulf. Upon return they would introduce many of the material items that were simultaneously the driving force and the symbolic benefits of modern consumer capitalism. In addition to new clothes, electrical appliances and tape decks, this included the regular recreational consumption of khat. As a social group, these deracinated returning migrants would join the ranks of the unemployed and under-employed in the rapidly expanding urban centres, to share social attitudes and individual aspirations that were often in collision with the austere values of traditional society and the prevailing doctrine of Somali state socialism. Khat chewing therefore became a way of passing time in a situation of severely limited entertainment options, of expressing a new 'cosmopolitanism', while enacting a vision of the 'good life' (Cassanelli 1986).

New commercial establishments dedicated to the purchase and consumption of khat opened in the urban centres of Somalia to cater for this demand. They were called *majiis*, or 'gathering places', where food, music and, in some cases, female company were provided. Significantly, many *majilis* were run by the wives of the migrant workers. These women had both the capital to set themselves up in business and the social freedom to operate independently. Already the rumoured – and in some cases probably valid – link between khat and prostitution gave expression to the social tensions encapsulated by khat. The rationale for the Somali government ban on khat introduced in March 1983 is that the use of khat was introducing alien values and subverting public morals (Elmi et al. 1987). This anxiety has to be seen in the context of a rapidly urbanizing society, with large numbers of pastoralists shifting into a sedentary lifestyle and new occupations. Concern focused upon the suspension of the established hierarchical order and the dissolution of established categories of conduct and association, and found expression in the stated concern over the declining propriety of women, and the assertiveness of the young. People were no longer behaving toward each other in ways assigned to them by tradition, or according to the interpretation of the custodians of these traditions. And the opening of public spaces allowed for a social intercourse across the boundaries that had structured Somali society so effectively. As a result, it was feared, collective identity and the pursuit of the common good was being replaced by individualism, and the search for material gratification. The government publications of the time – displaying, perhaps, a southern bias – represent khat as un-Somali. Less often explicitly stated, but certainly very important, was the fact that the khat consumed in Somalia was mostly imported from neighbouring Ethiopia, a country with which Said Barre's government had fought a war that had by the 1980s lapsed into a tense stand-off.

Anxiety over rapid social change and the inversion of existing power relations has been documented in other African countries in the post-colonial period (Comaroff and Comaroff 1993). Many nationalist politicians organized their followers as 'youth movements', as implicit criticism of an outdated status quo and the promise of a different and better tomorrow (Bayart 1993). These were often run alongside women's associations that sought to harness the 'soft power' of cultural authenticity and moral purity supposedly embodied by women, while soliciting more concrete support from the growing financial strength of female traders. Significantly, the involvement of women in the production and distribution of mind-altering substances, mainly alcohol, has provoked repressive responses from governments concerned over threats to the established order and the loss of morality. The distillation of 'native gin' in Ghana (Akyeampong 1996) and the brewing of beer in Uganda (Willis 2002) has been the target of successive legislative interventions designed to contain an incipient threat to cultural and moral values.

The sentiments and anxieties voiced by the Barre regime about khat consumption may seem to echo many of those we hear in the Somali diaspora today, but we must also recognize that the campaign against khat was prompted by the state's worries that khat gatherings provided an unwelcome opportunity for criticism of government policies. Khat gatherings could not be readily controlled either by the state or by traditional authorities, and were therefore politically threatening to the regime. As such, Said Barre's banning of khat can be read as a ban by an increasingly unpopular regime on public association, a strategy reminiscent of the banning of coffee houses in the Ottoman empire. Unable to reduce the burgeoning demand for khat, the government campaign against khat ultimately unleashed forces of criminality and corruption that would contribute to its own eventual demise. Today the flourishing khat markets of Mogadishu and Hargheisa provide a key source of government revenue and are one of few pools of capital accumulation.

Back in the UK, many among the immigrant Somali community think that the local *mafrish* plays a valuable role. A Somali male resident in Southall confessed that he had never been to the *mafrish* himself, and did not chew khat, but nonetheless he believed that the *mafrish* was important for his community as a mechanism for the preservation of Somali culture. For this commentator, and many others, the *mafrish* is a site of Somali public discourse, a way of preserving continuity between lives lived in exile in London, and that of their fathers and forefathers back in Somalia. And, very importantly, the *mafrish* allows men to come together to discuss the affairs of the moment. The *mafrish* is a very male place.

It is this issue that lies at the heart of the current debate over the use and status of khat in the UK. Khat chewing in the *mafrish* is principally a male activity, from which women are excluded, and where their participation carries the risk of being stigmatized as prostitutes. Perhaps unsurprisingly, therefore, it is invariably female informants who perpetuate the claim that many *mafrishes* double up as brothels. This unsubstantiated claim adds a strong moral slur to their criticism of the *mafrish*, and is doubtlessly seen as adding further weight to demands for their closure. No evidence of any kind could be collected to substantiate these allegations. At the same time, some of the proprietors of *mafrishes* are women, usually converting parts of their own rented homes or business premises for the purpose. Their clientele, however, is exclusively male, and these female proprietors conspicuously do *not* play a prominent part in the social life of the establishment. The role of the female seller of khat is another instance of the difficulty in coming up with definite accounts over the distribution of costs and benefits, support and opposition for khat and its uses in the Somali community.

When asked about their patterns of khat use at the *mafrish*, few chewers attach any importance to tradition and cultural continuity. *Mafrishes* are popular because they provide users with 'something to do', allow them to relax and, crucially, to express themselves in their own language. Significantly, the clientele in all the establishments canvassed were from their late twenties upward, in keeping with prewar Somali conventions where chewing was 'predominantly an adult male habit, where a woman and young persons were mostly discouraged to join' (Kujog 2001: 321). Participants in a young people's focus group confirmed that they would not be allowed into the local *mafrish*. While these young men also complained about the lack of social 'facilities' for their own entertainment and use, they were fluent in English and found it far easier to negotiate local services than their older compatriots.

For the older men who had to flee Somalia as adults, the language problems are often insurmountable. Many gain only limited proficiency in English and have to depend on children, spouses or community interpreters in their dealings with officialdom. Language difficulties compound the barriers of non-recognition of Somali qualifications reportedly suffered by so many Somali professionals (Bloch and Atfield 2002). This alienating difficulty serves to erase the meaning of previous achievements and life experiences. For Somali job seekers without networks of contacts or suitable references, and unfamiliar with the culture of work in England, the bar is invariably set high. Some professionals refuse jobs they perceive incommensurate with their qualifications (Harris 2004; Summerfield 1993). For many men, suffering the humiliations of benefit dependence and status loss, the *mafrish* offers a haven of familiar talk and contemplative companionship. Here they can employ their verbal dexterity, recapture something of their former status, and assume the titles and significance of their former lives.

The opening times of *mafrishes* vary from lunchtime onwards until evenings. The proprietor and staff are often weary from the previous night's session, which can draw on until the small hours. Closing times are determined by the customers, some of whom spend long hours and good money at their favourite establishments. The pattern of use in the UK, however, differs from the reported tradition of khat consumption in prewar Somalia. Back then, khat was chewed after lunch, on a full stomach and integrated into the rhythms of work and family life. As the pharmacological effect wore off, chewers would return to their domestic responsibilities or even their offices. In the UK by contrast, *mafrashi* become busy in the early evening. People drop in after work, not always to chew on the premises but to check on the arrival of fresh deliveries, to take away small bundles for home or just to socialize. While surveys (Fowzi 2005; Griffiths et.al. 1998; Patel 2005; Woods 2005) indicate a high level of unemployment among regular khat users, the daily routine is adapted to the cycles of working life, analogous to the use of alcohol by the mainstream. Therein, however, lies part of the problem. The pharmacological properties of khat act as a stimulant on the central nervous system. The chewer feels energized and becomes active. Even after the euphoria has faded, the stimulus continues, driving off sleep until the early morning. As the rest of the family rises for a new day of work and school the khat chewer slips into a torpor.

For chewers whose consumption escalates, this is part of a reinforcing pattern. As they shift their activities to a nocturnal cycle they become estranged from both their own family and mainstream society and become locked into a small community of *khateurs*. What appears normal, pleasurable and meaningful in the *mafrish* is the source of domestic friction and intensifying social marginalization. As one former users said, 'your world becomes smaller and smaller ... you get up and go to see the man, sit there with your bundle and start talking with your mates ... then you think you can stop it, but if there is nothing else happening and everything is such a big effort you end up going back and chewing some more.'

The very attraction of the *mafrish* as an oasis of the familiar Somali culture and language in the desert of exile only serves to raise the obstacles toward integration and self-realization within the UK context. The sharp and gendered divisions among UK Somalis over the status of khat have accentuated the dilemma of users, by precluding them from presenting their habit as a custom that is sanctioned by tradition and culturally integrated. Instead it is increasingly seen as an abject vice further victimizing women and children and abusing the generosity of the welfare state. *Mafrish* owners and staff have responded by lowering their profile and striving to keep below the radar screen of the authorities. Many Somalis are well travelled and well connected. Migratory behaviour over wide territories and multiple locales is rooted in the not too distant past, when the majority of the population were pastoralists. The experience of the war has forced many Somalis down circuitous routes of migration and exile. Following the collapse of the state, clan and extended family remain the principle form of social organization. With networks across East Africa, the Middle East, Europe, North America and beyond, many Somalis are well informed, and chewers particularly are acutely aware of the legal ban on khat in many countries. The low profile kept by many *mafrishes*, the secretive manner in which the trade is conducted, the refusal to speak to researchers and journalists – all are motivated by the fear that more information will only cause the UK government to follow suit and prohibit the substance. Many operators, in any case, are well in breach of local licensing regulation. In Hounslow, West London a number of mafrishes have sprung up catering for a large Somali community and benefiting from the short run to Heathrow airport – and consequently, high-grade fresh quality khat. They have become known as 'buur', meaning 'hill' in Somali, because they are often located in council flats on the second or third floor.

While measures can be taken against the misuse of social housing for trading activities, it is more difficult in the case of commercial premises – as the case of the Streatham *mafrishes* illustrates. An orchestrated campaign from the residents' association and the 'Streatham Society' eventually prompted Lambeth Council to take legal proceedings against three cafés (two of which were selling khat). The Council sought to prove that the operations of the cafés were detrimental to the amenity of local residents, because customers were congregating on the public footway outside the premises. Evidence for this, and for the noise and disturbance that was caused, was provided in the form of letters of complaint by local people and the members of the self-appointed Streatham Society. Also taken into account were planning objectives designating the area as a 'fringe location' of Streatham Major Centre, intended to avert the noise and congestion associated with the excessive concentration of cafés in or near a residential area. The London Planning Inspectorate must tread carefully in cases such as this, however, so as not to stifle the spirit of enterprise and to run into potential compensation claims. For the period 2001/02, for example, only 32 Stop Notices were served in all the 32 London Boroughs put together. In most cases of this kind, planners are keen to find alternative solutions and very willingly enter into discussions with the operator of the business. The outcome in Streatham was rather mixed. Following the public hearing on 12 May 2004, the Planning Inspectorate granted permission to one café but refused planning permission to another,[12] while no application was submitted for the third (Klein 2004b).[13] Overall, the decisions gave a little to everyone, and so represented a political compromise.

The formal process for *mafrish* owners, community protesters and local authorities alike is therefore long-winded, unlikely to result in a definitive decision and, accordingly, perhaps best avoided. In the meantime, the khat-distribution industry remains unregulated and includes a long list of players operating without licences, having little regard for the health and safety of their customers, and in some cases even engaging in sharp practice.

One egregious example is reported from a Somali-run establishment in Tower Hamlets, East London, one of the oldest Somali communities in the country. The owner provides khat on credit to cash-strapped customers against security of their benefit book. These are kept in the *mafrish* to ensure that khat debts are settled as soon as the welfare cheque is cashed. In this fashion the owner guarantees payment but also locks the chewer into his particular establishment. Customers paying in arrears are in a weak bargaining position when it comes to quality control, and old stock can more easily be offloaded onto them. By such mechanisms, the combined circumstance of poverty and psychological, if not physical, addiction can be exploited by businessmen seeking revenue streams and risk minimization on stock depreciation. To those involved in the trade, use of khat may be cultural, but it is first and foremost strictly business.

However, the cultural aspects of *mafrishes* seem to be emphasized in the fact that they tend to evolve in clusters. Much to the annoyance of the Streatham Residents' Association, Somalis would travel from the Elephant and Castle, from Lewisham and Greenwich to visit one of the four *mafrashes* in the Streatham dip area. In Camden too, there were five *Mafrishes*, the largest of which was receiving four weekly deliveries of 10 boxes containing 40 bundles each, the smaller ones receiving two boxes. This amounts to a total of 720 bundles per week, accounting for a Camden khat economy of £2,160 per week, or £112,320 per annum. Against the magnitude of either the illegal drug scene or the licit though rowdy night-time economy, this modest turnover can hardly be said to constitute 'big business'. Nor are profits large: retailers simply add £1 to the wholesale price. With margins as low as this it is not surprising that Somali informants did not regard the khat business as a road to riches, while conceding that money could be made higher up the market chain. Even the larger *mafrishes* depend heavily on sales from drinks, cigarettes and food to make their profit, while smaller establishments can at most hope to eke out a bare living.

As a consequence of the marginal economic position of khat retailing, few establishments have the capital to invest in facilities. Without interventions, this cycle of decay will only accelerate a race to the bottom, as the very absence of facilities ensures ease of entry for new competitors. There are already signs of a strangling competition, with *mafrishes* fighting each other, newsagents and greengrocers increasingly moving into the trade (even supermarkets in the King's Cross area of London now sell khat), and a growing band of 'mobile traders' dispersing khat from the backs of cars across the cities of the UK. It is easy for any would-be retailer to obtain a supply from the wholesale market in Southall, where khat is traded by the box. It is apparent that the 'mobile traders' deliberately target areas with *mafrishes*, where three factors are working in their favour: (i) benefit-dependent khat chewers are highly sensitive to price differences, and 'mobile traders' with no overheads other than petrol can easily undercut established mafrishes by a few pence, (ii) the 'mobile traders' can deliver straight from the market and thereby provide a fresher product and (iii) many chewers are loath to purchase second or third bundles from the same source for fear of being branded addicts, so those in the midst of a session tend to buy further bundles from outside the *mafrish*.

Ease of entry, negligible overheads and low profit margins, then, exert downward pressure on the khat retail sector. In the absence of clear trading standards, these factors contribute to the poor conditions observed in most commercial establishments (Fowzi 2005; Isse 2005). That this is not a necessary consequence is demonstrated by khat chewing in communal settings. At the Yemeni Community Centre in Sheffield, for example, regular khat sessions have been held for many years. Only in 2004, however, did the manager decide to withdraw permission to allow khat use on the premises. The reasoning is illuminating. First he lists the health and safety concerns because chewing is accompanied by heavy smoking, and the attendant fire risk raises the need for insurance, while lingering smoke requires a better ventilation system. These expenses in turn impact on core funding. More seriously still, chewing can generate conflicts: 'People have been out of order and have been banned; the discussion of the khat circle also has an impact on the community', not because the khat session has become a decision-making forum, but because the chewers gossip. Dr Abdul Sharif was concerned to put an end to khat chewing in the centre without losing those members – mainly middle-aged men – who were regular chewers. The solution was to rent premises in the vicinity where the chewers could gather safely and peacefully under the aegis of the community association. The atmosphere is relaxed and welcoming, and questions, at least at the beginning of the session, are welcomed.

Opinions divide on the value of khat, as some chewers are facing problems, particularly once they have switched from the Ethiopian *habeshi*, to the reportedly more potent Kenyan *miraa*. On the other hand it is asserted that 'khat brings us together'. What the association has achieved, however, in providing a bright, clean space with good facilities is to reduce both use and the risks associated with use, and to keep the *khateurs* within the community. In contrast to practice in many of the commercial establishments, visitors take their shoes off before entering the area with seating. One man cleans his bundle of khat at a sink to wash off residual pesticides and fertilizers. The toilet facilities are clean and well maintained. After the first wave of euphoria has washed over the gathering some of the chewers paradoxically support tighter controls on khat use. It is suggested to reduce the number of incoming flights and the number of days when khat can be sold, an echo of the South Yemeni law prior to the unification of North and South Yemen, allowing khat to be sold only on weekends. All agree, however, that the worst scenario would be to impose a ban that could not be strictly enforced. One chewer says, 'If I go to the US or Egypt I won't mind not chewing because there is no khat. But if I know that there is a place where khat is to be had I will find it.' Supporting the ease with which contraband can enter the country he lifts up a packet of Yemeni cigarettes. 'I bought this here for 50 pence. So let them ban it but then ban it properly.'

At present there are thirty outlets where khat can be bought, arriving fresh on Mondays, Thursdays and Saturdays. If the market went underground, it is feared, chewers would be looking for it all the time. Moreover, there is a belief that the Yemeni community has adapted well to life in Sheffield, keeping a low profile and staying out of trouble largely because of khat. Some fear that banning khat will lead to a clampdown on a community already under siege. According to the community manager, 'when they eat khat they discuss this and it helps them to understand their plight better; there is the idea that in the past they were persecuting the West Indians, and now they are after the Arabs; they worry about the rise of right-wing attitudes, the hostility of the press and incoming legislation'. And while it is admitted that some chewers face problems, and that there are issues around smoking and the spend on household budget, one regular chewer expresses an opinion widely held among Yemenis (Al-Osami 2001) that 'it is not like a drug, weed or cocaine. If it is not there, no big deal'.

At the Dire Flamingo café in North London a group of Ethiopians meet most evenings of the week to engage in 'constructive chewing'. On the premises of a former café they have access to the full facilities – toilets and washing facilities, refrigerator for storing khat and soft drinks, a bar for tea and instant coffee and a large seating area to accommodate up to fifteen people. Next to each cushion is a small plastic basket lined with a bag where chewers discard the residue. Shoes are left at the door and pairs of rubber slippers provided. Most impressively, smoking has been banned inside the room. Smokers now have to get up, put on their shoes and huddle in the doorway. Dire Flamingo is not run for profit and the takings on khat – selling for £5 a bundle – are used to pay the rent. There are three key holders and a management committee. The place thrives because it serves as a meeting place for the Ethiopian community, and the commitment of three key members. It demonstrates, however, that socially integrated chewing is possible and that khat-related harms can be successfully managed and contained.

Community self-help has been constructive in the examples cited from Sheffield and North London, but where commercial attitudes dominate it is evident that only through a regulatory framework will improvements be made in the facilities available for khat consumers. As long as the khat scene dwells in a quasi-legal but unlicensed twilight zone, chewers who have escaped a collapsing state and who feel themselves on sufferance in a strange land are unlikely to develop a strong sense of their own rights as consumers. Unwittingly, local authorities turning a blind eye to the unregulated *mafrish* are colluding parties to the low standards of facilities that khat chewers must endure. In an age when the smoking of tobacco has been banned in bars and clubs, it is reasonable to ask what provision is being made for the health of khat chewers.

By the summer of 2005, the market for khat in London was so dynamic that the product was by then available at a myriad of outlets. In the Edgeware Road area of West London, popular with tourists from Arabic-speaking countries, Arabic-language signs give directions to outlets were khat is available. Some of these are cafés, but there are also various shops stocking varieties of khat, and even a pizza takeaway unit that sells khat on the side. Even more convenient for visitors from other parts of London, or chewers wishing to preserve their anonymity, is one of the newsagents located in the underpass. You can buy your khat here while collecting your evening paper. Here the owner reports a brisk trade of 150–200 bundles a week, selling at £5 each. Slightly higher prices, and the more salubrious location in a prosperous quarter of the city, suggest that these outlets are catering to a more affluent and possibly more covert clientele. In Hounslow, Camden and Tower Hamlets, where the bulk of London's khat consumers are Somalis, the leaf trades at £3–4 a bundle, and is sold mainly by greengrocers. Across London, it is not unusual to find khat being kept in fridges, wrapped in banana leafs, like just another fresh vegetable. These retailers reach a clientele that is not catered for by the *mafrishes*, now often including non-Somalis and particularly Arabs from the Gulf. Consumers from the Gulf would face severe punishment if they bought khat back at home, where its sale and consumption are strictly banned. In the Edgeware Road, consumers also include the occasional British purchaser, perhaps experimenting with the substance. The scale of this trade is not easy to estimate, but the very availability of khat in these new urban markets suggests that there may yet be other consumers, beyond the Somali, Yemeni, Ethiopian and Kenya diaspora, who are keen to try 'the flower of paradise'.

–9–

Transnational Debates

Transport technology holds the key to khat's transnational markets. The alkaloids in khat degrade after the leaf has been plucked, so it is essential to get the harvested crop to the consumer as speedily as possible. The life of harvested khat is not more than 72 hours, and after 48 hours the quality, condition and potency of the leaves declines considerably. Chilling and sprinkling with water or wrapping moistly will assist the longevity of the potency of the plant, but none of these measures can completely disguise the steady decay of 'old' khat. Freshness is everything in this market, and the need for speed in delivery from farm gate to the consumer affects local, regional and international markets alike. Air freight is the most important medium of transport for khat in the international market. As we have seen, khat was first transported by light aircraft around eastern Africa and the Horn from the 1930s, allowing consumers within the production region to sample varieties from different localities and adding an exotic and cosmopolitan aspect to the top end of the market. Khat transported longer distances has always fetched better prices in its receiving markets, although it has not always been the best-quality khat that makes this journey. Over the past two decades, with the rapid enlargement of the Somali, Yemeni, Ethiopian and Kenyan diaspora communities in Europe, North America and even further afield, the transhipment of khat by air freight across the continents has become a lucrative and growing business. Like other trades in perishable commodities from produce in eastern Africa and the Horn, such as vegetables and flowers, khat's international market is highly organized to ensure the efficiency of movement that is necessary to get the crop to its consumers in good condition. But, unlike these other international trades, the khat market has stayed in the control of groups from the producing regions. The international khat market is controlled and run by Ethiopians, Somalis, Yemenis and Kenyans for the most part, with only a very small number of 'outsiders' having managed to break into the circle of exporters and wholesalers. In a context of increasingly globalized trade, it is notable that the khat market has remained in 'indigenous' hands.

This chapter begins with an account of the transnational marketing of khat into the United Kingdom, moving on to examine the anxieties that have emerged connecting khat to criminal activities of various kinds. The final section describes how this international market has generated concerns about khat's effects upon its consumers in the diaspora communities, connecting khat with debates about immigration, cultural integration and identity.

International Trade

The quantity of khat imported into London's Heathrow airport has risen dramatically since the mid-to-late 1990s. Accurate figures are hard to come by: khat is often simply described as a 'vegetable', and as it requires no special licence of authority there is no official record of its movement as a distinct commodity, making it peculiarly invisible. However, we do know that approximately eight cargo flights reach Heathrow each week carrying fresh khat, four from Kenya, two from Ethiopia and two from Yemen. Khat may enter the airport by other means also, of course, but these flights constitute the main exports to London from the region handled by the most important exporting agents based in Nairobi, Addis Ababa and Sennar. From information gathered from Customs officers, and from discussions with several of the major UK-based importers and distributors, it is clear that Kenyan varieties of khat now dominate this flow, accounting for some 5,000 kg per week. Table 9.1 summarizes the figures for these 'official' imports through Heathrow.

Table 9.1 Imports to London (2004)

Country of Origin	Daily Imports (kg)	Number of Flights	Street Name	Price per Bundle (£)
Kenya	5,000	Four times a week	Mirra or murungi	3–4
Ethiopia	500	Two times a week	Hereri	5
Yemen	175	Two times a week	Taizi	7

Source: Her Majesty's Customs and Excise.

The domination of Kenyan khat in the UK market is a relatively new phenomenon. Historically, khat grown in Yemen and Ethiopia has been available in the London market for many more years, and is still considered by many to be products of more reliable quality. According to one prominent Ethiopian importer, the London trade was dominated from the 1950s onward by Yemenis and Somalis of the Issaq clan.[1] Then, in the mid-1990s, Ethiopians broke into the market – probably galvanized by the revitalization of the khat traders' associations in Addis Ababa – to be followed by Somalis, who were dealing almost exclusively in khat grown in Kenya.

The shifts in the market over time have been reflected in changing prices, although not by a significant degree. Political factors sometimes also ramped up the price. In the 1980s, the price of khat in Whitechapel was increased to £4 a bundle, and proceeds channelled to the Somali National Movement (SNM), the paramilitary arm of the Issaq clan fighting against the Siad Barre regime and for the independence of the former British protectorate of Somaliland. There have also been many attempts by wholesalers in London to control the trade and keep newcomers out of the market. As the market began to expand at the end of the 1980s, some suppliers sought to keep out new rivals at this time by applying pressure on retailers to buy only through established channels. One failed importer described how retailers whom he supplied on credit would withhold payment claiming that the khat had not sold. When he came to collect his money he was shown old stock of khat that was hard to distinguish from his own stock. After two deliveries, this trader was unable to take the losses any longer and withdrew.

In the last few years it has become much harder to control the market in this way, as new traders have come in, content to ship relatively small quantities and slowly build up their businesses. The London market is thus highly fragmented, with the few larger wholesalers greatly outnumbered by an array of small-time traders for whom the trade is an adjunct to other kinds of activity. For example, in the Spring of 2004 one of our informants was importing two 120-kg consignments from Addis Ababa into Heathrow each week, these arriving on British Airways. His khat was purchased 6 months in advance, through agents at Addis Ababa's main khat market, and the money paid into a UK bank in sterling. The money was then transferred to the Ethiopian National Bank, having been exchanged into US dollars. The Ethiopian National Bank then paid the Ethiopian contractor in Ethiopian Birr. In London a clearing agent, H&M, settles the paper work and arranges the cargo for collection from their warehouses near to Heathrow. From there, the trader and his driver collect the khat by van and deliver it directly to their retailers all over London. This trader had a customer list of more than fourteen *mafrishes* and shops that he supplies, but explained that these premises were forever closing and new ones opening up. Any successful trader has to keep a keen eye on this, to ensure that supplies are paid for and that the market is secure. Most of this trader's clients are Ethiopians or Yemenis, with only a few Somalis.

As the number of khat-selling outlets in London has increased, the import business has fragmented, with new traders constantly entering the market. In the late 1990s there were a dozen importers working out of Heathrow, but now there are so many that the distribution to the retailers is highly competitive and often chaotic. Registered importers, wholesale traders and freelance distributors all turn up in the courtyard of the Customs clearing agents after the arrival of flights from Nairobi or Addis Ababa. Many bring friends or hangers-on with them to help them 'secure' a supply. There are frequent tussles over consignments, some of the more desperate even breaking open boxes to retrieve a few bundles and start chewing. The larger and better-established traders are distressed by such behaviour, as they know that it damages the image of the trade.

The volatile character of the trade and the sometimes aggressive behaviour of the traders is one of several disincentives to the clearing agencies at Heathrow, not all of whom are prepared to handle khat. The main player therefore is an organization called Air Connection Limited, which is well established in both Kenya, where the company organizes the packaging of khat bundles, and in the UK where it arranges customs clearance and provides a lorry to ferry the khat to its warehouse in Southall.

Here, those traders who are not registered importers can get access to supplies. The packing of khat bundles and the wrapping into banana leaves has profound implications for the importance of regulation, labelling and control, which will be explored below.

The freight charges, including all customs duty in the UK, are paid for in advance to Air Connection Ltd in Nairobi at the rate of £5 per box. Each box contains forty bundles of khat, each of which in turn is made up of about 30–40 twigs wrapped up in a fresh banana leaf, this weighing 150–200 grams. The packaging of khat into boxes has been a major innovation in the trade: Until the mid-1990s, khat was imported in sisal sacks, some of them pest infested, and charged at a flat freight rate of £32 for ten or more sacks containing forty bundles of khat each. The boxes make both handling and pest control much easier, and should also facilitate the administration of a more efficient tax regime. At the point of import, khat is presented as a raw vegetable, in the same category as beans. Although the UK Medicine Control Agency technically reclassified khat in 1998 as a medicine, which requires both importers and retailers to obtain a licence, and then necessitates the imposition of VAT and further import duties, not a single khat importer has in fact applied for such a licence and no one appears to have insisted that they do so. Instead, Customs and Excise collect VAT on the basis of CIF – the value of the khat based on a calculation of the original costs of the goods as quoted on the waybill, insurance and freight documents issued in Nairobi or Addis Ababa. The actual cost listed in this documentation is a closely guarded secret kept by each clearing agent. According to UK Customs and Excise, £0.26 per kilo of khat was the tariff being collected in 2005, or £130 per 500 kg of khat. At a rough calculation, this amounts to a tax of about £0.05 per bundle. Khat is therefore quite certainly the most 'under taxed' psychoactive substance in the UK. However, recent Customs and Excise investigations have revealed that several khat importers are registered with the UK Inland Revenue as khat importers and therefore pay income tax on their earnings. Despite this, it is clear that the regulation of khat imports through Heathrow is as yet woefully underdeveloped.

Customs officers working with khat will make occasional inspections to ensure that no illicit drugs have been hidden within the boxes. As they open boxes, they wear plastic gloves to protect themselves from the DDT that has been found on some consignments, particularly those of khat coming from Yemen. The presence of so toxic a chemical is worrying, especially as many khat chewers are entirely unaware that the harmful residues of pesticides used to protect the trees may be found on the leaves they will put in their mouths. Very few consumers wash their khat before chewing, although this would seem to be an easy health precaution that all should take.

The integration of processing, packaging, export and import by a single business, as in the example of Air Connection, allows for the complete commodification of khat. This substantially reduces the consumer's ability to make informed purchasing decisions. Back in the production regions, consumers are keenly aware of types and brands of khat, and will pay premium prices for the best varieties or those available only in specific seasons or through particular dealers. Yet in the diaspora, the bulking of khat by the exporters and wholesalers seems to be used to deliberately obscure the origin and brand identity of the khat. Indeed, exporters will often 'rebundle' the khat before loading the freight, mixing varieties and qualities in order to 'even out' any price inequalities between the local market and the export market, and thus maintain their profit margins against seasonality and local market fluctuation. This practice is very common in Nairobi, and is one of the reasons why the price of Kenyan khat in the international market remains so surprisingly stable and inelastic. In the UK market, it is only a few well known, popular and more expensive 'quality' brands, such as *'kangeta'* and *'giza bomb'*, that escape this homogenization – although consumers report that even these are sometimes subject to 'mixing' with other less prized varieties.

The bundles supplied to the UK are therefore not from the same tree, nor even necessarily the same source supplier, as would invariably be the case in local markets in Kenya, Ethiopia, Djibouti, Yemen or Somaliland. Analysis of UK-purchased bundles showed that the twigs vary in terms of taste, sizes and types within bundles, and that the method by which the bundles themselves are tied is also inconsistent. In some cases, the bundle contained a few pieces of good-quality khat tied together with a string, alongside other, smaller, low-quality samples which have been tied separately. In other instances, the leaves are much fewer and the bundle is bulked up with twiggy growth. This is more common from varieties of Kenyan khat, from which consumers strip the soft bark as well as chewing the leaves. A bundle of this kind might contain between 20 and 25 twigs, without much leaf. These manoeuvres allow traders to maintain profits more readily, but they are surely only practicable in a market where supply is to some extent constrained and individual consumers have little real choice. Importers are aware that consumers are conscious of quality, but that they are also sensitive to price, and some worry that consumers might buy less khat if they could readily obtain khat of a consistently higher quality.

The decision by some major airlines to suspend khat shipments has not stopped the trade, but it has added yet another anxiety for those involved in the export business. Kenya Airways stopped handling khat from Nairobi in August 2003, with British Airways following suit in May 2004.[2] The sudden disruption of what was at the time still a growing trade (Gordon Opiyo 2004) caused a temporary khat drought in London. Traders at first brought in supplies from the Netherlands, and then greatly increased their imports from Ethiopia. But stability was soon restored to the Kenyan market when other airlines came in to take up the market share. These charter airlines, including East African Safari Air, Excel Airways and DAS, already deal in fresh flowers and other horticultural products exported from Nairobi and have welcomed the opportunity to get involved in the khat business. Based in East Africa, these companies also seem more tolerant of the idiosyncrasies of the trade at the Nairobi end, where suppliers compete ruthlessly with one another to supply the export traders at the airport depots, and where the wholesalers often try to load more khat than is allotted on the flight or more than they have paid for. It was the difficulty of handling this situation that led the local freight manager of British Airways to withdraw from khat shipments.

Customs officers[3] believe that the scale of khat imports into the UK is in very large part motivated by the profit differential in the re-export trade. According to their calculations, khat sales in the UK yield a profit of about £10 per kilo, compared to a profit of £200 per kilo to be made in the USA. With this considerable incentive in sight for those prepared to smuggle khat into those countries where it has been prohibited, it is not surprising that so much khat finds its way from London to the USA, Canada and the Scandinavian countries. This is a frantic business, requiring the rapid trans-shipment of khat before its psychoactive properties decay. Those conducting the re-export trade are fully aware that their activities are illegal in the receiving countries. This is a criminal trade (see Table 9.2). When it arrives in London the khat is offloaded, treated with water and ice to prolong its freshness, and then repackaged. The leaves are rewrapped into smaller bundles before being placed inside whatever container is to be used in the trafficking. There are three principal methods of 'trafficking' khat. The first, and most widely publicized, is the so-called 'suitcase trade', involving the packing of up to 40 kg of khat to be carried as personal luggage by a courier who is simply a passenger on a regular flight. Smugglers generally avoid employing nationals from the khat-producing countries as couriers, for fear they might attract the attention of the Customs authorities. Instead, the couriers are almost invariably white citizens from the target country or from the UK In most cases, the couriers do not know precisely what they are carrying, only that they must deliver a package at the other end. They are paid in cash, or have their air ticket subsidized by the contractor.

Less spectacular, but probably of much greater significance in terms of bulk carried, is the parcel trade. Parcels of khat are made up to between 5 and 40 kg in weight, made out to fictitious names, and classified on the Customs dockets as

Table 9.2 Seizures in Countries where Khat is Illegal

Year	Khat Seizure (kg)				
	US	Denmark	Sweden	Norway	Finland
1999	22,100				
2000	33,800	2,329			462
2001	37,200	5.761			616
2002		3,100			1,050
2003		4,565	6,900	6,350	1,888

Source: Nordic Police Liaison Officer and US Drug Enforcement Administration.

'books', 'spices', or some other seemingly innocuous gift. The major international parcel shippers operating out of London, such as FedEx, UPS, DHL and Royal Mail, have systems in place to sample and check packages sent through their services, yet this is by no means comprehensive, nor is it always conducted with the necessary diligence. Moreover, as khat is not illegal in the UK, there is no immediate reason for workers here to treat the commodity with suspicion. Customs staff believe that khat consignments shipped by this method are significant, a view informed by occasional operations to target the parcel shippers. One such Customs operation in 2004 revealed some 100 khat-filled parcels waiting to be shipped out to the US. This discovery posed a dilemma for all involved. UK Customs officers could seize these packages on the grounds of false declaration, which is an offence under UK law, but they were reluctant to embark on the heavy paperwork involved for what is, in essence, a relatively trivial offence. The courier company was very reluctant to act against its customers: as khat is a licit substance in the UK, the contents of the packages presented no legal difficulty for the customers of the company. However, parcel companies can be fined by the US authorities for knowingly carrying a controlled drug, so having identified the contents of the 100 packages, they reluctantly took the decision to destroy them.

As far as the UK Customs service is concerned, they do not want the UK to gain a reputation as a transit country for an illegal drug. In the nature of their work, they also need to maintain good working relations with colleagues in other countries, and for the UK the USA connection is especially important. UK Customs have in the past given intelligence to the authorities in the US, Canada or Scandinavia about khat consignments leaving from the UK. However, the passage of the 2001 European Human Rights Act within the European Union has outlawed this practice and it has stopped. Another previous strategy of the UK Customs officers, of seizing a shipment of khat leaves for inspection and then releasing it only after it has decayed, has also now been halted. Perhaps surprisingly, the USA Drug Enforcement Administration[4] is apparently unconcerned by these developments. According to British Customs officers, their USA counterparts have asked them not to convey further intelligence on khat to the USA as it is simply too cumbersome to seize every shipment. Already overstretched, and with bigger problems than khat smuggling to confront, the DEA lack the resources and the will to deal effectively with khat: 'we are swamped … don't tell us any more', was one DEA senior officer's response.

Khat and Crime

In the skies above the Atlantic, the status of the leafy bundles of khat turns from harmless vegetable matter into a Class 1 narcotic, and that of the traders from greengrocer to international drug trafficker. In the UK the emphasis has fallen on the plight of couriers, as hapless individuals lured into crime by the promise of a free ticket and some pocket money.[5] The smuggling case that has received the widest publicity was that of David McCann, a seventeen-year-old from Deal, in the English county of Kent, who was arrested by US Customs officials in 2003, when he was caught at New York's JFK airport with a suitcase full of khat. The story made it into the British press and was featured in the BBC Television investigative news programme *Inside Out*. Viewers were treated to a luridly sensationalized account of Britain's 'khat smugglers' who regularly took consignments in luggage on flights to the USA. News reporter Paul Ross was filmed as he bravely decided to chew some khat for himself – entirely in the interest of research, of course, and under the 'close supervision' of a doctor. 'I feel trembly and a bit hyper, like I've had too much coffee', said Ross, 'Take it from me, khat tastes disgusting. My blood pressure has shot up and my head aches.'

This television programme, scheduled in peak-time viewing, described khat simply as a 'Class 1 narcotic', without any explanation of what this meant in the USA. Viewers were left with the inference that khat was therefore as potent and as dangerous, as heroin or crack cocaine. Other worries were more explicit still: Much was made of the suggestion – entirely uncorroborated by evidence of any kind – that 'profits from khat may go to terrorist groups'. It was claimed that khat fetched ten times its UK price in the USA, and that 'highly organized gangs are making £150 million a year smuggling khat into the States'. These claims were based upon an interview with Thomas E. Manifase, a special agent with the US Department of Homeland Security. Mr Manifase said nothing about his evidence, but he was keen to speculate on the international dangers inherent in khat smuggling:

> I can tell you we are taking a real hard look at the people who smuggle this into the US. We are trying to find out who these people are and who is behind this. We are looking at the funding, the money, where's it going? It could be being used to fund terrorism because it's being sent back to countries that support terrorism like Yemen and others. (Manifase 13/10/2003)

Paradoxically, while this sensationalist reporting hinders a better public understanding of what khat is and what its effects are, it also portrays the British couriers, like David McCann, as respectable individuals with no blemish to their record who suddenly finding themselves unwittingly in the maw of the American criminal justice system, arrested, handcuffed, computerized and deported along with other international drug traffickers. It is interesting how strongly this contrasts with the depiction of drug couriers bringing cocaine and heroin into the UK, who may often be just as naive about the potential consequences but are nonetheless cruelly exposed to the full force of the law (Green 1990; Klein 2004). Yet according to the National Criminal Intelligence Service,[6] British khat couriers are being 'duped' into committing an offence against their better knowledge. The pattern of courier recruitment suggests the work of organized syndicates, working from specific parts of Britain. In May

2003, the *Observer* reported that half of the khat couriers detained in New York, like David McCann, originated from Deal in Kent,[7] and in February 2005 it was reported that the DEA had apprehended 'at least five mules recruited in Milton Keynes'.[8]

Public alarm over the connections between khat and crime was also provoked by the case of the murder of Amarjit Chohan, the owner of CIBA Freight Services, an importer of perishable foods and flowers from Africa. With twenty-two employees in west London and a turnover of £4 million, CIBA was also a major player in the importation of khat. When Mr Chohan and his family were brutally and mysteriously murdered in April 2003, rumours immediately linked the killing to his involvement in the khat trade. This immediately raised concerns about khat to a new level, entangling khat in the UK's hard-drug debates, and invoking fears of organized and international criminal connections. The significance of this can be seen if we examine the causal links between khat use and crime in the UK within the framework developed for other psychoactive substances (Bean 2002). Criminologists conventionally use a threefold typology to distinguish the connections between criminal violence and drugs (Goldstein 1985). These are:

i.   Psychopharmacological – violence due to the effect of the drug itself
ii.   Economic compulsive – acquisition crime or 'fund raising' to finance drug purchases
iii. Systemic – violence to protect turf, enforce contracts, establish reputation, etc.

The reports suggesting that trafficking syndicates operated out of towns in Kent, or from Milton Keynes, were seen as further proof of the invidious but pervasive criminalization of the khat trade in the UK, while the case of Mr Chohan was cited to support the suggestion that systemic violence was taking root in the upper end of the khat market, at import and distribution levels. Such concerns turned out to be grossly misplaced, since there is no evidence of anything remotely akin to systemic violence in the khat trade. The murderers of Amarjit Chohan and his family turned out to be members of London criminal networks with a history of drug dealing. Their interests lay not in the modest returns of the khat trade, but in using Chohan's legitimate and successful company as a front for the exponentially more lucrative importation of heroin.

Despite the facts of the case, reporting of the Chohan murder seems to have irredeemably smeared the khat trade, and continues to be cited in conjunction with other anxieties about the social harms brought about through khat. At street level, these suggestions have chimed with rising anxiety over the depredations of Somali youth gangs in some British urban areas. With these issues to the fore, there were deeper concerns implicit in the initial reporting of the Chohan case: would an internationalized smuggling industry for khat turn Somalis into Britain's new 'Yardies'?

Fears about localized Somali urban violence in Britain centres upon the main immigrant areas, and almost invariably links the problem to that of khat use, even when there is no evidence to substantiate such a connection. In Streatham, South London, for example, shopkeepers reported that large groups of Somali youths 'swamped' their premises, stealing anything they could get hold of. The owner of one newsagent's store reported systematic targeting by a group of up to twelve Somali youths, who would enter his shop on successive weekends and remove items without paying.[9] The character of the ethnic-monitoring forms used by statutory services, including the police and the National Offenders Management Service,[10] make it difficult to enumerate contributions to overall crime by Somali groups. According to the senior police commander in the London borough of Lambeth, a notable feature of Somali involvement in street robberies has been the high degree of 'unnecessary violence inflicted even after the goods they wanted to steal had been obtained'.[11] These remarks are tempered, however, by the Operational Manager at Streatham Police Station, according to whom 'Somalis as crime generators are no more and potentially less than other groups'.[12] The local police officer responsible for the stretch of Gleneagle Road where a brisk khat trade takes place points out that the young Somalis involved in robberies and shoplifting have nothing whatsoever to do with the khat trade. This officer went on to caution the members of the local residents' association against 'blaming all the problems in the area on the khat trade'. According to police analysis of crime patterns in the Streatham Sub Command the area around Gleneagle Road, where the local khat trade is concentrated, there is no evidence of increased criminality nor of crime being especially linked to khat.

If khat cannot be linked to urban crime, is it then responsible for the violence of Somali youths? Muna Deria, a researcher from the Somali community, provides a different explanation for the use of violence by Somali gangs. As relatively recent arrivals on the UK street scene, Somali kids came with few cultural attributes 'cool enough' to be of value in this urban mileau. According to Deria, they eventually found their sharper identity and a 'place' on the street after the release of the successful Hollywood film of the US operation in Somalia in the early 1990s, *Black Hawk Down*.[13] Taking up images from this movie, Britain's Somali youths embraced a 'guerrilla chic', turning the violent past that had driven them or their parents out of Somalia into a cultural asset. In sociological terms, this allowed them to find a symbolic fit between the values and lifestyles of the group, and to create a homology between the subjective experience of dislocation, exile and marginalization and the consequential internalization of patterns of violence (Hebdige 1979). Within a street culture of 'guerrilla chic', the subjective experience of trauma and emotional disturbance could be put into subcultural context and the violence instrumentalized as a means to an end. It allowed Somali gangs to rise in the pecking order of subgroup cultures in urban Britain, soon rivalling the status of the previously dominant West Indian gangs who were notorious for their ruthlessness. Indeed, this is not a new phenomenon in criminal markets where newcomers often have to employ violence to enter into closed 'markets', and where the use of excessive force is in fact a sign of weakness (Ruggiero and South 1995).

While these developments have profound implication for local crime and antisocial behaviour profiles, they are deeply flawed when employed as an argument for the control or prohibition of khat. Among Somali youths born in this country, khat use is at best occasional, as will be discussed below. The Somali-youth street gangs have no involvement whatsoever in the khat trade, and individual members only very rarely develop the habit of khat consumption. For Somali youth in Britain, khat is simply not cool.

Immigrant-Somali khat use is in fact located in older age cohorts, among persons who have no dealings either with youth gangs or with criminal markets. Even avid khat consumers with a daily habit still manage to fund their purchases through perfectly legal means. The ratio of price to potency for khat has thus far saved them from the debt/crime trap encountered by so many opiate or crack cocaine addicts. Chewing twice a day, seven days a week, keeps a khat consumer 'under the influence' for the equivalent price of a rock of crack cocaine, whose fleeting pleasures evaporate within 20 minutes. Even five bundles of khat consumed in a binge over three days will cost less than a single gram of heroin in London.[14] While the expenditure may place enormous stress on the modest budgets of immigrant households, it remains affordable without resort to crime. Rather than being compared to buying cocaine or heroin, khat purchases fall more obviously into the same category as nicotine and alcohol. Though habit forming in many individual cases, khat chewing remains sufficiently affordable to spare users and victims from the acquisition crime associated with class A drugs.

A more genuine worry about criminality and khat focuses upon the alleged formation of syndicates in the 'suitcase trade'. Fear of prosecution shrouds this part of the khat trade in secrecy, but anecdotal information and second-hand reports, combined with intelligence from the Customs authorities, provides an outline of recent developments. Organized criminals have entered the suitcase trade not from the main centres of initial importation in the UK and Holland, but from those countries where the legal supply of khat has been eliminated, predominantly the USA, Canada and the Scandinavian countries. In a classic pattern familiar to many other histories of smuggling, criminal groups are thus forming around the very opportunities created by legislators having moved to ban the commodity *without* having eliminated the demand for it.

The Social Issues

The social issues raised by khat consumption in the UK, and in other countries where there are large diaspora communities from the Red Sea region, are driven by the apparent psychoactive effects of chewing. Since 1987, among the Somali community there have been several isolated incidents of violent assaults, and even the occasional murder, in which khat has been cited as a contributing factor. Hussain Yusuf, for example, an immigrant living in Sheffield who attacked a Somali mental-health worker after he refused to lend him money, is reported to have been addicted to khat.[15] A body of case reports of this kind has been built up in the psychiatric literature to document and discuss cases of actual and potential violent behaviour by khat-using patients (Cox and Rampes 2003; Critchlow 1987; Gough and Cookson 1984; Nielen et al. 2004; Pantelis et al. 1989; Yousef et al. 1995). This kind of attack fits in perfectly with the first category of drug-related violence cited in the typology above, that triggered by the psycho-pharmacological influence of the drug on the user. The analogies drawn between khat and crack cocaine in the British press, and between amphetamine use and khat chewing by some pharmacologists and research chemists, lends plausibility to the image of wired-up, highly volatile individuals posing a danger to society and themselves through their khat consumption. It is also suggested that many chewers unleash their aggression at home, connecting khat consumption to 'invisible violence' directed against spouses and children in the home (Fowzi 2005).

Informants have indeed described scenarios where domestic disputes deteriorate into violence related to khat. The one that best fits the typology of the drug-driven violence is the gradual erosion of domestic harmony as husbands, fathers, sons return from their 'khat spree' feeling tired, irritable and morose. They no longer have either the energy or the confidence to contribute to running a household or raising their children. Instead, they lock themselves in their bedrooms to catch up with sleep. Fights often ensue over the sharing of tasks, or getting families to keep quiet. Such disagreements may come to revolve around the notion of authority and command within the home, and the distribution of responsibilities and privileges.

Whether ending in violence or not, this scenario of domestic conflict over khat consumption has motivated a very vocal debate within the immigrant Somali communities over the efficacy of chewing. Somali women's groups in some British cities have organized campaigns to raise public attention to their plight, and this has at times resulted in their calls for a ban on the importation of khat. In Sheffield, for example, a petition with 5,000 signatures was submitted in 2001 calling for a ban on khat, and workers at the Bromley office of the drug-treatment charity Turning Point launched a nationwide campaign for prohibition during 2003. Bali Kaur, an outreach worker and the campaign coordinator, has been trying to give a voice to the women who 'were very, very frightened to raise the issue with their husbands'.[16] The victimization of women and children by men trading their family responsibilities for the fleeting pleasures of intoxication has touched a raw nerve in a country with a history of social mobilization around drug control going back to Hogarth and Gin Alley, the Temperance Movement and the campaign against the opium trade. Stephen Pound, Labour MP for Ealing North, for example, fulminated against khat in a parliamentary debate in January 2005, telling the House of Commons that 'large numbers of people in west London who chew khat all night long, becoming increasingly aggressive [then] come home in the morning, beat up the wife and try to sleep through the day'.[17] Such generalizations carried greater weight precisely because they were backed by the campaigning of those within the immigrant community.

Yet in spite of the numbers of signatures on petitions and statements in parliament, tales of khat-triggered domestic violence are by no means consonant with the experience of all Somalis. One young informant, who had tried khat but not liked it, reported that he looked forward to his father and uncle returning home from a chewing session, because the potency of the leaves made them relaxed and indulgent. Moreover, he and many other Somali informants pointedly distinguished khat's tranquil pleasures from effects of alcohol and other 'drugs' which made you incapable and aggressive. Khat, by contrast, was presented as a substance that brought people peace and energy, even giving inspiration to musicians and poets.[18] As was pointed out in the introduction to this book, the psycho-pharmacological consequences of khat use are widely held to depend on the circumstances of the users and their families, on the actual locale where the khat is chewed and on the general pattern of consumption. Generalizations about the behaviour of consumers can be grossly misleading. In the khat scene, much depends upon whom khat is used with and in what frequency.

A second social issue that is frequently discussed in relation to the domestic impact of khat consumption is the financial burden that chewers place upon the family budget. This was a recurring theme in all our interviews and public discussion about khat with members of immigrant communities. One can sum up this discourse in one pithy sentence: Khat chewers spend scarce funds on a luxury that only reduces their chances of finding employment. Even moderate use makes a dent in the family budgets of immigrants, many of whom rely upon state benefits: The price of the bundle (£3), when combined with that of the cigarettes, tea or soft drinks that are consumed at the same time, and taking account of the transport costs of getting to the venue, can easily tot up to £6–8. When occasional indulgence turns into a regular habit, the impact on household finances can be severe. With no other sources of income, chewers divert benefits intended for family necessities or try to extract funds from other family members.

It is important, however, to appreciate the diversity of Somali families and the heterogeneity of the community. Even among the wave of refugees fleeing the civil war from the 1980s onward, significant differences obtain, all of which impact on the relationship with khat and the negotiation of problems at home. One Somali anthropologist has noted how the breakdown of the extended family system among earlier immigrants forced men and women to share childcare and domestic chores. Men also had to spend more time in the home because they spoke better English (Ahmed 1994). This changed from the mid-1990s onward. According to Harris (2004: 60), the majority of Somalis arriving in England in that period were single mothers with their children. In some cases the men would follow after several years, by which time the women had established themselves, learnt to operate within the system and improved their language skills. There is, therefore, some discussion over the extent to which Western culture has impacted on gender relations. One informant, for instance, maintained that the opportunities to Somali women in the UK dramatically altered the power relations between sexes.[19] Others, however, maintained that in Somalia, and particularly in rural areas, women enjoyed even greater autonomy, largely controlling their own resources. Ethnographic accounts of pastoral society in Somalia also speak of a division of spheres, where women enjoyed great decision-making powers (Lewis 1962). The idea of Westernisation as a 'liberating force' for Somali women may therefore be overplayed, motivated in part perhaps by a cultural narcissism among social-service agencies in the host community.

A general consensus obtains among informants and researchers, however, that there is something akin to a 'crisis of masculinity' among Somali immigrants. In traditional Somali society men stood at the apex of the domestic unit, as figureheads combining protective, symbolic and economic functions. In the UK, where security is guaranteed by the state, the welfare services maintain the family, and the honour of clanship is meaningless now that the role has become redundant. This has had consequences for internal power relations: 'The problem is … because they have no work [women] don't see men as any longer responsible … for family income … So women are saying, "you have no right to shout at me, to tell me what to do. I am being looked after by the British government so what the hell are you controlling me for?"' (Harris 2004). This situation can be exacerbated where welfare cheques, tenancy agreements and other legal contracts are made out to women. As a consequence of this, men can be quite literally displaced as heads of their households, their place taken in popular imaginary by the welfare state. One informant recalled sitting in a community and watching a woman walking past, dropping her social-security book. A Somali man called to her, 'Madam, you have just dropped your husband on the floor'[20] (see also Griffith 2002).

But how can we be sure that khat is in fact the cause of these social ills? A professional with close experience of working with a range of refugee communities in London reminded us of a more basic reality about the Somali diaspora: 'The families were not functional in the first place, people lose sight of that. The women came first and had to fend for themselves to establish themselves. The men came later and no longer had a role. Some young women arrived with their siblings. Many of the children were extremely disturbed by what they had seen.'[21] She adds that some Somali community groups have shown themselves to be adept at playing up the khat issue to attract funds. An even more vivid example is provided by a social worker working in a supported housing scheme for homeless Somali men in Bristol. Commenting on the sharp increase in the number of homeless Somalis, she contends that 'many women now call in the police when they have serious crises at home and accuse the men of domestic violence. And when they tell the officers that they are also chewing khat they [the men] have no chance'.[22] Gender relations in the Somali community are therefore just as complex and contested as in any other community. Somali refugees, relatively recently arrived, have no model of harmonious, cohesive, functioning family units to look back to. Life in the UK is radically different from anything they experienced 'back home'. In the UK, Somali families are nuclear, not extended, and men and women are permanently co-resident. Add to this the high unemployment rate among Somalis, and the continuing anxiety over family and friends left in the war-torn country or scattered in the diaspora, and it becomes clear that the pressures are immense. Khat use has certainly become a factor in family relationships and in community identity, but to regard it as the 'corrosive, vicious, and pernicious' driver of family breakdown in the Somali community, to quote MP Stephen Pound, is an absurd and potentially very damaging generalization.

In the public discourse about khat in the UK there is much that has not been said. Because of the gender politics that has driven the involvement of Somali women's groups in the debate, one issue that has been overlooked is the use of khat among Somali women. In contrast to practices in Yemen, where both men and women chew equally avidly, in Somalia it has never been the norm for females to chew (Green 1999). These attitudes have transferred with the diaspora, forcing Somali women in the UK to chew their leaves in secret (Turning Point 2005). Those from both sides of the divide on khat collude in an exercise of suppression and denial about this practice: Khat supporters emphasize the taboo on female khat use so as to underline their social responsibility and their adherence to 'traditional values', while prohibitionists build their case upon the message of female victimization. The spreading of khat among UK Somali women is, however, an open secret and represents a thriving segment of the khat market. Could it be that the much larger percentage of women than men supporting a ban on khat (Patel et al. 2005) is explained, in part at least, by their exclusion from the *mafrish* and the stigmatization of their consumption? And for Somali men, is khat consumption and its distinctive patterns of male association the last preserve of a social seniority lost in all other spheres?

Unable to purchase in the *mafrish*, and risking exposure and opprobrium by purchasing at a shop, most khat-chewing women depend on trusted males to supply them. While women are therefore more likely to be solitary users, they also chew at 'women-only' khat parties. Research among khat-chewing Somali women in the north London borough of Camden offered an insight to the particular difficulties faced by women chewers, and revealed some of the issues that members of the Somali community are less keen to air in public. Let us consider the case of Sabia.

Case Study – Sabia[23]

Sabia, a single mother with her 4 children, came to the UK 10 years ago, having witnessed the murder of her husband in Somalia. With only a basic education and a limited knowledge of English, Sabia is having a hard time with her adolescent children. One of the boys is having problems at school and has been in trouble with the police, giving her constant worries over his safety and future. Sabia spends most of her nights chewing khat with a group of female friends and neighbours. These khat sessions typically go on until the early hours of the morning, but sometimes Sabia will go through 36 hours without catching any sleep. Especially if she has some important appointment to go to in the mornings, Sabia does not bother to go to bed. She feels constantly exhausted, though, to the extent that she cannot carry out the normal day-to-day duties, such as cooking meals for her children.

Upon arriving at her house at 4.00 pm, I rang the doorbell but got no reply. After 15 minutes one of the children arrived home and was able to use his key to let me in. I was shown into the dining room, where Sabia was sleeping on the floor. At first I thought that she had been dozing in front of the TV, but later discovered she had spend all of the previous night chewing khat and was unable to go to her bed. Realizing I was in the room, she slowly roused herself, looking extremely tired and behaving irritably. She was unwilling to talk much. Her daughter made an effort to tidy the room, and Sabia announced that she would not prepare any food and that the children should get a takeaway instead. After the children had left to get their meal, Sabia used her phone to call someone about a khat delivery. But the delivery had not arrived: Sabia was told to call again later. Half an hour later she got the same news, and now Sabia had to call her eight friends, all of whom had planned to join the session. When one friend declared that she would not come because of my presence [the researcher], Sabia reacted angrily. Having finished her calls, Sabia went back to sleep. After another hour or so she re-emerged, called the supplier again and placed an order for 40 bundles. The news that the khat had arrived prompted an almost instantaneous change in her behaviour. She became hyperactive and almost hysterical, laughing, giggling and talking constantly. With her energy renewed, Sabia rose to wash her face and then went to the kitchen to prepare a meal.

Sabia now repeatedly looked at the mirror to check her appearance and eventually went to her room to shower and dress. She gave the supplier another call to check when the delivery would be made. Reassured, she continued talking. Being turned down by one of her friends no longer affected her mood. She prepared the seating, fixed the drinks (sweet tea and water), put on make-up and perfume, and lit the incense burners. She then called the khat delivery agent once again, this time to ask him to bring cigarettes. He at last arrived, with the cigarettes and 40 bundles of fresh khat. When he asked for payment, Sabia haggled over the price, but then paid in full. Around 6.00 pm the first guests arrived, each carrying her own bundle of khat. Each made a payment to Sabia. The room quickly filled with smoke, but the windows remained firmly shut as fresh air was believed to spoil the khat effect. When I left at 3.00 am, the khat session was still in full flow.

In female gatherings such as that at Sabia's home, discretion is of paramount importance to safeguard the reputations of the participants. As women are the primary carers of children they also bear the risk of compromising their parental responsibilities in the eyes of neighbours and social services if their pattern of use becomes public. Yet, as is apparent from Sabia's story, women often suffer the same post-traumatic stress disorders, and the pressures of exile and adaptation to a new life, as so often appear in accounts of male khat use. According to the director of the Orexis drug treatment centre in Deptford, South London, many Somali clients have been victims of torture and rape and use khat to self-medicate against past trauma.[24] Somali women seem to be especially reluctant to contact the available outreach services, however, and Orexis has therefore depended on community workers already engaged in the cases of Somali families introducing them to the drug-treatment centre.

Such outreach services targeting highly vulnerable and hard to reach groups are extremely rare. Khat has only recently been included in national drug strategies in the UK, which hitherto concentrated on class A substance users. The recent shift by the National Treatment Agency to a policy of 'every drug matters', regardless of its classification, indicates an emerging broader social conception of drug-related problems. Work funded by the Home Office (Turning Point 2005; Patel 2005) has also underlined the need for service provision for users of khat, as pioneered by Orexis in Deptford, Project Liban in Tower Hamlets, Somali Mental Health in Sheffield, or Hounslow DAIS. The problem with many conventional treatment centres is that they are medicalized, when what Somalis need is a more comprehensive social service.

Language skills and the perception of agency relevance to individual needs are crucial in determining patterns of access. A survey among Somali residents in Streatham found that 56 per cent were reluctant to contact services because of language difficulties (Ahmed et al. 2004). The language barrier would be higher still for issues as delicate as drug problems, and where the process of counselling and treatment are so language-centred. Other problems to be overcome are issues of definition and stigma. An early approach by the director of a Streatham-based drug-treatment service to members of the Gleneagle Road community was brushed off. Khat was not a drug, they contended, and the services offered were therefore quite inappropriate.[25] Yet among the customers visiting Nura and the other *mafrishes* in this area there is a body of opinion that regards their own pattern of khat use as problematic. Several admit to spending too much time and money on khat, but plead lack of alternatives as their excuse. Chatting and chewing informally, a surprising number of khat users will support the idea of regulation, or even prohibition of khat imports.

This paradoxical response has been reported in several larger surveys of khat chewers (Fowzi 2005; Salam 2004). With reference to a larger sample of systematically interviewed users in Sheffield, it was found that

> a majority of khat users felt that khat was a problem within their community, had a negative effect on their family, and should not be brought into Britain. This suggests that complex relationships between personal attitudes, cultural norms, socio-economic factors and 'psychological dependence' contribute towards individuals' use of khat. (Woods 2005)

Part of the complexity feeds into the question of classification. This is not merely a taxonomic exercise: It is decisive for individual and community approaches to resolving problems. Hence, the recognition that personal khat use is problematic or even shameful can be much more difficult to deal with if we insist upon labelling khat as a drug. Many Somali in the UK have strong opinions about drugs, and are keen to stress that khat should *not* be put in this category (Griffiths 1998). Their definition is not drawn from science, but from scripture. Islamic teaching clearly forbids anything that intoxicates a person.[26] Drug use, then, is not merely a breach of man's imperfect law, but defiance of divine will: Those who persist, including drinkers of alcohol, run the dual risk of social isolation in this life and damnation in the next. The polemic claim by some Somali members of the anti-khat movement that khat is a drug therefore carries a ferocity that is often lost on their British campaign allies.

The pathos of guilt, the admission of powerlessness and continued use is explored by Woods (2005) with reference to the mental health profiles of the khat users he surveyed. A quarter of the informants reported sufficient emotional distress to suggest that they were experiencing a minor psychiatric disorder, and 72 per cent had suffered trauma. A number of studies have identified a high incidence of mental-health problems among Somali immigrants in the UK and across the diaspora (Bhui et al. 2003; McCrone et al. 2005). There is a growing body of work on the particular mental-health issues in refugee communities, and the link of migration itself and the genes of mental disorder mediated through such stressors as acculturation, unemployment and the experience of violence, bereavement and separation from family. Against this background, Woods suggests that we should view khat use as a form of self-medication (Woods 2005), reviving the role played by the plant in the pharmacopoeia of pre-colonial Somalia (Beekinghuis 2001).

In the classical khat-using countries the leaves of *catha edulis* have long been prized for their medical properties. In Harar, for instance, it is believed that khat can affect 501 different cures (Zaghloul et al. 2003), and has widely been used for treating melancholia and depression (Alem and Shibre 1997). Most popularly used, perhaps, were the performance-enhancing properties of khat, allowing the user to stave off fatigue and suppress hunger (Elmi 1983; Kalix 1984). Many khat-chewing informants explain their habits as a way to 'forget' and to console over the losses of the past and the problems of the present. The psychiatrist at St Clement's Hospital in East London, Eleni Palazidou, who deals with a large caseload of Somali clients, quotes the case of one patient who escaped a massacre of an entire village by lying under a pile of corpses. To the consternation of the hospital staff in London, some patients even bring khat into the psychiatric wards.[27] Mental-health practitioners confronted with severe cases of disturbance are therefore faced with a diagnostic problem: should they view khat use a consequence of such trauma, as suggested by Woods (2005), or is khat to be seen as the trigger that produces the condition?

The conditions associated with khat range through anxiety, dizziness, impaired concentration, insomnia, headaches, migraine, midriasis, conjunctival congestion, impaired motor concentration, fine tremor and stereotypical behaviour, depression, hypnagogic hallucinations, schizophrenia and psychosis. These adverse mental-health effects provide the backbone to the medical argument for tighter controls on khat. But how convincing is the evidence? A recent literature review of khat and mental-health issues (Warfa et al. 2006) has identified 41 English-language research papers including, *inter alia*, 5 clinical case-report papers and 26 epidemiological studies. This review finds that the authors of the case reports used routine mental-state assessments and history-taking methods to obtain baseline information about inpatients with severe psychiatric conditions and khat abuse. Although mental-state examination can vary from one clinician to another in terms of both cross-cultural content and length of examination, the authors generally provided comprehensive case details and reported a causative relationship between khat use and psychosis or psychotic symptoms. Several authors proposed that their case findings warranted a policy change that would restrict the use of khat. In contrast, none of the epidemiological studies found, or claimed to have found, a causative relationship between the consumption of khat and any psychiatric disorders. Researchers in the largest study on khat and mental disorders are clear that their work 'could not determine the existence of a causal relationship between khat and psychosis' (Odenwald et al. 2005: 21). Indeed, none of the numerous studies in the UK and elsewhere have so far been able to establish a causative link. The medical evidence marshalled in support of tighter controls on khat is therefore based exclusively upon the case notes of clinicians, and not on epidemiological research (see Table 9.3).

This inevitably raises serious doubts as to the veracity of the judgements reached by the clinicians. As Kalix observes, khat use is self-limiting because the plant material is so bulky, and the mode of administration so lengthy that khat-induced psychosis is an infrequent occurrence (Kalix 1984). Even where a relationship is established, the evidence suggests at best that khat acts as a trigger in 'dual diagnosis'[28] patients: 'Khat users with psychosis frequently present to general adult psychiatry services' (Cox and Rampes 2003). Moreover, the diagnostic tools used in

Table 9.3 Khat and the Literature on Health

Study	Hypothesis Related to Khat Use and Mental Health Reported?	Sample Size Representative of Population?	Validity and Reliability Issues Discussed?	Controlled for Known Confounders Explained?	Causative Link between Khat Use and Psychiatric Disorders Found?	Other Associations between Khat Use and Mental Health Found?
Kennedy et al. 1983	yes	yes	yes	yes	no	P
Dhadphale and Omolo 1988	no	no	no	no	no	yes
Elmi 1982	no	yes	no	no	no	no
Litman 1986	yes	yes	yes	yes	no	yes
Griffiths et al. 1997	no	no	yes	no	no	yes
Woods 2005	no	N/A	P	yes	no	yes
Odenwald et al. 2005	yes	yes	P	no	no	yes
Kebede et al. 1999	no	yes	no	yes	no	no
Bhui et al. 2003	no	yes	yes	yes	no	yes
Numan 2004	no	yes	no	no	no	no
Alem et al. 1999	no	yes	no	no	no	
Bhui et al. 2003	no	yes	yes	yes	no	yes

psychiatry are subject to limitations. One community worker warns that perceptual change may be seen as a fact and that the labelling of such change as psychotic is a matter of opinion. Using another kind of language, this could also be termed a mystical experience (Leech 1994). In the treatment of immigrants from different cultural backgrounds, statements about hallucinations are 'easily mistaken for schizophrenia' (Granek et al. 1988).

It becomes clear, then, that the actual evidence for a link between khat and mental-health disorder is yet to be established. What we can safely say is that khat, when used in excess, can adversely affect the mental health of clients suffering mental-health disorder. This holds for any other psychoactive substance, including alcohol. The campaign against khat, then, is largely precautionary, concerned with the rapid spread of a substance unknown to professionals in the UK and other Western countries worried about both the possible consequences for the emerging communities of new migrants and the crossover to the main population.

Is khat likely to break out of the realm of diasporic consumption? In one of the most sensitive explorations of regular khat use, the writer Kevin Rushby, back in the UK after a long period of residence in the Red Sea region, recalls his longing for the khat-chewing sessions of the Yemen. Unable to find comparable pleasures at home, he embarks on a journey through the khat heartlands of Ethiopia and Djibouti with Yemen as its final destination, chewing avidly and regularly along the way. As a connoisseur, he enjoys all stages of the khat experience, from the selection and purchase to the civility and ritual surrounding consumption:

> I passed the hours listening to the gentle lubalub of the hookah and whispered conversations about dead poets and fine deeds. In Sana'a, Khat governs. Each day at three, climbing the steps to a smoky room with a bundle under the arm; then closing the door to the outside world, choosing the leaves, gently crushing them with the teeth and waiting for the drug to take effect. No rush, just a silky transition, scarcely noticed, and then the room casts loose its moorings. (Rushby)

There are few other English-language accounts as evocative of the experience produced by khat. Rushby's appreciation and indulgence is predicated, however, upon his acculturation and adjustment to this very non-English setting. He is proficient in Arabic and feels affection and admiration for the host culture.

Perhaps it was the surrender to a chemically produced tranquillity described so vividly by Rushby that alarmed a number of medical professionals into pressing for preventative scheduling of khat in the 1980s. Citing newspaper reports of khat use by Westerners,[29] and seemingly unaware of early international attempts to prohibit khat, they proposed immediate action as a precautionary measure (Pantelis et al. 1989). Other authors at this time speculated that a second generation of immigrants growing up with khat would inevitably become more integrated with British culture and would transmit khat use to the main population (Mayberry et al. 1984). Occasional reports of indoor cultivation of *catha edulis* also raised the (faintly ridiculous) fears of a new, domestically produced drug crop spreading in Western countries (Giannini et al. 1986).

In the early 1990s the first appearance of khat on the club scene seemed to suggest that these concerns may have been justified after all. Stalls and shops in London's Kensington Market, in fashionable Brighton, and in the country's then capital of youth culture, Manchester, were reportedly selling bags of khat for £8, representing a mark-up of more than 400 per cent on the imported bundles.[30] But the trend proved brief. Chewing bitter leaves and twigs for hours on end did not hold much appeal in Britain's hyped-up youth drug culture. Within another year, khat was reportedly being served in small 25 ml bottles as a tincture, but this did not catch on either.[31] Then, with the emergence of 'head shops' catering for a young party-going crowd around the country, a network of retail outlets emerged for the sale of 'herbal highs' as alternatives to MDMA and amphetamines. One company, Cybertonics, developed a product named K2, containing pseudo ephedrine, one of the constituents of khat, among other ingredients. But the best-known khat-based product at this time was marketed by 'Keith the Khat Man', who sold small bottles containing cathine and cathinone at £3–4 each. Business was briefly brisk.[32]

Although the law-enforcement agencies seemed to take a relaxed view of these developments, they should perhaps have been more diligent. While khat leaves are legal in the UK, any process of producing the controlled active ingredients of cathine and cathinone is a crime. In 1998, a case was brought in Lewes Crown Court against one producer of khat tinctures. Ignorance constituted part of the defence, as the accused purported not to have known that he was producing cathine or cathinone until one of the bottles was analysed. The jury acquitted him, but the case also marked the high point of the UK khat-tincture experience. Israel is still the only country where the sale of synthesized cathine and cathinone to non-traditional users has been reported. Apparently popular at weddings, parties and on the Tel Aviv club scene, they are known as *hagitat* – a play on khat with the Hebrew word *hagiga,* meaning celebration (Avrahami 2004). In the UK, khat-based preparations have at best enjoyed a novelty value or a niche market as an organic product. The majority of drug users are neither experimental nor adventurous, preferring to stick to known products – as the widely practised 'branding' of ecstasy tablets demonstrates. And while there is great demand for mind-altering substances, particularly among the 16–29-year-old age group, the market is already saturated with well-established substances that have similar but far more powerful stimulating properties than khat and its principal alkaloids.

Despite the dire predictions of some, khat has remained firmly anchored in the diaspora communities. The process of acculturation has, if anything, run the other way. Among the Somali, many young men have taken khat, some will indulge occasionally, but the regular visitors in the *mafrishes*, and the bulk of the 'chronic' chewers, are in the 25–45-year-old bracket. These men have picked up khat chewing either in Somalia or along the journey of exile, and imported the habit into the UK. Younger immigrants, and those in later generations, are less likely to be khat consumers.

This finding has important implications for the regulation and management of khat use. It is thus apparent that youths in the diaspora communities can substitute a range of other substances for khat. However, the idea of 'Gradual process of degeneration from socially sanctioned, controlled drug use to socially detrimental drug abuse' (UNDCP 1997) is the master narrative and foundational myth of the modern drug-control regime and the international bureaucracy that supports it. It conjures a notion of socially integrated drug use which was essentially problem-free and associated with a minimal level of harm. Through processes too complex to be explained or analysed, the nature and the level of drug use has changed to become socially destructive and in need of control. This narrative of modern degeneration tries to appear culturally sensitive and to appreciate the value of diverse consumption patterns, while at the same time imposing negative value judgements on a cultural product. It conjures an image of unchanging cultural patterns in a static past, corrupted and rendered non-functional by the intrusion of modernity. Yet we know that the Said Barre government sought to ban khat in Somalia before the war, that patterns of khat consumption within the Red Sea region have undergone significant changes since the 1960s, and that there is a deeply contested history of debate over the use of khat throughout the Horn and Eastern Africa.

The arguments made for cultural tradition in the defence of khat, and for modern degeneration in the campaign for prohibition for its ban, each having to be thoroughly qualified. Several points should be made. First, it is important to note that many khat chewing Somalis picked up the habit during the war or in refugee camps, in circumstances of situation, of societal dysfunction and individual dislocation. They were initiated into a pattern of khat use that was not embedded in a reproducing and organic social structure, was not culturally sanctioned and was never subject to time-proven rituals of harm minimization. A pattern of use driven by the individual's search for gratification, aided by the workings of a fragmented market, has continued in the UK. The oft-repeated sentiment of UK Somalis that 'khat use is different here' refers not so much to the physical properties of the leaves themselves as to the redefinition of its social, cultural and commercial value. In London, khat is treated and traded like any other vulgar vegetable and always available. Society is indifferent, the community fragmented, and the pattern of use in the hands and mouths of the consumers themselves. As long as they can pay, and regardless of the protestations of the anti-khat lobby, vices do not come cheaper than the price of a bundle of leaves.

These stories of khat consumption in the Somali diaspora are connected to debates 'back home', and especially in Somaliland, where efforts are being made to construct a new nation state out of the rubble of the old Somalia. Here, too, the debate about khat use is shaped by anxieties and fears that have little to do with an understanding of the pharmacological effects of chewing the leaves of catha edulis. Let us conclude this chapter with a tale from Somaliland that illustrates the connections between local and global discourses on khat consumption.

On 5 October 2003, a 60-year-old Italian doctor and aid worker, Annalena Tonelli, was murdered in the Somaliland town of Borama. Tonelli was a respected and much loved local personality. She had worked in Somaliland for six years, running the TB hospital and raising awareness of communicable diseases, including HIV/AIDS. Her funeral and memorial service was attended by Somaliland's Vice-President, and several Ministers, as well as representatives of the UN and other aid organizations. Among those present was Rakiya Omaar, director of the humanitarian agency Africa Rights. Writing in the Somaliland Times, Omaar explained that the Somaliland government had attended the ceremony 'in a show of force, both to express their appreciation for the work of Dr Tonelli, but also to send a message to the international community that her murder will not go unpunished' (Omaar 2003). Two men had been arrested in connection with the murder, Omaar told her readers. Speculating as to the motive for the murder, she wondered about rumours that the killer was mentally deranged. 'Why are there so many mentally disturbed people walking on the streets of all our towns?' Omaar asked. 'We have as yet no statistics on the extent of the problem, but it is undeniably prevalent.' She continued,

> Whether you live in Berbera, Hargeisa, Burao or Borama, you come across them every day. In fact you live in fear of them. They are mainly men, many of them in the prime of life, and often armed with knives, swords or heavy rocks. But there is a troubling increase in the number of women who are evidently in mental distress. And even more tragic are the far greater numbers we don't see – chained to beds in their homes by desperate relatives who do not know where to turn to for help. Some families are looking after more than one patient.
>
> Every Somalilander who reads this article knows an individual with some form of mental health problem; they are our relatives, friends, colleagues, classmates and neighbours. We also know the terrible price each family is paying in the absence of even the most basic services – the psychological trauma, the economic burden and the social consequences of looking after disturbed and sometimes very violent people … This phenomenon is not only a tragedy for the individuals and families concerned, but is likely to undermine stability and growth on a national level.

In Somaliland, the explosion in mental illness since the 1990s has customarily been blamed on the war that devastated the country, and the consequent social disruption of the multitude of Somali exiles in the refugee camps in Ethiopia and Kenya. But Omaar had another explanation to offer: 'the surge in mental distress is a direct consequence of the dramatic increase in the consumption of *qat* [khat].' Describing khat as 'a potent and addictive drug', Omaar chastised Somalilanders for their unwillingness to confront the harm that it was doing to their society. Unless khat was controlled, there would be 'many more senseless deaths on our streets'.

Warming to her theme, Omaar now provided a litany of evils associated with khat consumption – evils that hindered the social and economic development of the country:

> You only need to look at the absurd economics of qat, with vast amounts of cash leaving our borders every day into Ethiopia. Don't expect to see civil servants, including senior officials, attend a meeting in the afternoon, no matter how important the subject under discussion is to the prospects of Somaliland. The dirt in our towns, littered with thousands of the multi-coloured plastic bags used to wrap qat, would be a sufficient reason to ban it. Not to mention the destructive impact on family life and our educational system where it is not uncommon to see secondary school students more interested in qat than in their studies. It is not, in fact, possible to measure the cost of qat to our society.

To underline the point, Omaar explained that young Somali males in Britain registered the second-highest level of suicide among any immigrant group, 'no doubt while under the extreme and prolonged influence of qat'.

Calling for prohibition of khat in Somaliland was unlikely to gain much support, Omaar conceded, for the trade generated tax revenues for the government, was popular with the majority of people, and would be protected by 'powerful businessmen who have invested in this lucrative sector'. Indeed, in Somaliland's elections of 2003, shrewd politicians stockpiled khat for distribution to their potential voters. Both the government and its opponents 'literally chewed over their options while under the influence of qat'. Khat consumption in Somaliland is therefore by no means restricted to deranged young men roaming the streets, but its use is all too easily deployed in any emotive discussion of the social and economic issues of the day. The questions that Rakiya Omaar wanted to ask were not really about the death of an Italian doctor, then, but about the death of a country.

–10–

The Politics of Khat Control

Lobbying for Identity and Recognition

Over the past few years the interests and agendas of various social actors have coalesced around a set of issues in which khat figures as the common denominator. By locating the root cause of the various problems in the substance, and declaring it a drug, the door opens to a process of control. There is machinery for driving this process in place, a vocabulary for dangers and remedies, and a set of roles for participants and players. Most importantly, there is a destination which, once reached, allows the passengers to disembark and pass on the responsibility for dealing with the consequences to a different set of professionals.

Prominent among the anti-khat campaigners in the West are members from the Somali community, whose voice from the 'inside' ring with authority and authenticity. Their direct experience of living with a problematic khat user can lend a sense of purpose to the campaigns and provide a source of energy. Some of the most outspoken campaigners have been working in local government, in health- and social-care agencies or in education. They have used their position to highlight a problem within a marginal and not very visible group. At the same time, they have been able to inject the community into the work programmes of local and national agencies and raise awareness. Harris points to the plethora of investigations and research reports on the Somali community, particularly when compared to other, sizeable immigrant groups, as for example the Yoruba (Harris 1994: 12). She suggests that the Somalis as refugees are far more dependent on government-funded initiatives and that the dramatic problematization of issues is one way of attracting attention. Amplifying the problems associated with khat has secured many community groups the interest of the authorities and funds.

It is important to note that among Britain's larger immigrant groups, Somalis are among the most socially and economically disadvantaged. The established community of migrant workers whose roots stretch back to the 1950s and 1960s are now a minority. Most UK Somalis arrived as refugees, with no resources, and are often poorly qualified in conventional and locally appropriate skill sets. The considerable social distance from the indigenous British culture has exacerbated this comparative deprivation. Though a positive stance toward diversity has allowed Britain to develop a dynamic self-image, and to integrate cultural icons like reggae music or chicken tikka masala, there are no markers with which Somalis can readily identify, and in turn be recognized.

In the existing patterns of multiculturalism, UK Somalis see their identity submerged within wider reference groups, such as Afro-Caribbean or Islam. At the same time, the pressures for assimilation are considerable. Once again, the Somali experience is at odds with that of Commonwealth immigrants, in that their colonial encounter with the British was comparatively short. Somalis have little experience in adapting their culture and customs to the imperial design, of finding a role for traditional structures within the wider system. The first- and second-generation migrants, having found a haven and established a foothold in the UK, are now struggling to maintain an identity in the face of multiple pressures to conform and adapt. For many, then, the sprig of khat so popular with the older males may serve as an icon for group recognition in a multicultural Britain that seems to be taking only scant interest in yet another group of dark-skinned immigrants. To others, however, the very same sprig symbolizes a hangover of a past that they have run away from. It encapsulates images of a past marred by arrested development, categorical discrimination and an amphetamine-fuelled violence spiralling out of control. As an image, then, khat is as powerful as it is contested.

Constructing a Consensus on the Pathology of Khat

The different groups engaging in debate are looking for allies among decision-makers, and seek to establish their view as the dominant model for understanding khat. In seeking to understand how a particular consensus is being arrived at with regard to psychoactive substances, we follow Bergeron and Kopp (2002) in looking at two effects. The first positional effect is the cognitive perspective. Most of the UK professionals supporting a ban are psychiatrists who come into contact with deeply disturbed clients who happen to be khat users, and hence identify khat as the source of the problem. The campaign leaders in the community are usually either women who are living as single parents or those whose husbands are not economically active. Moreover, as women they suffer social stigma if seen chewing khat and are excluded from the *mafrish*. Finally, there are politicians concerned about 'drug markets' and immigration. Few among these campaigners have ever experienced the pleasures and benefits of a khat chew or appreciated the social function of the *mafrish*.

The second positional effect is the process by which ideas harden and turn into a cognitive frame. As the case studies of khat-induced psychosis build up, albeit slowly, they establish a necessary association that is then developed into a causal relationship. As the view of khat as a problem drug becomes institutionalized, it is increasingly immune to the accumulation of anomalies. The supporting networks of policy-makers, practitioners and researchers allow the model to withstand sustained criticism by referring to one another, and by explaining away anomalies with secondary theories.

The causal relationship between khat use and psychiatric conditions, for instance, is severely compromised by the large number of casual and socially functioning khat users or the long history of khat use in the Horn of Africa. As objections to the advocated prohibition of khat, these arguments are neutralized by further hypothesis, holding for example that disturbances and measurable disorders occur to all users along a continuum – that khat was used to pay militias in the Somali civil war and hence perpetuated the cycle of violence; that khat use in the UK is not socially integrated; and that the khat is more readily available and stronger.

Far more difficult to contain are political accusations pointing to the ulterior motives behind a particular policy. There is a school of thought suggesting that drug control has long been used in multicultural societies as an instrument of minority control. For instance, Himmelstein (1978)

> repressive controls are a response to the drug user, not drug use. Drugs associated with groups low in the privilege structure are the ones that get proscribed and stigmatised. Groups high in the privilege structure are the ones who do the proscribing and stigmatising.

In the United States the prohibition of opium, cannabis and the differential of penalties between powder cocaine and crack cocaine is steeped in the politics of race. At the same time a closer analysis of the antecedents to drug-control legislation in the US shows that 'the relationship between hostility towards minority groups and legislation against the drugs they are believed to use is rarely simple and direct (Giffen 1991: 16). Thus, for instance, many Afro-American community leaders were in full support of the war on drugs of the Republican administrations of Reagan and Bush Sr. Congressman Charlie Rangel, for instance, a founding member of the Congressional Black Caucus, was an architect of the drug policies in the 1980s, chairing the Committee on Narcotics Abuse and Control, drafting legislation to increase penalties for drug dealers and instrumental in taking the fight into drug-producing and -transiting countries.

Equally, when the first municipal ordinances against opium distribution were issued along the western seaboard of nineteenth-century America, Chinese-community spokesmen could always be found and cited in support. In the case of khat in the UK, the Somali campaigners provide an indispensable alibi for the coalition of professionals, researchers, bureaucrats and politicians of all colours that their intentions are for the greater good of vulnerable populations, untainted by the cynical politics of race.

If community members are needed to legitimize the campaign and to document the pathologies of khat use, and practitioners volunteer to explain them, no theoretical model can be elevated into orthodoxy, and become adopted as policy, without the support of politicians. Khat opponents can take heart from the alacrity with which members from both sides of the House of Commons have taken the floor to call for a ban on khat, often echoing the concerns of local councillors and community activists. In the frenetic atmosphere of parliamentary politics, khat has provided an opportunity for politicians to display their concerns for community welfare and talk tough on 'drugs'. Few topics have provided a similar bandwidth in appealing to integrationist and racist opinion alike than the campaign against khat.

In the various parliamentary debates, there has been scant reference to the experience of other countries where khat has been brought under control. Yet for an assessment of potential implications of such a policy for the Somali community, a comparison may prove instructive.

Comparative Experience: The United States

In the United States and Canada, khat is a prohibited substance. In law this is not always straightforward, as in the United States it is not khat that is banned but the two known active ingredients, cathine and cathinone. Dried khat, where both compounds have disintegrated, should therefore technically fall within the law but individuals have been successfully prosecuted for possession and distribution of dried leaves.[1] The ambiguity extends to live plants that are not intended for ingestion. While the Drug Enforcement Administration operatives may take the view that khat is an illegal plant, the Federal Register of banned substances lists cathinone and cathine but not khat. It is important to remember that the agency's views are not law, even though in practice they can amount to much the same. There has been some activity at points of entry as discussed above, and within areas with concentrations of Somali, Yemeni and Ethiopian populations. There have been concerns that the bulky nature of khat should give opportunity for officers to make self-serving claims about seizing '100 pounds worth of Schedule I narcotics', but in the event, there has been only limited activity around khat. Indeed, so little information has been available that one lawyer claimed to have won acquittals by arguing 'lack of fair notice'. In American law people must be duly informed that a substance is illegal, and with khat appearing on neither federal nor state lists of banned substances, this was not done.[2]

While khat has not been awarded high priority by US enforcement agencies, the very process of classification has in itself been characteristic. The scheduling of cathine in 1988 and cathinone in 1993 was not preceded by consultation of the communities most affected. It followed very much as a routine fulfilment of the country's obligation to the 1971 Convention on Psychotropic Substances. This treaty is an undertaking by international partners to prohibit the importation, sale and distribution of listed substances. The US government was one of its principal architects and is widely seen as the unofficial guardian of this and subsequent drug-control instruments. Every year the State Department runs a certification exercise for countries suspected of involvement in drug production or drug trafficking. Where governments are deemed to be complicit to such activities, economic sanctions can be applied at the discretion of the US President. The US in turn does its utmost to live up to the spirit and the letter of the conventions, including the pre-emptive scheduling of substances like khat.

An additional justification for the ban came from an unexpected quarter, namely the US military entanglement in the United Nations peacekeeping mission to Somalia. To many Americans the attack on their troops in Mogadishu was difficult to understand, since the main purpose of their mission had, ostensibly, been to feed the Somali people. Khat provided a ready explanation, the Somali militias were high on drugs, their reasoning impaired by a powerful and exotic psychoactive substance. This theme was most graphically developed on the website of the 'supporters of the US Border Patrol'. This showed a picture of a young Somali militiaman armed with a rifle above the caption 'Khat eater waiting for a new target'. There is also a video clip of the dead US soldiers in the streets of Mogadishu with the text

> Almost all of the barbarians who attacked the UN peacekeepers and the barbarians who hacked them into chunks and the barbarians who attacked our troops and the barbarians who then – by the thousands – attacked our rescue forces all chewed a narcotic called khat.[3]

The site expounds the conjunction of xenophobia and prohibitionism by claiming that the number of 'violent and illegal aliens in America' can be calculated from the amount of khat entering the country. Though this is in itself at best an exercise in speculative guesswork, the point is made in stigmatizing an ethnic minority and denigrating their culture. The 'othering' is complete by the conclusion that 'the narcotic is an acquired taste and certainly not for an American palate'.

Comparative Experience: Canada

Until the 2006 election, Canada's drug policy was clearly and provocatively out of step with its southern neighbour's march to war. In contrast to the abstinence-centred US approach, Canada began to implement a set of policy measures bundled together under the euphemism 'harm reduction'. These include the decriminalization of minor drug offences, the provision of clean injecting equipment, methadone-maintenance provision for chronic users and the establishment of a safe and supervised consumption site in Vancouver. The underlying ethos of Canada's drug policy has been the promotion of public health, even where this meant tolerating modest levels of illicit drug abuse. Against this history of loosening restrictions, the country experienced an exponential growth in the semi-clandestine drugs economy, fronted by so called 'head shops' offering drug-use paraphernalia, and backed by extensive marijuana cultivation.

It is all the more surprising, then, that Canada has followed the US in the prohibition of khat. Some commentators suggest that this was in an attempt to prevent cross-border trafficking (Anderson and Carrier 2006). An alternative explanation is proffered by a Toronto-based Somali-born journalist, who claims that the ban was the product of a historical accident. In Canada, khat was a legal substance under the Food and Drugs Act, and could be imported with a licence. Undeclared consignments were confiscated. This state of affairs aroused the ire of a number of Muslim clerics who embarked on a letter-writing campaign to the Canadian media from the early 1990s onward demanding a ban on khat. This caught the attention of the Association of Canadian Chiefs of Police, as they were pushing for a tightening of the drug laws and an extension of police powers.[4] The officers succeeded in putting it on the agenda, and in 1995 a process of public consultation was begun for Bill C-7 in which members of the Somali community and prominent drug researchers were able to make depositions. Strong warnings came from expert witnesses from the Toronto-based Addiction Research Foundation. One area of concern was informed by the experience of drug control in general, where: 'to criminalise it [khat] is to risk starting down a well worn path towards greater problem'.[5] The other area of concern related to the impact such a ban would have on the relationship between the Somali community and the law-enforcement agencies, because 'criminalizing khat could create a new form of dangerous drug and criminalize a whole community'.[6]

Notwithstanding these objections, the Controlled Drugs and Substances Act came into force on 14 May 1997, making the possession and importation of khat illegal. While the ban on khat has played into the hands of police forces, by extending their powers and furnishing them with new instruments for proactive policing, it has increased the burden for their fellow officers at the Canada Customs and Revenue Agency. Their work is guided by a risk matrix that calculates drug prices and an actuarized value of human life and illness. In 2003, khat was upgraded from Cdn 40 cents to 50 cents a gram. Though exorbitant compared to London street prices, this still is low down on the list of enforcement priorities. Next to other threats, from class A drugs to terrorism, the ban on khat is seen as a nuisance. Each seizure is taking away two officers for 4–8 hours at a time and 'interfering with important stuff we could do … every agency works within the constraints of manpower and resources … We work on the basis of risk management and where we get the biggest bang for our buck … khat does not even figure …'[7]

The officers express a clear sense of frustration at having their hands tied by legislation that is forcing them to act. Often, it is customs clearing agents who alert customs officers to suspicious consignments. Any drug will then be seized and the people arrested and handed over to the Royal Canada Mountain Police for processing. In the case of khat, the Customs and Revenue Service rarely proceed with prosecutions. Ironically their success rate with khat is believed to be far higher than with any other prohibited substance, because khat is so bulky and easy to stop. This has had precious little impact on the flow of khat. One officer says provocatively:

'We have prohibited it, but has it had any impact on the market? I don't know' – and that every shipment that is taken out is just as easily replaced.[8]

The trade comes mainly out of London, and to a lesser degree out of Amsterdam. This is quietly played down, as there is no mileage in branding the UK as a 'transit country'. Khat arrives both as cargo and in the luggage carried by couriers, often Canadians recruited in the UK or sent over from Canada, carrying three suitcases and with their personal items in a backpack. So far there is no evidence of Somali diversification into other drugs, and all khat seizures were single-substance seizures. The only traces of cocaine and heroin were found on the couriers, in every case white Canadians.

The officers at the Intelligence and Risk Management Division are puzzled by the prohibition of khat. 'I do not know, it does not make any sense. If you look at other substances and see what damage they do and compare it to khat ...' The team speculate that there could have been pressure from members of the Somali community, especially from women, and that the government would act if there were a breakdown of family values.

Table 10.1 Total Khat Seizures, Canada Border Services

Year	Number of Seizures	Quantity (kg)	Value (Cdn$)
2004	1,331	14,539,341	7,269,673
2003	1,694	21,375,014	9,929,474
2002	692	20,094,086	8,037,641
2001	554	12,223,499	3,594,666
2000	517	9,984,793	1,996,963
1999	524	6,309,316	1,261,856
1998	310	7,945,048	1,589,011
1997	97	1,707,596	341,519
Totals	5,719	97,178,693	34,020,803

Source: Canada Border Services.

Impact

The passage of the Controlled Drugs and Substances Act had two immediate consequences for the community of khat users. First it led to the demise of socially integrated chewing by Somali men. Secondly it pushed the trade underground, turning traders into 'drug pushers'. While the criminalization of the import trade has not, as yet, led to criminal diversification and the injection of violence into khat transaction, it has had other predictable and deleterious effects. This includes the dehumanization of the khat sellers. With regard to the widely reported use of violence by police officers against suspected khat sellers, one commentator found that the police were entitled to use whatever force necessary to eliminate a threat when 'they busted a bunch of drug dealers' (*Toronto Star*, 25 July 2001). The identification of 'drug dealers' as legitimate targets of police violence feeds into xenophobic alarm over Somali migration. (The expatriate Somali population is estimated at 50,000, mainly concentrated in the Toronto area.)

It is alleged by members of the Somali community that these prejudices are shared by some police officers. The particular incident which gave rise to these comments occurred in a derelict shopping mall called Banaadir Plaza on Lawrence Avenue in July 2001. The complex had become popular with Somalis, who came to the unused facilities to trade, swap stories and socialize. A mini bazaar economy had grown up, with stalls, barbershops, money-transfer banks and catering services. On Saturday, 21 July 2001, four undercover police officers went in to arrest a man accused of khat selling. According to some witnesses he was kicked and beaten before a crowd ringed the officers who then fired shots in the air before retreating to their vehicle. A mob threw bottles and cans, damaging the car, and then moved on to the police station (*Toronto Star*, 23 July 2001). The matter was settled in subsequent meetings between community leaders and senior police officers, and similar breaches of the peace have been avoided.

According to informants, the behaviour of individual officers or units is straining the relationship between the community and the police. Some officers, for instance, have taken to walking into Somali restaurants and cafés and demanding that patrons open their mouths to be checked for khat.[9] While these spot checks have driven the last remaining *mafrishes* underground, they only reinforce the self-image of the Somalis – a community under siege, who have to prove their innocence.

Even more familiar is the opportunity for extortion that the khat ban has opened up. A number of officers from the Toronto drug squad have been charged with a range of offences against members of the Somali community. In one well-publicized case, non-uniformed officers broke into a house by force and used excessive violence against one Somali man, before framing up charges of khat possession (Grayson 2004). While reports of corruption among police officers investigating khat rings have not as yet been substantiated, they are widely perceived as plausible by Canadian Somalis. As immigrants with sometimes-insecure residence status, they are extremely exposed to police pressure and any suggestions of criminal activity.

Interestingly, the prohibition of khat seems to have achieved little in improving the opportunities for Somalis to become more closely integrated into Canadian society. On the contrary, the sudden criminalization of some has cast an aspersion over the entire community and compromised relations with law enforcement. Though unsuccessful in eliminating khat, it has dramatically changed the culture of khat use. In Canada there are no longer any *mafrishes* where men can go to buy their bundles and chew together. Users now come to the seller to score and take their khat away. This can be a long-winded process, as khat arrives with great irregularity.

One informant admits to spending two or three hours driving around looking to score, and often having to wait until after midnight. One consequence is that the life of chewers is disrupted by sudden arrivals or cancellations. While these men may chew less than their relatives in the UK, they spend as much time away from their homes chasing the chew. And even a more moderate khat habit knocks a large hole into the family budget. After the introduction of the ban, the price per bundle jumped from Cdn$20 to Cdn$60. For this greatly inflated price, customers have ended up with a poorer service. It seems that since criminalization the actual transaction has become a sordid backstreet affair. Dealers who have become furtive, hard and ruthless, no longer giving credit and threatening violence, are increasingly a feature of the khat trade. The customers cannot discuss the quality or argue over price but are left with what is on offer. To students of illicit drug markets this all sounds depressingly familiar. The experts from the Addiction Research Forum have at least the satisfaction of having rightly predicted the negative fallout from the prohibition on khat.

Khat in Sweden

The civil war in Somalia has dispersed a large refugee population all over the world. One of the largest Somali communities in Europe, estimated at some 15,000 strong, can be found in Sweden. There has been growing concern among social services and the police about the use of khat among Somali men. Some community groups have appealed to the authorities to take preventive action, arguing that khat use further impedes the successful integration into mainstream society. The Swedish authorities have proved receptive to these demands, which fit into a general policy that is intolerant of drugs and disapproving of alcohol use. In clear contrast to most other EU countries, Sweden has eschewed so-called harm-reduction policies, and makes no distinction between hard and soft drugs, nor any concessions to so-called non-problematic drug users. These resource-intensive measures are predicated on the policy objective that the use of illicit drugs can be eliminated from Swedish society.

While the overall objectives of Sweden's drug policy are strongly reminiscent of the US zero-tolerance approach, the methods are very different. Sweden is not waging a war on drugs, hence the emphasis falls less on fighting criminals than on extending the reach of state authority into this occluded sphere of private life. Treatment is mandatory for all offenders who are a danger to themselves or to society. The overall policy is seen as therapeutic and one more instance of the welfarism that characterizes the country's social model (Levitt et al. 2006).

By the same token, Somali refugees to Sweden enjoy a wider range of benefits and a higher quality of support than almost anywhere else in the Diaspora. The munificence of state paternalism is evident in Rinkeby, a suburb of Stockholm with an estimated 6,000 Somali residents. It is also the home to other immigrant groups from the Balkans, Turkey, Africa and the Far East who share generously proportioned apartment blocks with good facilities all kept in good order. Entrance halls, pathways, the open spaces between the blocks are well maintained, and furnished with playgrounds and wheelchair- or pram-friendly ramps. The settlement is laid out around a central square with an underground station providing easy access to the city centre and a number of shops. Significantly, not a single one of these is owned or even staffed by Somalis. The general lack of commercial activity – contrasting sadly with the hustle and bustle of cafés and restaurants, money-transfer and telephone services, and trading emporiums that characterize the Somali neighbourhoods in Lambeth, Camden, Tower Hamlets or Hounslow – is palpable. In Rinkeby, shops and cafés are concentrated in the market square and run by members of earlier immigrant groups. The main outlet for Somali enterprise, it seems, is illegal and underground.

In Sweden, khat-prevalence statistics are hard to come by, and vary between 15 per cent for Upsalla[10] and 30 per cent of all Somali men across the country.[11] According to police sources, there is a sizeable population of regular users, chewing a bundle a day. Swedish police refer to the banana-leaf-wrapped bundle as 'marduff', weighing an average of 200 grams and costing 150–400 Skr. There is even a market for old khat, at 50 Skr a bundle, which is suggestive of a strong placebo effect working on regular users.

Without business premises at their disposal, some Somali entrepreneurs have in the past used their residences to sell khat. This is a risky strategy, however, as neighbours do inform readily, and the police will raid on suspicion. The local CID officer remembers coming into the area a year ago and raiding a flat on the first floor: 'Lots of Somalis jumped out of the window leaving behind a big bag of khat.'[12] In 2003 the trade evolved into an open market in the pedestrianized zone around the central square. One popular trading place lies between the outward-facing wall of a council estate and a row of low buildings for businesses and amenities. When the weather permits, crowds gather for shopping and socializing, and the dealers can mill around unnoticed, taking cover in shops and the café while stashing their khat behind the bushes. The police promptly requested the council to cut back the bushes so that nothing can be hidden behind them. Once this had been done the retail trade shifted to the car parks.

As in Canada, the clandestine Swedish khat market is taking on the characteristics of other illicit drug markets. Gone is the social bond linking the customer and khat user to the seller, as can be found in the London *mafrishes*. The communal atmosphere of the chew, with its ritual of greetings, finding a suitable place to sit in, the rounds of soft drinks, the sharing of sweets and cigarettes is all gone. There is no inspection of the wares, no discussion of quality nor haggling over price. The relationship is entirely functional and brusque in a sellers' market developing structures reminiscent of cocaine and heroin street markets. Often, for example, the khat buyers meet their connection in a public place like a car park, and hand over the money to one man, from whom they get directions for the pick up place where the khat is held by someone else. In some instances customers pay well in advance to the arrival of the khat. At the appointed hour, groups of Somali men can be seen hanging around waiting for the 'man'.

Khat Use and Importation

Sweden was one of the first European countries to impose strict controls on it, but khat remains available. Law-enforcement officers readily point the finger to the UK and the Netherlands as the entrepôts for their khat supply. For years the main mechanism was the 'suitcase trade'. Many of the couriers are ethnic Swedes or Britons, many repeat offenders and with a drug habit to support. Typical is the case of a man arrested in 1999 with two suitcases containing 35 kg of khat. He was sentenced to four months in prison but came to the attention of the police again in 2001 when two suitcases bearing his name were found in Vasteras, a small airport used by Ryan Air and only sporadically covered by Customs officers, hence attractive to traffickers. On this particular day a team was checking the incoming passengers and the courier simply left the suitcase on the conveyer belt and walked through. Later that same year he was arrested in Oslo and was sentenced to prison for two months.

The suitcase trade is an ongoing irritation for Swedish officers, but constitutes a mere trickle of the overall flow of khat into the country. Since the completion of the Oresund Bridge linking Copenhagen, Denmark and Malmö in the south of Sweden, khat is coming into the country literally by the vanload. Most of the 9 tons of khat seized in 2004 was found on cars and vans driving up from the Netherlands where the khat is loaded, through Germany and Denmark to Sweden, and sometimes on to Finland. In 2005 a car with 54 kg was intercepted going out to Finland on a ferry. The Finnish driver was not charged but the two Somali passengers were sentenced to 6 months' imprisonment. The most severe punishments on the record are 8-month sentences, but the average is 4–6 months.

The officers confess an element of frustration, at what they regard as mixed messages from the policy-makers. On the one hand khat has been put under control, on the other the law seems toothless and the methods and resources made available inadequate. Putting it simply, one officer states, 'we have no experience fighting khat'.[13] As only operations involving more than 400 kg of khat are considered a felony, most operations are reactive. Only rarely does the drug squad initiate investigations, or employ the more sophisticated instruments in the arsenal of modern policing, such as observation, surveillance, controlled delivery or wire-tapping. Some police offices have been pushing for a reduction of the weight limit from 400 to 100 kg, so as to redefine these offences from misdemeanour to felony.

It is hard to say if the reluctance by lawmakers to accede to these demands is motivated by concern or inertia; the response of some Somali campaigners is definite: 'They do not care because it is only Somalis who suffer.' If there were a similar problem among the mainstream Swedish population, goes the argument, the authorities would have taken strong measures long ago. And for a large number of Somalis, khat is no innocent pastime but the most serious threat to the Somali community. This view is particularly strong among former users who have themselves grappled with a 'habit'. One man relates how he began chewing as a teenager while sitting with adults in Somalia, then he started using it with his friends first at weekends and then every day. Khat is bad, he claims, because it reduces people to pawning their possessions and even to begging (*shahat*). After experiencing problems with his health, his teeth, his sex life and his family, he gave up.

These stories of addiction, personal calamity and official indifference provide a constant theme in the discourse around khat among Sweden's Somali community. There is little help for problem users, as treatment service are not geared up for this new drug and are probably too interventionist to attract many clients. Given that the objective of all treatment provided in Sweden is abstinence, and the usual methods are residential treatment with detoxification, khat users trying to kick a problematic habit therefore have no one to rely on but their families.

This is only one of a number of trends emerging in Sweden that may ring a cautionary note to UK campaigners. One concerns the consumption trends within the community, possibly occasioned by the difficulties and costs involved in negotiating the black market for khat. Older khat users are reported to be turning to alcohol, with devastating consequences for their social inclusion. Among the Islamic Somalis, drinking is simply not tolerated, leading to the expulsion from families, support networks and social isolation. Both khat and alcohol are increasingly cited as factors in Somali family disputes, with social workers reporting a high rate of divorce and second marriages. When marrying for the second time, most Somali women choose Swedish men. If this suggests that substance abuse may contribute, perversely, to the partial integration of Somalis into mainstream Swedish society, it also indicates a growing disparity between Somali men and women. While women are marrying into the majority population and finding employment with government agencies or the service sector, men are left on benefit and criminalized. Raising the transaction costs for khat traders through interdiction, seizure, arrest and prosecution has removed one incentive against the diversification of smuggling operations.

In 2004, Customs officers made their first seizures of mixed consignments of khat and cannabis, and more worrying still, of khat and cocaine. Somali importers are evidently making a calculated decision to maximize the returns on their trafficking operation. The shifting pattern is reflected on the retail side where there have also been arrests of Somali hashish dealers. Khat importers and dealers are adding value to their sale by switching product lines. In part this will be stimulated by demand from their traditional Somali customer base. In Sweden, the crossover from khat to other illicit substances is far more gradual in terms of price than in the UK, where the differential between the licit and the illicit substances remains dramatic.

The high prices and restrictive consumption opportunities have also contributed to the regular cross-border visits to Denmark, where khat is banned but chewing itself is not considered 'possession' and therefore no offence. On weekends, Swedes and Somalis travel to their more permissive southern neighbour on the same ferries to indulge in alcohol and khat respectively. This is possibly one indicator to suggest that by devising ingenious methods of beating the illiberal regime, they are at last becoming acculturated.

–11–

Conclusion
Mapping the Future of Khat

This exploration of the production, distribution and use of khat across different continents has brought up the complexities that bedevil the search for an appropriate control regime. There is considerable pressure to impose a ban on khat. At international level, these efforts are championed by the International Narcotics Control Board (INCB), the body established within the UN system with a quasi-judicial function to promote compliance to drug-control treaties. In its last Annual Report, recommendation 45, the Board states:[1]

> The Board notes with concern the abuse of khat (*Catha edulis*), which is currently not under international control, in countries in Eastern Africa and elsewhere. The Board calls upon WHO to expedite the review of this substance to determine whether it should be recommended to be placed under international control. (INCB 2006: 96)

It is clear from the wording that the Board has already decided on the way forward. Khat is being 'abused', a term that is normally associated with the consumption of substances which either are illicit, are considered harmful to the health of individuals and society or have no recognized medical benefit. The Board is resolutely positivist in its assessment, giving no quarter to the economic benefits, cultural or social significance of use, the benefits of simple pleasure or the medical claims of traditional practitioners. The scientific assessment will analyse the pharmacological composition of a substance and review the evidence on the impact on physical and mental health. This prepares the way for legal controls recommended by the Board. The mechanisms for international prohibitions exist in the UN Single Convention on Narcotic Drugs of 1961 and the Convention on Psychotropic Substances of 1971, which have already scheduled cathine and cathinone, the main active ingredients of khat, and made their extraction illegal. Inserting the plant matter into this schedule is not technically difficult.

For the INCB and the other agencies involved, principally the United Nations Office on Drugs and Crime (UNODC), the extension of controls over other substances is of clear institutional interest. New substances falling under international control will automatically extend the remit of these agencies and may well attract new functions and funds. But agency professionals already regard it as their duty to apply their expertise to substances outside the immediate controls set by the Convention. They have been monitoring khat for many years, and find the measures employed against illicit substances effective and appropriate (UNDCP 2000). Khat, according to this line of reasoning, is a mind-altering, habit-forming drug with no proven medical benefit, inflicts more harm than good and should be brought under control.

Perversely, large numbers of khat chewers in Ethiopia, Kenya and the diaspora support a ban on khat. They attribute all manner of negative medical and social consequences to it and place it at the root of both personal and community misfortunes. In the diaspora, some of the severest attacks on khat are launched by critics sucking a tight wad of leaves in the other side of their mouth. Having condemned the mindless pursuit of pleasure, the strain on finances and family life, the wasted energy and time, they often go on to say that a ban would have to be perfectly watertight. Because, if just one leaf were to get past the checkpoints they would find it, and worse, spend all their energies in hunting it.[2] It is difficult to take the stated support for a putative khat prohibition, when qualified by these unattainable conditions, at face value. It is more an expression of idealism, that the world would perhaps be better off without khat, but that this is not a realistic option because the chewer, having had one taste, will always want more.

What we learn from Canada and Sweden, where tough restrictions are in place, is that some users will invest significant amounts of time in sourcing khat underground. This echoes the experience of other drug markets, where chronic users turn scoring into an activity invested with emotional significance, and replacing work, study and relationships. Where drug-using groups are already marginalized because of employment status, race and religion, the prohibition on what is not only a major pastime and source of pleasure but also a symbol of collective identity only reinforces the sense of exclusion. A recreational pattern of khat use within the strictures of custom and tradition, punctuated etiquette and embedded in the rhythm of daily life, can then slip into a dysfunctional obsession that is exacerbated by stringent control measures.

Caution is advised when pressing the case against khat as a source of dysfunctional behaviour. Some of the most extreme khat abusers have exhibited paranoia, episodes of psychosis, cravings, anhedonia and dysphoria. But these symptoms are highly exceptional, affect primarily Somalis and not other ethnic groups, and are usually associated with post-traumatic stress disorders contracted during conflict situation, for instance Somalia's protracted civil war. As for the long-term medical effects, study after study concludes that in contrast to many other psychoactive substances in use globally, and in particular alcohol and tobacco, khat is a rather benign substance. Cessation after long-term use may result in disturbed sleeping patterns, agitation and the onset of cravings, but these will all pass relatively quickly and with little discomfort.

The possible medical consequences of khat use and the associated policy conundrum is nicely encapsulated by Rushby:

It is a substance that an initiate can quite calmly sit and chew while calling for it to be banned. Qat sits on the fence of our preconceived ideas and on either side of it too, challenging our conception of what a drug is, of what addiction is, of what an addicted society should be like. It questions where we draw the limits and makes those limits look as ridiculous as those straight-line colonial borders on maps of Africa. (Rushby 1998: 7)

It is therefore interesting to look at some of the key problem areas where khat has been mentioned. In Kenya, the civic-minded elders of Lamu protesting against the public sale of khat in their town have identified 'divorce, prostitution, begging and abandonment of families' as key problems caused by khat. These claims in the war against khat have in essence been echoed in faraway London, where khat is again blamed for the break-up of families and the loss of female honour. The Ethiopian anti-khat association, Rouh, also highlights the ill effects of khat mainly related to indolence and recklessness that have been mentioned as one of the causes for the spread of HIV/AIDS.

It is important to give recognition to the grain of truth in these arguments, the sincerity of the protestors and the magnitude of the problems they have identified. In Kenya, Somalia and Ethiopia as in much of Africa, ongoing urbanization is having serious implications. The fragmentation of extended families, the emergence of nuclear households and individualism are constant themes in contemporary African studies. In parallel runs the continuous discussion over the moral economy and the questions of identity and loyalty. Rapid change driven largely by external factors has placed great stress on traditional institutions and social structures, resulting in the breakdown of marriages, the reconfiguration of families and changes in gender roles. Transport modernization, the integration of labour and commodity markets within nation states and at regional level have created challenging new situations of inter ethnic contact.

Khat may well exacerbate many a consequence of rapid social change, but it is difficult to credit claims of causality. Or, turning the argument, would any of these deleterious consequences have occurred if khat were not in the equation? This is one of the most pressing issues to pursue in the discussion over khat regulation. There is an inherent danger in penalizing the victim, in this case the khat user who derives enjoyment from chewing as an interlude from the daily struggle to make ends meet. Khat users may not be helping themselves in taking on a drug habit, but persecuting either them or the sellers will not alleviate either their private troubles, or the underlying social and economic problems.

This is perhaps most evident when we look at the populations with the most problematic pattern of use. In the refugee camps of northern Kenya, idle men start chewing early in the morning. Khat is no longer a pleasure to punctuate the labours of a working day, but becomes a route of escape from a meaningless void. It is one of a repertoire of substances – including cannabis, distilled spirits and prescription medication – that are cheap and effective as a means of altering consciousness. It is arguable that the use of any of these cheap and easily available drugs makes it more difficult to summon the personal and financial resources which will allow one to escape the harsh conditions of camp life. On the other hand, the majority of refugees who are not using any substance are facing the same intolerable conditions and are locked into a life of deprivation, with little prospect of moving on to a new life any time soon. Khat use may not be helping the individuals concerned, but it is not a causal factor in their plight and should not be confused with the structural impediments faced by African refugees.

A similar situation is observed in the diaspora. Once again there is a strong case to be made against khat use. It does take up time and money, and holds users in a culture of exile that does not facilitate integration and advancement in the new country. Yet, for many of the older migrants particularly, the chances of finding employment, learning foreign languages and acquiring appropriate skills are slim in any case. The experience from Sweden is striking. While khat has been banned, the majority of Somali refugees are unemployed, and even seek to move on to the UK, where it is easier to start businesses – including, of course, the khat trade.

The financial burden on khat users is sometimes considerable, but the high cost of khat in both Sweden and Canada has been brought about as a consequence of prohibition. Chewers now spend much more on purchasing their irregular arrivals of khat than their relatives in the UK and the Netherlands – who chew more, but at a fraction of the illicit market price. Nor does prohibition result in Somali men in either Canada or Sweden investing their freed-up time in their families. Instead, driven by hope and rumour, they are cruising all over town in search of contraband consignments.

One of the consequences that few of the pro-ban campaigners in the UK ever considered has been the deterioration of Somali relations with the police. In Canada and Sweden, officers have been issued with a khat profile. Somali men are often automatically suspected and, on occasion, subjected to random searches. The onus is on the community of users and traders to prove its innocence. A trickle of traders are finding their way into the criminal justice system for khat-related offences. Increasingly, however, traders at local and middle market level are diversifying into other substances. For these at least, the ban on khat has only given them a vigorous push into criminality. The formation of Somali criminal networks pioneered in countries with illicit khat markets with serious consequences for their community and the host nation. In the UK officers from many UK law-enforcement agencies have warned of the benefits accruing to organized-crime groups from a ban on khat. One senior officer from the Metropolitan Police dismissed the idea of prohibiting khat as taking a sledgehammer to crack a nut.[3] But in the UK there were serious concerns about how a ban could foster the emergence of Somali crime groups and the potential links with terrorists. Another officer said, 'We do not want to create a situation that provides opportunities for organized-crime groups.'[4]

Given the controversy surrounding khat, as well as over other substances that are subject to control, it is important to be aware of the perverse consequences of poorly designed policies and keep an eye on the big picture. One such instance relates to findings concerning drug use among street children. The survey quoted in this book (see Chapter 4) found that up to a third of Ethiopian children interviewed were light to heavy users of khat. Children were being introduced and initiated into use by their peers. Khat use may have serious implications for the development of these children. In the circumstances, this is a minor concern, however, and the efforts of national and international agencies should not be directed at repressing the supply of the drug but into getting these children into protected shelters. There is always a danger that marginal populations are further penalized by policy decisions taken in pursuit of unachievable ideals.

A coherent policy on khat regulation should be informed by an understanding of the realities on the ground, including how individuals, communities and wider society are affected. The debate in most countries has been influenced by claims that khat is a harbinger of social damage and dire medical consequences, even though the former accusation is conjectural and the latter inconclusive. The economic argument for khat, however, is rarely stated – let alone propounded forcefully. The analysis of the Ethiopian khat production provides compelling evidence of the benefits reaped by rural households, and the significance of khat in maintaining sustainable livelihoods. What is further demonstrated is the knock-on effects in terms of processing industries, transportation and distribution systems, and the creation of a regional trading system with economic benefits for all participants. Somali nationalists often argue against the khat trade because they witness the cash flow into the producing countries of Ethiopia and Kenya. It is rarely conceded by khat detractors that Somali transporters and trading groups have established leading positions in regional and international markets. And, given the lack of multinational competitors within the khat trade, it is fast becoming one of the principal vehicles for Somali financial accumulation and economic growth.

Some of these points were brought to the attention of the UK government when it was deliberating on the status of khat in 2005. The Kenyan exporters' association sent presentations listing the benefits for all involved. Interestingly, the UK importers and distributors, particularly the *mafrish* owners where khat is consumed, and who have the highest stake in the continuation of the trade, kept a low profile. One informant explained that 'as a culture we are good at crisis management, but bad at planning. This comes from the days of pastoralism – when the rains fail we have to improvise, but when things go well we enjoy'.

Beyond such cultural determinism lies a further point with regard to the general position, first, of khat in society, and of the Somalis in the UK. In Somalia khat was banned, and in Ethiopia and Kenya the sale of khat is subject to only limited regulation. Somalis of the khat-chewing generation – that is, people who are in their late twenties and older – often exist in a state of limbo. They live in the UK, often have been there for many years, but are still thinking about returning home. The UK sojourn is a necessary stage before resuming life in Somalia. Chewing khat helps keeping that dream alive, and holding on to a quasi-Somali presence. Critics have argued that it prevents the chewers from integrating into UK society. One rarely considered aspect of this argument is that khat chewers do not enjoy the protection and benefits of UK legislation for consumer protection. Across the UK, many of the *mafrishes* where Somali men go to chew are dark and dingy places, with no ventilation, no fire escapes and poor hygiene. Chewers visit anyhow because they do not know their rights, and in any case, prefer not to attract attention. For the *mafrish* to find a place among the range of entertainment venues of twenty-first-century Britain, these facilities need to be put into place. The sale of khat has to become properly regulated, licensed and, regrettably for some, taxed. It is doubtful that the khat sale in the current legal twilight zone can continue indefinitely.

In the UK, at least there is an opportunity for setting up the use and distribution of khat on a solid footing. After a careful appraisal of the evidence, the Home Secretary decided to leave the status of khat unchanged, based on the advice from the Advisory Council on the Misuse of Drugs. The ACMD stated:

> The ACMD believes that it would be inappropriate to classify khat under the Misuse of Drugs Act 1971. The prevalence of khat in the UK is relatively low and isolated to the Somali and Yemeni communities. There is no evidence of khat use in the general population. Furthermore, the evidence of harm resulting from khat use is not sufficient to recommend its control. (ACMD 2006: 28)[5]

The technical committee of the World Health Organization, who found no reason for recommending the scheduling of khat, confirmed this conclusion later in 2006. With these statements of support it will be possible to resist the pressures for control and establish a workable system of regulated distribution and consumption. The alternative is an almost inexorable slide into control and prohibition. For the UK Somalis it would spell the end of a lifestyle and mark a slide into criminality and further marginalization. For the rural producers in Ethiopia and Kenya the consequences are far graver.

Notes

Chapter 1 Going Global: The Khat Controversy

1. This book will mainly use the term khat; however, other spellings will be used in citations and where appropriate in the context. Also, because of different plant sources for khat leaves, the terms 'tree', 'bush', 'shrub', 'plant', 'seedling' are used intentionally throughout.
2. Acknowledgment goes to Nebiyou Getachew for sharing this story.
3. For instance, the BBC reported on 10 December 2003 that 'Ethiopia swaps Coffee for Drugs', *BBC News World Edition*. According to the report, farmers in Deder, Harerge have uprooted coffee and planted khat, mainly because the price of coffee fell from US$3 per kg to US$1 and down by half to US$165m in total value, while Khat production doubled to US$58m. It was estimated that Ethiopia lost US$830 million in export earnings in the years 1998–2002.

Chapter 2 Devil's Cud or Farmers' Boon?

1. The research is based on field visits covering East Harerge and West Harerge Zones of Oromia Region; Dire Dawa City; Harari Region of Western Ethiopia; Sidama and Gurage Zones in Southern Ethiopia; Bahir Dar in Northern Ethiopia; Addis Ababa; Djibouti City; and Hargeisa in Somaliland.
2. On the way from Addis Ababa to eastern Ethiopia one passes through towns such as Welenchiti where *teff* fields are extensively in sight. Just past the Awash valley and entering Meiso, however, khat fields occupy a large proportion of cultivated land. The geography beyond the Awash valley is highland, and intercropping of khat, coffee and sorghum stretch along Bike, Dabeso, Metakesha, Hirna, Zigita, Addes, Boroda, Karamile, Kobo, Kulibi, Langee, and Keksa towns.
3. Interview with Abduresak Abubeker and Abeba Alemayehu, Finance and Economic Development Office of East Harerge Zone.
4. Calculated from figures published by Dire Dawa Foreign Trade Office (2004).
5. Gebissa (1997) argues that the land policies of Haile Selassie had implications for the changes in agricultural production. First, land became concentrated in few hands because of the patrimonial state. Officials and the gentry owned vast tracts of land. Second, the rulers controlled access to land despite population

growth, thereby increasing concentration of population per land and diminishing availability. Tenancies were broken up and landholdings became fragmented.

6. See Hailu (2005) for a review.

7. In 1990, the Derg announced a series of new measures focused on encouraging private-sector participation while abolishing producer cooperatives and marketing parastatals (Hansson, 2001). In 1992, the EPRDF signed a loan agreement with the IMF and began implementation of stabilization and adjustment programmes, which reversed state control of agricultural marketing.

8. Interviews with farmers revealed that increasing production on grazing and fodder land meant they kept fewer cattle. This in turn has led to decline in manure used as fertilizer and a rise in use of chemical fertilizers.

9. Interview with Abduresak Abubeker and Abeba Alemayehu, Finance and Economic Development Office of East Harerge Zone.

10. There is a mosquito-like pest called *berrari*, which attacks khat leaves. *Adoba*, a fungus-like disease, and *Terba* insects also damage about 80 per cent of the khat.

11. Farmers remove the leaves during drought until the rains come as protection against excessive transpiration. The dry season makes it impossible to harvest khat more than twice. The water shortage in the city of Harar has been linked to 'tragedy of the commons' where khat farmers around Lake Alemaya, which is the source of piped water, are said to have diverted water reservoirs to irrigate their khat farms. Conversation with Mr Mesfin Tegene, Vice Minister Water, Ministry of Resources, Ethiopia.

12. Of the total labour expended in crop production 45 per cent is on khat night guarding, bringing the average total labour per acre of crop land to 548 hours (Miller and Mekonnen 1965, cited in Getahun and Kirkorian 1973).

13. Interview with Tadesse Lala, Negusse Degefa, Girma Gofa, Gemechu Admassu, West Harerge Zone Finance, Planning and Economic Development Office.

14. Interview with Yunus Hassan, Taddesse Esubalu, Wegayehu Gashaw and Tesfaye Alemayehu, Agriculture Development Office in Dire Dawa.

15. Interview with Demeska Tamiru, Finance and Economic Development Office of East Harerge Zone.

16. Interview with Dr Abebe Fanta, Dr Tesfaye Behsah and Dr Tesfaye Lemma, Alemaya University Ethiopia. Hospitality by Professor Desta Hameto is acknowledged.

17. The dry khat seasons are November, December and January (bad harvest); the wet seasons are February, March, and April (good harvest); and the mild period is over May, June and July. During high-demand periods traders purchase khat from Aweday, Garamuleta, Deder, and Arawacha.

18. This is what makes khat farming a lucrative business in Oromia region.

19. Interview with Sheriff Ahmed Adem, Harari Agricultural Bureau, Ethiopia.

20. Interview with Yohannes Shiferaw, Bureau of Statistics and Population, SNNPR Region, Ethiopia.
21. Conversation with Dr Kebede Kanchula, Molla Tegene, and Tedla Wolde Michael, Sidama Zone Rural Development and Coordination Department, Ethiopia.
22. Interview with Semayehu Tesfaye, SNNPR Agricultural Bureau, Ethiopia.
23. Interview with Yilma Bekele, Gurage Zone Planning Bureau, Ethiopia.
24. However, farmers in Silte are currently in negotiations to start irrigating their khat farms.
25. Interview with Berhanu Benti, SNNPR, Finance and Economic Bureau.
26. Interview with Dr Danial Dauro, Director General, Southern Agricultural Research Institute, Ethiopia and Walta Information Centre on-line report, 31 May 2005.
27. The project aimed to achieve the following in 2005: 1,939 demonstrations and variety trails; 53 irrigation schemes; 20 watershed management sites; 1,981 hectares planted with 13,958,213 trees; Training for animal husbandry technicians; 9 animal-health clinics established; 11 animal-health posts set up; 13,325 animals fattened.
28. Interview with Jamal Kerga and Heru Hasen, Gurage Zone Agricultural and Natural Resources Desk, Ethiopia.
29. Interview with Teshome Wale, Rural Development and Agricultural Bureau, Amhara Region Ethiopia.
30. In this sector 29 NGOs have 62 projects in 67 districts participating in various extension support programmes.
31. Up to April 2004, there were 13,352,800 kg of vegetables, 661,900 kg of coffee, 225,540 kg of fruits and 3,812,300 kg of sweet potato seeds distributed.
32. Quoted in Milich and Al-Sabbry (1995).
33. The amount exported and the value declined dramatically in 1991/92, reflecting political uncertainty during the years of transition and change of government.
34. The foreign-exchange earnings from khat and volume of exports are underestimated and sometimes reported as miscellaneous earnings. This is mainly because of khat's association with drugs
35. The Khat economy supports beyond recurrent budget and covers capital spending too, particularly. For instance, each local administrative area (Kebele) has a school; out of 35 Kebeles, 21 have health centres. There are three hospitals in rural areas. Clean-water coverage is 40 per cent in rural areas and 68 per cent in urban areas. There is an 80-kilometre all-weather road. The Dire Dawa economy was mostly related to contraband trade in an area colloquially known as 'Taiwan'. The government's drive to wipe out contraband has resulted in a shift to the khat economy. Officially the Dire Dawa economy is said to be in 'transition' from contraband to private-investment-driven economy. However, there is little investment and the khat economy strives. Interview with Tebebu

Belay, Assefa G. Giorgis, and Alemayehu Bekele, Eastern Zone Customs Office, Dire Dawa and Abraham Sahilu (Head), Lishan Tsehay, and Abeba Alemayhu of Dire Dawa Planning and Economic Development Bureau.

36. Interview with Kedir Sirage and Feleke Gebre Michael, Gurage Zone Revenue Desk, Ethiopia.

37. For processed khat the tax is 4 birr per kilogram. The issue of packaging is also a problem because the tax is on total weight rather than net weight. The total weight includes packaging in usually heavy water-soaked grass wrappings. Therefore traders complain that they are actually taxed for waste including the thick stems of the khat which will be thrown away during final processing.

38. Interview with Haile Niru, Bureau of Revenue, SNNPR Region and Tesfaye Wolde Michael, Matheos Rike and Abraham Daniel, Sidama Zone Finance and Economic Development Department, Ethiopia.

39. Interview with staff of the Revenue Bureau, SNNPR (Mr A. Matusala and colleagues).

40. Interview with Assey Kebede, Revenue Bureau, Amhara National Regional State.

41. Interview with Akalu Geneme and Tilahun Eshete, Revenue Bureau, Amhara National Regional State.

42. Interview with Ebrahim Amadu Hassan, Director of Customs Authority, Djibouti.

43. The profession of the khat importer is exclusively reserved to Djibouti citizens only, who must as a prerequisite obtain the consent of the Department of Commerce and Industry.

44. Confirmed by Mohammed Ahmed Ducale and Khadar Mohamed Abdi Customs Office, Somaliland.

Chapter 3 Trading the Dollar Leaf

1. Interview Omar Abdulali, farmer; Ziad Jibri and Hussein Abdurahmen, agents.

2. Interview with Ahmeddin Muktar, trader and Abdulaziz Mohammed, Tajudin Abdurhman and Asman Jibro, from Eastern Harerge Agricultural Bureau, Ethiopia.

3. Interview with Abebe Mekonnen and Abiy Teferra, Jerusalem Children Community Development, Dire Dawa, Ethiopia.

4. Interview with Tamrat Kebede, Dire Dawa Foreign Trade Office.

5. Interview with Akalu Geneme, Bureau of Revenue, Amhara Region Ethiopia, and Assey Kebede, Finance Bureau, Amhara Region Ethiopia.

6. The project was initiated and put in place in 1982 by the former Minister of Commerce and Industry, M. Aden Robleh Awaleh, who wanted to favour and facilitate the creation of small- and medium-scale enterprises. According to the

recollections of the Financial and Administrative Director of SOGIK, M. Sahal, SOGIK employs 38 people including 18 workmen and drivers, 2 managers of administration and finance, 2 secretaries, and others responsible (Araita 2004).

7. At this time, the Ethiopian government had even, by way of gratitude, given the former Minister of Commerce, M. Aden Robleh a medal (according to the President of the UDT [Democratic Union of Djiboutian Workers] M. Oubouleh).

8. SOGIK has suffered financial difficulties, particularly between 1994 and 1997, and accumulated financial debts with banks, which, according to its management, is the result of political-judicial influences. Insider information reveals that post-1997 tightening measures such as the suspension of the distribution of khat to politicians or shareholders has contributed to the improvements of the society's accounts.

9. This development was introduced following the arrival of the new autonomous management, which took over the running of the airport and the international port of Djibouti.

10. Translated from French by Neil Carrier.

11. Interview with Abdela Hassen, Ethiopian Chat and Agro – Industrial Products Manufacturing Import and Export Share Company (ECAIPMIESC); Berhanu Deres, Berwako General Trading and Construction Works Share Company (BGTCWSC); Esmail Adem, Kulmiye Trading Share Company; and Solomon Tefera, BIFTU-DINSHO Share Company.

12. Interview with Yunus Hassan, Agriculture Development Office in Dire Dawa.

13. Interview with Zerihun Ashebr, Finance Bureau, Dire Dawa Ethiopia.

14. Interview with Zewdu Girma, schoolteacher in Jijiga.

15. Interview with Ubah Mohammed and Abdibasid Ahmed, Investment Bureau as well as Mohammed Ahmed and Abebe Kebede, Somali Region Finance Bureau, Ethiopia.

16. In 1998 the government announced that khat exported by road to be priced at US$3 per kg fob.

17. Interview with Ahmed Abdulahi Oamr, Mohamed Ahmed Ducaale, Ahmed Daud Jedi and Abdirhaman Jama Elnu, Ministry of Finance and Ahmed Abdulhasin Nadif, Planning and Coordination Department at the Ministry of Planning and Coordination, Somaliland.

18. BBC On-line Monday, 15 August 2005.

19. Interview with Murad Zekaria, Bureau of Finance and Economic Development, Somali Region, Ethiopia and Naasir Moxald Aadan and Wegayehu Wolde Senbet, Revenue Bureau, Somali Region, Ethiopia.

20. Khat distribution became faster and easier after 4 private airlines and 4 private telephone companies were established in Somaliland.

21. The US$6,000 charter-flight fee is also required to be paid in dollars by the Ethiopian Civil Aviation Authority, which exporters complain about because the

price at US$ 6.00 is supposed to be Cost and Freight, while the khat which goes to Djibouti is also priced at US$ 8.00 and US$ 6.00 while they are FOB prices.

22. SOMETH in return agreed to supply the Ethiopian company with fish and sea products, gums, semi-processed hides and skins as well as edible salt. Puntland has a population of 2.5 million.

23. Interview with Zerihun Ashebr, Finance Bureau, Dire Dawa Ethiopia.

24. Interview with Metmiku Yohannes and Workiye Wendimu, Eastern Region Post Office, Dire Dawa, Ethiopia.

Chapter 4 Consuming Habits along the Red Sea Littoral

1. Interview with Ayachew Kebede, Bureau of Finance and Economic Development, Amhara National Regional State.

2. Another study among street children also found that poor level of knowledge about drugs and peer pressure contribute to the spread of khat use (FSCE 1999).

3. Abdul Malik, Aragaw Wedeyes, Samel Shifa, and Beredin Seid are the founding members of Rouh Anti-Khat Office, Addis Ababa, Ethiopia.

4. The Republic of Djibouti has an area of 23,000 square kilometres and borders Ethiopia, Somalia and Eritrea. Its port has become an important outlet for Ethiopia. Since 1887, the town of Djibouti has developed around the actual port and the railway connecting it to Ethiopia.

5. Hassan (2004) observes that to achieve his ends, the broke unemployed man invents incredible tales to try to extract a few coins from his parents or friends. The chewing session thus begins at 2.00 pm. All around the room, every fifty centimetres, are placed two or three cushions on which the future 'grazer' will lean. People arrive at almost the same time, and as they are familiar with the place, each finds his own place and installs himself comfortably. Moreover, it is a special day, for it is Thursday. In effect, in Djibouti it was decided to break with the custom of colonial times by instituting a Thursday/Friday weekend.

6. Interview with Abdisalam Mohamed Shabeeleh, Minstry of Tourism and Culture, Somaliland.

7. Interview with Abdi Haybe Elmi Awad, Mohammed Farah and Yusuf Aineb Muse, academics at the University of Hargeisa, and Abdirizak Dahir Salam, student, University of Hargeisa.

Chapter 5 Made in Meru: A Market History

1. Interview with Fatouma, Maua, 12 February 2004.

2. Interview with Robert, Maili Tatu, Nyambene, 12 February 2004.

3. Interviews carried out by Nuur Sheekh.

4. Interview with Stephen on his farm near Karama, 11 February 2004.
5. Interview with Peter, Laare, 12 February 2004.
6. Interview with Abdi in Maua, 13 February 2004.
7. Interview between Nuur Sheekh and Adan Kheir.
8. The term *kilos* will be used throughout this chapter in its local usage, and should not be confused with the weight measure of a kilogram.
9. During 2006 British Airways cargo management in Nairobi briefly halted khat haulage, owing to difficulties experienced in the loading of agreed quantities of khat through the agents. At this time, exports shifted to other international cargo handlers.
10. Interview with Nuur Sheekh.
11. Mbithi in interview with Nuur Sheekh and Susan Beckerleg.
12. Interview between Nuur Sheekh and Adan Kheir.
13. Interview by Nuur Sheekh with Abdulkadir Araru, former journalist with the *East African Standard.*
14. Interview by Nuur Sheekh with Abdulkadir Haji Osman, who supplies Duale with the cartons.
15. Interviews with Kirithi Nabea and 'Balckie', Malindi, August 2004.
16. Interviews with Martin in Lamu, 2 August 2004 and James in Nakuru, 20 August 2004.
17. Interview with Halima, Isiolo, 14 February 2004.
18. Interview with Saidi, Isiolo, 15 February 2004.
19. Interview with Aiysha, Namanga, 6 February 2004.
20. Interview with Ahmed, Namanga, 7 February 2004.
21. Interview with market traders, Thika, 9 February 2004.
22. On the Kenyan side of the border there are no paved roads for hundreds of kilometres, and newspapers arrive only twice a week. Somali and Borana traders dominate the commercial life of Moyale.
23. Interview in Moyale, 13 April 2004.
24. Informal interviews, Dongoni trading post, 4 February 2004.
25. Interview with Winnie, *chyulu* retailer, Mtito Ndei, 4 February 2004.
26. Interview with Fatouma, 19 August 2004.
27. Interview with John, 15 February 2004.
28. Interview in Timau, 16 February 2004.
29. Dixon guided the team around theTaita Hills on 3 February 2004.
30. Interview with Maina, 3 February 2004.
31. Estimated by Caxton, Embu, 10 February 2004.
32. Interview with Caxton, Embu, 10 February 2004.
33. Interview with Abdulalihi, Moyale, 13 April 2004.
34. Interviewed, Kimana, 8 February 2004.

Chapter 6 Kenya: Culture, Controversy and Cooperation

1. Interview with Mahmoud Abdelkadir, Lamu, 2 February 2004.
2. Interview with Martin, Lamu, 30 July 2004.
3. Interview with Mahmoud Abdelkadir, Lamu, 2 August 2004.
4. Interview with Noor and customers, Chagamwe, Mombasa, 28 January 2004.
5. Interview with Mohammed Dekow Kossar, Gerissa, 17 February 2004.
6. Interview with Blackie, Malindi, 24 January 2004.
7. Goldsmith (1997: 463) notes that 'Kenya's North Eastern Province is one of the regions of greater Somalia represented by the five-pointed star imposed on the blue background of the Republic of Somalia's flag. Ninety per cent of the region's inhabitants voted for unification with Somalia in a 1960 referendum on the issue prior to Kenyan independence.'
8. Interview with Ali and colleagues, 4 April 2004.
9. During visit to camps, 4 April 2004.
10. Interview in Eastleigh, 19 April 2004.
11. Interview with Mishal Ismael, Ifo Camp, 4 April 2004.
12. Interview with Halima, Dadaab, 4 April 2004.
13. Interviews with Rukiya Omari, Garissa, 16 February 2004.
14. Interview with Amina, Garissa, 13 February 2004.
15. Interviews with Andrew and Omari, Wajir, 6 April 2004.
16. Interview with Officials of the Dawa Women's Group, Mandera, 7 April 2004.
17. Interview with Abdul Rahman, Mandera, 15 April 2004.

Chapter 7 On the Khat Frontier: Uganda

1. Interview with Robert, Kabale and Rangara Chabakazi, 8 October 2004.
2. Interview with Shaban, 22 August 2004, Mbale and the slope of Mount Elgon.
3. Interview with Balgis of Taufiq Hotel, Mbale, 21 August 2004.
4. Group of male farmers in Bubulo, 22 August 2004.
5. Interview with group of consumers, Moroto, 14 December 2004.
6. Interviews conducted while travelling with Mahmoud, 15 December 2004–17 January 2005. Mahmoud's father settled in Uganda in the 1940s after fighting in the Second World War as a soldier in the King's African Rifles.
7. Interview with Omari, Nakapiripirit, 15 December 2004.
8. Interview with Lopilipili, 15 December 2004.
9. Interviews with farmers, Kasenge, 26 August 2004.
10. Interviews with Semakula's wife and grandson, 27 August 2004.
11. Interviews in Kiti, 2 September 2004.
12. Interview with Yusuf Kator, 11 October 2004.

13. Interviews and visit to Mabira Forest in company of Umaru Sendi, 24–25 August 2004.
14. Interviewed at his farm in the Mabira Forest, 24 August 2004.
15. Interview with Siraj, son of Byarufu who has inherited his father's farm, 30 August 2004.
16. Interviews with Musa and Mohamed, Kasese, 31 August 2004.
17. Interview with Bright Mfitimpano on his farm in Kigezi, Nyakabande Sub-County, 10 October 2004.
18. Interview with Ali, Kabale, 8 October 2004.
19. Interview with Fred, Kabale municipal market, 8 October 2004.
20. Interview with Moses, Kabale, 9 October 2004.
21. Interviews with Salim Brek and his wife Fatuma, Kisoro, 10 October 2004.
22. Interview with Musa, Kasese, 31 August 2004.
23. Interviews with Looku Peter and Hassan Auren, Hirihiri, 17 December 2004.
24. Interview with Mama Mbale, Mbale, 22 August 2004.
25. Interviews with Zainab, Farida and James in wholesale depot, Kasenge, 26 August 2004.
26. Interviews in Master Coffee, Jinja, 24 August 2004.
27. Interview with British Harrison, near Lugazi, 25 October 2004. British, whose grandfather was English, rents his khat crop to Mama Fatuma. He disapproves of khat chewing and says he could not indulge because he is a former schoolteacher with a reputation for respectability to maintain with his local community.
28. Interview with Salima, Kigali, 25 February 2005.
29. Interview with Rajab, 27 February 2005.
30. Reported in *New Vision*, 30 May 1998.
31. Interviews with traders and consumers, Mubende, 31 August 2004.
32. Interviews with traders and consumers, Bugembe, 24 August 2004.
33. Interview with trader in Mpugwe, 2 September 2004.
34. Interview with Sh. Yusuf Kator, Kiti, 11 October 2004.
35. The enumerators who conducted the survey were named Mzee Hassan and Musa Almasi.
36. Colette Jones assisted in the manipulation of the data using SSPS12. Jason Dowling was responsible for the data entry.

Chapter 8 The Ambivalent Amphetamine

1. This banking service arranges for the transfer of funds from the UK to Somalia or Kenya. It is based on trust, and requires no identification other than a number for the receiving partner. The transfers are instant, can be delivered to the recipient's door, and the charges of 2–5 per cent are lower than those for comparable bank services.

2. *The Post* 18/03/04. On Somali money remittances, see Lindley 2005.
3. www.bnp.org.uk/freedom/streatham.html
4. The website justifies its campaign against khat because it produced spitting: '... a stimulant with similar effects to [those of] amphetamine. It comes from a leafy green plant of the same name. Used mostly in Africa, Khat is getting more common in Europe particularly in immigrant communities'. As of 2003, Khat was not an illegal drug in the UK. One of its side-effects is the stimulation of saliva, meaning that the user must spit regularly – an aggressive and anti-social action.
5. Concept developed by Howard Parker with reference to heroin use. It suggests that substances are used in cycles and leave 'footprints' that allow the next epidemic to break out.
6. See Cassanelli (1986: 249) on the role of ex-Saudi workers in establishing khat use in Somalia.
7. *Mafrish* is an Arabic term that refers to a place in households specially decorated to entertain khateurs. *Mafrish* is inspired by this term and is currently used by the Somali community to refer to khat cafés. We use the anglicized form *mafrishes* for the plural.
8. There are a small number of British khat aficionados, but they typically adopted the habit after working in Yemen, Ethiopia or Kenya (Rushby).
9. Interview with Sado O.
10. http://www.unhcr
11. The difficulty of breaking through the mistrust is underscored by the fact that neither of the two Home Office research exercises undertaken by Turning Point and NACRO respectively could generate any data from inside commercial mafrashi.
12. Appeals Decision APP/N5660/A/03/1131211 and APP/N5660/C/03/1130989; 24/05/04.
13. It should not come as a 'bolt from the blue' to a small business of a self-employed person. It should be preceded by informal discussion about possible means of minimizing harm to local amenity caused by the business activity PPG 18 Briefing Note 'Planning Enforcement'.
14. http://neighbourhood.statistics.gov.uk

Chapter 9 Transnational Debates

1. Somalilanders who came to Britain as seamen, army veterans having served in the King's African Rifles during the World Wars or in search of work.
2. The airlines cited irregularities by cargo handlers and corruption by agencies at Jomo Kenyatta airport as the reason. Other airlines that have stopped shipping khat are Lufthansa and MK Mauritius. *Daily Nation*, 21 September 2004.

3. As of 2005, officers working on khat have been moved to the newly formed Serious and Organized Crimes Agency (SOCA).
4. Drug Enforcement Administration.
5. For example, see the khat-smuggling report in the *Daily Mirror*, 28 April 1998.
6. As of 2005, merged into SOCA.
7. *Observer*, 11 May 2003.
8. *Milton Keynes Citizen*, 3 February 2005.
9. Interview with MF, 7 August 2004, London.
10. A new agency as of 2005 incorporating the probation service.
11. Interview with RQ, 20 July 2004, London.
12. Interview with RA, 22 July 2004, London.
13. Film about the shooting down of US helicopters and ensuing firefights between Somali militia and US troops in Mogadishu.
14. Rocks of crack and grams of heroin are trading in London at £40–60.
15. *Star*, Sheffield, 27 March 2003.
16. *Guardian*, 4 September 2002.
17. Hansard, 18 January 2005.
18. Focus Group in Waaberri, 7 September 2004, London.
19. Interview with Sado Omar, 9 January 2004, Sheffield.
20. Interview with MD, 9 January 2005, Sheffield.
21. Interview with Lambeth Crime Prevention Trust officer, 8 June 2004, London.
22. Interview with Sado Omar, 10 January 2005, Sheffield.
23. Field notes from Warsan Fowzi. The name of the informant has been changed.
24. Interview with DW, 13 October 2004, London.
25. Interview with RO, 23 August 2004, London.
26. Interview with MM, 8 April 2004, London.
27. Interview with Eleni Palazidou, 26 March 2004, London.
28. 'Dual diagnosis' describes drug-using mental-health patients presenting respectively to mental-health or drug services.
29. *Sunday Times*, 20 January 1985.
30. *Observer*, 27 November 1994.
31. *Sunday Times*, 30 April 1995.
32. *Observer*, 24 March 1996.

Chapter 10 The Politics of Khat Control

1. A US Drug Enforcement Administration news release of 10 October 2002 reports the case of a resident from Portland, Maine being found guilty of trafficking khat, and facing a maximum sentence of 20 years. www.usdoj.gov/dea/pubs/states/newsrel/maine101002.html

2. www.al-bab.com/yemen/data/news00.htm#QAT 25/11/2000. Changes in the disposal of immigrants found in breach of the law since 9/11 have eliminated this particular defence.
3. (Accessed 26 March 2005): http://www.borderpatrol.com/borderframe901.htm
4. Interview with Mohamed, Toronto, 12 January 2005.
5. Robin Room (1997), *ARF Journal* 26(5) (September/October).
6. Perry Kendall, President and CEO of the Addiction Research Foundation, Toronto, Addiction Research Foundation response to Bill C-7, 13 December 2005).
7. Interview with Michael Crichton, Manager of Intelligence Development, at the Intelligence and Risk Management Division, Contraband and Intelligence Services, Ottawa, Canada, Customs and Revenue Agency, 14 January 2005.
8. Interview with officers from Canada Customs and Revenue Agency, Ottawa, 14 January 2005.
9. Interview in Toronto community centre, 15 January 2005.
10. Stig Hellander, personal communication.
11. English-language summary of Swedish Police Academy Report.
12. Interview with Rinkeby (CID officer), 21 May 2004.
13. Interview with Swedish drug-squad officer, 13 May 2004.

Chapter 11 Mapping the Future of Khat

1. INCB (2006) Report of the International Narcotics Control Board for 2005, Vienna: United Nations.
2. Various interviews in both London and Stockholm.
3. Interview with Chief Superintendent Richard Quinn, Borough Commander, Lambeth, 7 June 2004.
4. Interview with Metropolitan Police Officer, 6 June 2005 – name and rank withheld.
5. Advisory Council on the Misuse of Drugs (2006), *Khat (Qat): Assessment of Risk to the Individual and Communities in the UK*, London: Home Office.

Appendix: People Interviewed for *The Khat Controversy*

In Ethiopia, Djibouti and Somaliland

Abdela Hassen, Ethiopian Chat and Agro-Industrial Products Manufacturing Import

Abdi Haybe, Elmi Awad, Mohammed Farah, and Yusuf Aineb Muse, Academics at the University of Hargeisa, and Abdirizak Dahir Salam, Student, University of Hargeisa

Abdul Malik, Aragaw Wedeyes, Samel Shifa and Beredin Seid, Staff at Rouh Anti-Khat Office, Addis Ababa, Ethiopia

Abdulaziz Mohammed, Eastern Harergi Agricultural Bureau, Ethiopia Export Share Company (ECAIPMIESC)

Abduresak Abubeker and Abeba Alemayehu, Finance and Economic Development Office of East Harerge Zone

Abebe Mekonnen and Abiy Teferra, Jerusalem Children Community Development, Dire Dawa, Ethiopia

Abraham Sahilu and Abeba Alemayhu, Dire Dawa Planning Bureau, Ethiopia

Abraham Sahlu, Head, Planning and Economic Development Bureau, Dire Dawa, Ethiopia

Ahmed Abdulahi Oamr, Mohamed Ahmed Ducaale, Ahmed Daud Jedi and Abdirhaman Jama Elnu Ministry of Finance, and Ahmed Abdulhasin Nadif, Director of Planning and Coordination Department at the Ministry of Planning and Coordination, Somaliland

Ahmed Daud Jedi (Director General) and Abdirhaman Jama Elnu, Ministry of Finance, Somaliland

Ahmeddin Muktar, trader and Abdulaziz Mohammed, Tajudin Abdurhman and Asman Jibro, from Eastern Harerge Agricultural Bureau, Ethiopia

Akalu Geneme, Assey Kebede and Tilahun Eshete, Bureau of Revenue, Amhara Region Ethiopia

Assey Kebede, Finance Bureau, Amhara Region, Ethiopia

Ayichew Kebede, Bureau of Finance and Economic Development, Amhara Region Ethiopia

Berhanu Benti, SNNPR, Finance and Economic Bureau

Berhanu Deres, Berwako General Trading and Construction Works Share Company (BGTCWSC)

Dr Daniel Dauro, Director General, Southern Agricultural Research Institute, Ethiopia

Demeska Tamiru, Finance and Economic Development Office of East Harerge Zone

Professor Desta Hameto, Dr Abebe Fanta, Dr. Tesfaye Behsah and Dr. Tesfaye Lemma, Alemaya University, Ethiopia

Ebrahim Amadu Hassan, Director of Customs Authority, Djibouti

Esmail Adem, Kulmiye Trading Share Company

Faysal Ali Sheiku, Hassan Said, Musa Ahmed, Jamahariya (*The Republican*), Newspaper, Somaliland

Gami Ahi, Deputy Governer, Central Bank of Somaliland

Haile Niru, Bureau of Revenue, SNNPR Region, Ethiopia

Ibrahim Ahmedu, Vice Minister of Finance, Djibouti

Jamal Kerga and Heru Hasen, Gurage Zone Agricultural and Natural Resources Desk, Ethiopia

Dr Kebede Kanchula, Molla Tegene, and Tedla Wolde Michael, Sidama Zone Rural Development and Coordination Department, Ethiopia

Kedir Sirage and Feleke Gebre Michael, Gurage Zone Revenue Desk, Ethiopia

Matusala, A., Revenue Bureau, SNNPR

Mr Mesfin Tegene, Vice-Minister, Ministry for Water Resource, Ethiopia

Mohammed Ahmed Ducale and Khadar Mohamed Abdi, Customs Office, Somaliland

Mohammed Ahmed and Abebe Kebede, Somali Region Finance Bureau, Ethiopia

Murad Zekaria, Bureau of Finance and Economic Development, Somali Region, Ethiopia

Naasir Moxald Aadan and Wegayehu Wolde Senbet, Revenue Bureau, Somali Region, Ethiopia

Omar Abdulali, Farmer

Semayehu Tesfaye, SNNPR Agricultural Bureau, Ethiopia

Sheriff Ahmed Adem, Harergi Agricultural Bureau, Ethiopia

Solomon Tefera, BIFTU

Taaddasa Lalaa, Negusse Degefa, Girma Gofu, and Gemechu Admasu, West Harerge Zone Finance and Planning Office, Ethiopia

Tadesse Lala, Negusse Degefa, Girma Gofa, Gemechu Admassu, West Hararge Finance, Planning and Economic Development Office, Ethiopia

Tamrat Kebede, Dire Dawa Foreign Trade Office

Tebebu Belay, Assefa G. Giorgis, and Alemayehu Bekele, Eastern Zone Customs Office Dire Dawa, Ethiopia

Tesfaye Wolde Michael, Matheos Rike and Abraham Daniel, Sidama Zone Finance and Economic Development Department, Ethiopia

Teshome Wale, Rural Development and Agricultural Bureau, Amhara Region, Ethiopia

Ubah Mohammed and Abdibasid Ahmed, Investment Bureau, as well as Mohammed Ahmed and Abebe Kebede, Somali Region Finance Bureau, Ethiopia

Wegayehu Gashaw, Yunus Hassan, Tesfaye Alemayehu, and Taddesse Esubalu, Agriculture Development Office, Dire Dawa, Ethiopia

Workiye Wendimu and Metmiku Yohannes, Ethiopian Customs Authority at the Dire Dawa Post Office, Ethiopia

Yilma Bekele, Gurage Zone Planning Bureau, Ethiopia

Yohannes Shiferaw, Bureau of Statistics and Population, SNNPR Region, Ethiopia

Yunus Hassan, Taddesse Esubalu, Wegayehu Gashaw and Tesfaye Alemayehu, Agriculture Development Office in Dire Dawa

Zerihun Ashebr, Finance Bureau, Dire Dawa Ethiopia

Zewdu Girma, School teacher in Jijiga

Ziad Jibri and Hussein Abdurahmen, Agents

In Kenya, Uganda and Rwanda

Below are listed the names of people interviewed who were happy to provide their names. In the majority of cases, especially where people were nervous about outsiders 'spying' on the trade, no names were asked and none was given

Kenya

Guides/Key Informants

Ali Swaleh	Malindi	throughout
Abduba Galgalo	Changamwe, Mombasa	28/1/04
Dixon	Taita Hills	3/2/04
Winnie	Mtito Ndei	4/2/04
Caxton	Embu	10/2/04
Fatouma	Maua	12/2/04
Robert	Maili Taty, Meru	12/2/04
Saidi	Isiolo	13/2/04
Harrison	Timau	15/2/04
Saif	Mwingi	16/2/04
Omari	Garissa	16/2/04
Mohammed Dekow Kossar	Garissa	17/2/02
Abdul Rahman	Mandera	8/4/04
Imam Mahmoud Abdlkadir	Lamu	1/8/04
Mohammed Mahazi	Lamu	3/8/04

Khat Traders

Jackson	Shela, Malindi	25/1/04
Kimathi Zakayo (Blackie)	Omega Brothers, Malindi	24/1/04
Geoffrey	Kongowea Wholesale Market, Mombasa	26/1/04
Mzee 'Hitler'	Mwembe Tayari, Mombasa	26/1/04
Kirithi Nabea	Barani, Malindi	27/1/04
Habiba	Old Market, Malindi	27/1/04
Halima	Old Market, Malindi	27/1/04
Margaret	Vipingo, Kilifi District	28/1/04
Noor	Changamwe, Mombasa	28/1/04
Fatuma	Changamwe, Mombasa	28/1/04
Khadija	Old Town, Mombasa	30/1/04
Salimu	Watamu	31/1/04
Pius	Voi market	2/2/04
Abdulahi	Kaijado	5/2/04
Jennifer	Namanga	6/2/04
Peter	Laare	12/2/04
Halima	Isiolo	14/2/04
Rukiya Omari	Garissa	16/2/04
William	Garissa	17/2/04
Amina	Tea stall between Garissa and Dadab	4/4/04
Mishal Ismael	Ifo refugee camp	4/4/04
Andrew	Wajir	6/4/04
Amina	Wajir	6/4/04
Halima	Wajir	7/4/04
James	Wajir	7/4/04
Officials, Dawa Women's Group	Mandera	9/4/04
Amina	Moyale	12/4/04
Tesfaye Alemayehu Firew	Eastleigh, Nairobi	8/4/04
Martin	Lamu	30/7/04
Treasurer of Miraa Traders Welfare Society	Lamu	2/8/04
Fatouma	Missionary (Mombasa–Nairobi Road)	19/8/04

Farmers

Maina	Lushangoni Location, Wundanyi Division	3/2/04

George	Murugha Location, Wundanyi Division	3/2/04
Mzee Mganga	Murugha Location, Wundanyi Division	3/2/04
Mohammed	Kimana	8/2/04
Stephen	nr. Karama, Meru District	11/2/04
John	Timau	15/2/04

Consumers

Mohammed Saleh Awke	Namanga, TZ (visiting from Arusha TZ)	6/2/04
Ahmed	Namanga	7/2/04
Ali, Soldier	Tea stall between Garissa and Dadaab	4/4/04
Mohammed, Administration Police	Moyale	12/4/04
'Addis', Café owner	Moyale	12/4/04

Uganda and Rwanda

Guides/Key Informants

Abu Famau	Kampala	throughout
Mzee Hassan	Kampala	throughout
Musa Almasi	Kasese	throughout
Mzee Hedi	Kasese	29/8/04
Said Sulemain	Fort Portal	31/8/04
Bablo	Kabale	8/10/04
Ali Karama	Kabale	8/10/04
Umuru Sendi	Mabira Forest/Jinja	22/8/04
Family of the late Mtajazi	Matjazi, Kampala	28/8/04
Mohammed Ali 'Clay'	Kabale	9/10/04
Salim Brek	Kisoro	10/10/04
Saleh Ali	Kisoro	11/10/04
Said Amar	Kisoro	11/10/04
Balgis	Mbale	21/8/04
Jamaa Yusuf	Mengo, Kampala	11/12/04
Mohammed Ali Hajji	Mengo, Kampala	11/12/04
Mahmoud Abdi Jama	Moroto	14/12/04
Mohammed Abdi Ismael	Moroto	11/12/04
Hassan Abdi	Moroto	16/12/04
Sh. Yusuf Kator	Kiti	11/10/04

Khat Traders

'Mama Mbale'	Mbale	22/8/04
'Uncle Best'	Mbale	21/8/04
Mama Fatouma	Jinja	22/8/04
Zainab	Kasenge	26/8/04
Farida	Kasenge	26/8/04
Mama Abdul	Kisenyi, Kampala	26/8/04
Saddiq Umaru	Soroti	14/12/04
Yahya Shaban	Soroti	14/12/04
Juma Saidi	Kangole, nr. Moroto	14/12/04
Omari	Nakapiripirit	15/12/04
'Mjomba'	Kasese	28/8/04
Fred	Kabale	8/10/04
Moses	Kabale	9/10/04
'Ssenga'	Lyantonde	11/10/04
Abdi	Kisenyi, Kampala	10/12/04
Peter Looku	Hirihiri	17/12/04
Auren Hassan	Hirihiri	17/12/04
Salima	Kigali, Rwanda	25/2/05
Halima	Kigali, Rwanda	25/2/05

Farmers

Shaban	Mbale	22/8/04
Kizito	Mabira Forest	24/8/04
British Harrison	Lugazi	25/8/04
Wife of Sheikh Semakula	Kabasanda	27/8/04
Siraj Byarufu	Fort Portal	30/8/04
Robert	Kabale	8/10/04
Bright Mfitimpano	Kigezi	10/10/04
Lopilipili	Namalu	15/12/04
Rajab	Rohanga, Rwanda	27/2/05

Consumers

Ronald	Bugenbe	24/8/04
Muammir	Rukungiri	11/10/04
Mohammed	Kisenyi, Kampala	10/12/04
Khalid	Kisenyi	10/12/04
Anwar	Old Kampala	19/2/05
Aisha	Old Kampala	19/2/05
Rashid	Kigali, Rwanda	24/2/05

In the UK (Informants who gave consent to being cited)

Muna D., community researcher in London	26/01/04
Ali, *mafrish* owner, Tower Hamlets	28/01/04
Abdi Hassan, drugs worker at HOTS drop-in on Mile End Rd	26/03/04
Chief Super Intendant Richard Quinn, Borough Commander, Lambeth	07/06/04
Rick Algar, Operational Manger Streatham Police Station	22/07/04
Joe Onofrio, HMCE, National Coordinator, Synthetic Drugs and Precursor Chemicals National Intelligence, Custom House, London	14/01/04
Eleni Palazidou, Psychiatrist, St Clements Hospital	26/03/04
Jean Carpenter, Lambeth Crime Prevention Trust	23/03/04
Muntaz Malik, Imam, South London Islamic Centre, Mitcham Lane, Streatham	07/04/04
Dean Whittington, Director, Orexis	13/10/04
Dr Louise Ryan, resident Hopton Road	13/10/04
Michael Freeberne, Lambeth Community Police Consultative Group	07/08/04
Abdila M, khat importer	26/03/04
Abdil H, khat distributor	26/03/04
Beatrice Vaessen, Nurse Practitioner in Refugee Clinic, Hostel Barry House, London	06/04/04
Helen Watts, Street Care Officer, Lambeth	29/09/04
Mohamed Deria, journalist	08/06/04
Keith Hill, MP	07/05/04
Farah Mohamed, café owner, Lambeth	09/05/04
Abdulai, community organizer, Lambeth	09/05/04
Keith Naish, Operations Manager Street Care, Lambeth	29/09/04
Roby Tobrun, businessman, Lambeth	07/04/04
Dr. Abdul Sharif, community leader, Sheffield	18/03/04
Said, khat chewer, Sheffield	18/03/04
Nasir, khat chewer, Sheffield	18/03/04
Abdullah Mohamba, khat chewer, Sheffield	18/03/04
Abdullah, khat chewer, Sheffield	18/03/04
Mohamed Nasir, khat chewer, Sheffield	19/03/04
Ali, khat chewer, Sheffield	19/03/04
Saleh, khat chewer, Sheffield	19/03/04
Hizam Dubes, khat chewer, Sheffield	19/03/04
Yussuf, khat chewer, Sheffield	19/03/04
Nasir Mohamed khat chewer, Sheffield	19/03/04
Fuad khat chewer, Sheffield	19/03/04
Said Ahmed, journalist and community activist	25/03/04
Susan Doran, Community Safety Officer, Lambeth	02/09/04

Suzanne Maher, Gleneagle Road resident	12/10/04
Amerit Chanion, Community Development Officer, Lambeth	08/06/04
Dave Francis, Camden Drug Action Team, Camden	06/07/04
Omar Yusuf, Somali Community Centre activist, Camden	10/08/04
Fuad Ismail, New Roots, Camden	10/08/04
Asha kin Duale, Community activist, Camden	10/08/04
Hamdi Abdulle, Community activist, Camden	10/08/04
Khadija Shire, Community activist, Camden	10/08/04
Asha Jama, Community activist, Camden	10/08/04
Mohamed Hassan, Community activist, Camden	10/08/04
Adam Hassan, Refugee Link and Training Agency, London	07/10/04
Saeed Abdi, Somali Mental Health Project, Sheffield	02/03/05
Sado Omar, Community Health worker, Sheffield	02/03/05

In Canada

Michael Crichton, Manager, Intelligence and Risk Management Division, Contraband and Intelligence Services, Ottawa	15/02/05
Sylvia Bartlet, Intelligence Analyst, Contraband and Intelligence Services, Ottawa	15/02/05
Patricia Begin, Director, Canadian Council for Substance Abuse, Ottawa	16/02/05
Karen Cumberland, National Coordinator, Canadian Council for Substance Abuse, Ottawa	16/02/05
Anne-Elyse Deguire, Senior Research Analyst, Canadian Council for Substance Abuse, Ottawa	16/02/05
John Weekes, Senior Research Analyst, Canadian Council for Substance Abuse, Ottawa	16/02/05
Gerald Thomas, Senior Policy Analyst, Canadian Council for Substance Abuse, Ottawa	16/02/05
Mahdi Ali, Community Outreach Worker, Regent Park Community Health Centre, Toronto	17/02/05
Ahmed, journalist, Toronto	17/02/05

In Sweden: Stockholm, 17/05/04–20/05/04

Jan Eric Karlberg, Detective Inspector, National Criminal Intelligence Service	17/05/04
Gunnar Hermansson, Detective Inspector, National Criminal Intelligence Service	18/05/04

Lars Granstrom, Intelligence Officer, Swedish Customs	17/05/04
Stig Thelbert, police officer, Stockholm	18/05/04
Rick Wasserstein, film-maker	19/05/04
Stig Hellander, researcher	19/05/04
Dr Yakoub Aden Abdi, Drug Addiction Clinic at Danderyd Hospital	19/05/04
Abdulkadir Nuur, Somali League Sweden	19/05/04

Bibliography

Abebe, S. (2004), 'Khat in Dire Dawa', Paper for a Workshop Organized by Institute of Ethiopian Studies on Khat and the Ethiopian Reality: Production, Marketing, and Consumption, Addis Ababa, 16 April 2004.

Adam, H. M. and Ford, R. (1997), *Mending the Rips in the Sky: Options for Somali Communities in the 21st Century*, Lawrenceville and Asmara: Red Sea Press.

Advisory Council on the Misuse of Drugs (ACMD) (2006), *Khat (Qat): Assessment of Risk to Individual and Communities in the UK*, London: British Home Office.

Afrah, M., 'The Dark Side of Somalia', accessed online 26 March 2005 at www.banadir.com/the_dark_side.shtml

Ahmed, H. (2004) 'The Traditional Ritual of *Chat* Consumption in Wallo', Paper for a workshop organized by Institute of Ethiopian Studies on Khat and the Ethiopian Reality: Production, marketing, and Consumption, Addis Ababa, 16 April 2004.

Ahmed, M., Spencer, M. and Wintersteiger, L. (2004), 'Report into the Advice Needs of the Somali Community'. Report to the Streatham Town Centre Office.

Ahmed, S. (1994), 'Proceedings of Seminar on Khat and Health at St Margaret's House', St Margaret's House, Bethnal Green, London.

Akyeampong, E. (1996), *Drink, Power and Cultural Change. A Social History of Alcohol in Ghana, c.1800 to Recent Times*, Portsmouth, NH and Oxford.

Alem, A. and Shibre, T. (1997), 'Khat Induced Psychosis and its Medico-legal Implication: A Case Report', *Ethiopian Medical Journal* 35(2), pp. 137–41.

Alem, A., Kebede, D. and Kullgren, G. (1999), 'The Prevalence and Socio-demographic Correlates of Khat Chewing in Butajira, Ethiopia', *Acta Psychiatrica Scandinavica* 100, pp. 84–91.

Al-Hebshi, N. N. and Skaug, N. (2005), 'Khat (Catha edulis): An Updated Review', *Addiction Biology* 10(4), pp. 299–307.

Ali, E. (2001), 'Somali Women in London: Education and Gender Relations', Unpublished Ph.D. Thesis. London: Institute of Education.

Allen, J. de V. (1993), *Swahili Origins: Swahili Culture and the Sungwaya Phenomenon*, London: Eastern African Studies, James Currey.

Almedon, A. M. and Abraham, S. (1994), 'Women, Moral Virtue and *Tchat*-chewing', in M. MacDonald (ed.), *Gender, Drink and Drugs*, Oxford: Berg.

Anderson, D. M. and Carrier, N. (2006), 'Flowers of Paradise, or Polluting the Nation? Contested Narratives of Khat Consumption', in J. Brewer and F. Trentmann (eds), *Consuming Cultures, Global Perspectives: Historical Trajectories, Transnational Exchanges*, Oxford: Berg, pp. 145–66.

Anholt, S. (2005), *Brand New Justice: The Upside of Global Branding*, Oxford: Butterworth Heinemann.

ANRS-BOFED (2002), 'Annual Statistical Abstract, the Amhara National Regional State', Bureau of Finance and Economic Development.

Araita, A. (2004), 'Documentary and Bibliographic Analysis of the History and Arrival of Khat in the Republic of Djibouti' (in French), Unpublished.

Avrahami, I. (2004), 'A Qat above the Rest', *Haaretz*, 15 November 2004.

Awassa Finance-Bureau (1996), 'Khat Tax Improvement Law' (in Amharic), Finance Bureau, SNNPR, Awassa.

Bayart, J.-F. (1993), *The State in Africa: the Politics of the Belly*, London: Longman.

Bean, P. (2002), *Drugs and Crime*, London: Willan.

Beckerleg, S. (2006), 'What Harm? Kenyan and Ugandan Perspectives on Khat', *African Affairs* 104(418).

Beckerleg, S. and Sheekh, N. (2005), 'A View from the Refugee Camps: New Somali Khat Use in Kenya', *Drugs and Alcohol Today* 5(3), pp. 25–7.

Beekinghuis, A. (2004), 'Chewing Khat Together: From Indigenous Practice to International Issue', www.leda.lycaeum.org/documents/chewing_khat_together

Bennett, N. R. (1986), *Arab versus European: Diplomacy and War in Nineteenth-century East Central Africa*, New York and London: Africana Publishing.

BFED (2002) 'Annual Statistical Bulletin', Bureau of Finance and Economic Development (BFED), Amhara National Regional State, Bahir Dar.

Bhui, K. et al. (2003), 'Traumatic Events, Migration Characteristics and Psychiatric Symptoms among Somali refugees – Preliminary Communications', *Social Psychiatry and Psychiatric Epidemiology* 38, pp. 35–43.

Bloch, A. and Atfield, G. (2002), *The Professional Capacity of Nationals from the Somali Regions in Britain: Report to Refugee Action and IOM*, London: Goldsmiths College and Refugee Action.

BOPED (1998), 'Southern Nations nationalities and Peoples' Regional Government: A Socio-Economic Profile'. Bureau of Planning and Economic Development, Awassa.

Boxberger, L. (2002), *On the Edge of Empire: Hadhramawt, Emigration, and the Indian Ocean, 1880s–1930s*, New York: State University of New York Press.

Brenneisen, R., Fisch, H. U., Koelbing, U., Geisshusler, S. and Kalix, P. (1990), 'Amphetamine-like Effects in Humans of the Khat Alkaloid Cathinone', *British Journal of Clinical Pharmacology* 30(6), pp. 825–8.

Burton, R. F. (1966/1956), *First Footsteps in East Africa or, An Exploration of Harrar*, New York: Schuster (reprint).

Cabdidaawuud, M. W. Q. (2004), *Chat Surveys* (in Somali), Saudi Arabia: Saad Suubban Publishers and Distributors.

CACC (2003a), 'Ethiopian Agricultural Sample Enumeration, 2001/02: Results for Amhara Region, Statistical Report on Area and Production of Crops Part II.B',

Central Agricultural Census Commission (AACC), Federal Democratic Republic of Ethiopia.

CACC (2003b), 'Ethiopian Agricultural Sample Enumeration, 2001/02: Results at Country Level: Statistical Report on Socio-Economic Characteristics of the Population in Agricultural Households, Land-use and Area, and Production of Crops, Part I', Central Agricultural Census Commission (CACC), Federal Democratic Republic of Ethiopia.

Carothers, J. C. (1945), 'Miraa as a Cause of Insanity', *East African Medical Journal* 12.

Carrier, N. (2005a), 'Under any Other Name: the Trade and Use of Khat in the UK', *Drugs and Alcohol Today* 5(3), pp. 14–16.

Carrier, N. (2005b), 'The Need for Speed: Contrasting Timeframes in the Social Life of Kenyan Miraa', *Africa* 75(4), pp. 539–58.

Carrier, N. (2005c), '"Miraa is Cool": the Cultural Importance of Miraa (Khat) for Tigania and Igembe Youth in Kenya', *Journal of African Cultural Studies* 17(2), pp. 201–18.

Carrier, N. C. M. (2003), 'The Social Life of Miraa: Farming, Trade and Consumption of a Plant Stimulant in Kenya', Department of Social Anthropology, University of St Andrews.

Cassanelli, L. (1986), 'Qat: Changes in the Production and Consumption of a Quasi-legal Commodity in Northeast Africa', in A. Appadurai (ed.), *The Social Life of Things: Commodities in Cultural Perspective*, Cambridge: Cambridge University Press, pp. 236–57.

CBDSZ (1997), 'Short Study on Khat Production and its Problems in Bahir Dar City' (in Amharic), Council of Bahir Dar Special Zone Office, Amhara National Regional State.

Comaroff, J. and Comaroff, J. (1993), *Modernity and its Malcontents: Ritual and Power in Postcolonial Africa*, Chicago: University of Chicago Press.

Commercial Bank of Ethiopia (2002), Annual Report, Addis Ababa, Ethiopia.

Cox, G. and Rampes, H. (2003), 'Adverse Effects of Khat: a Review', *Advances in Psychiatric Treatment* 9, pp. 456–63.

Critchlow, S. (1987), 'Khat-induced Paranoid Psychosis, *British Journal of Psychiatry* 150, pp. 247–9.

Croppenstedt, A., Demeke, M. and Meschi, M. M. (2003), 'Technology Adoption in the Presence of Constraints: the Case of Fertilizer Demand in Ethiopia', *Review of Development Economics* 7(1) (February), pp. 58–70.

CSA (2000), 'Household Income, Consumption and Expenditure Survey. Central Statistical Authority', Addis Ababa, Ethiopia.

Degefe, B. and Nega, B. (eds) (2003), 'The Role of Urbanisation in the Socio-Economic Development Process', Ethiopian Economic Association.

Deslandes, P. N., Pache, D. M. and Sewell, R. D. (2002), 'Drug Dependence: Neuropharmacology and Management', *Journal of Pharmacy and Pharmacology* 54(7), pp. 885–95.

Dhadphale, M. and Mengech, H. (1987), 'Khat-induced Paranoid Psychosis', *British Journal of Psychiatry* 150, p. 876.

Dhadphale, M. and Omolo, O. E. (1988), 'Psychiatric Morbidity among Khat Chewers', *East African Medical Journal* 65(6), pp. 355–9.

Dhadphale, M., Mengech, A. and Chege, S. W. (1981), 'Miraa (catha edulis) as a Cause of Psychosis, *East African Medical Journal* 58(2), pp. 130–5.

Dire Dawa Foreign Trade Office (2000), 'Study on Khat production Expenses for Exports to Djibouti and Somalia' (in Amharic).

Dire Dawa Foreign Trade Office (2002), 'Eastern Ethiopia Khat Trade: Exports and Current Activity' (in Amharic).

Dire Dawa Foreign Trade Office (2004), 'Eastern Ethiopia Foreign Trade Overall Progress, 1994–2001' (in Amharic).

Drug Enforcement Administration website, accessed online 26 March 2005 at www.dea.gov/pubs/intel/02032/02032dt1.html

EDRI (2004), 'Agricultural Extension, Adoption, Diffusion and Socio-Economic Impact in the Four Regions [Tigrai, Amhara, Oromia and the South] of Ethiopia, Paper I-V', Paper presented to the National Workshop, Ethiopian Development Research Institute, Addis Ababa, Ethiopia.

Eggeling, W. J. (1951), *The Indigenous Trees of the Uganda Protectorate*, London: Government of the Uganda Protectorate.

Elmi, A. S. (1983), 'The Chewing of Khat in Somalia', *Journal of Ethnopharmacology* 8, pp. 163–76.

Elmi, A. S., Ahmed, Y. H. and Samatar, M. S. (1987) *Experience in the Control of Khat Chewing in Somalia*, Mogadishu: Somalia National University.

Everything about Qat/khat/kat http://www.sas.upenn.edu/African_Studies/Hornet/qat.html (accessed 9/1/04).

Fallers, L. A. (1964), *The King's Men: Leadership and Status in Buganda on the Eve of Independence*, Oxford: Oxford University Press.

FAO (2002), 'Ethiopia – Special Report', 30 December 2002.

FAO (2004), 'On-line Statistical Database', Food and Agricultural Organization.

Finance-Bureau (1996), 'Khat Tax Improvement Law', Finance Bureau, Southern Nations Nationalities and People's Region (SNNPR), Awassa, Ethiopia (in Amharic).

Fine, B. (2002), *The World of Consumption: The Material and Cultural Revisited*, 2nd edn, London and New York: Routledge.

Fowzi, W. (2005), 'Patterns of Khat Use among Somalis in Camden', Camden Drug and Alcohol Team.

FSCE (1998), 'Some Correlates of Poly-Drug Use Behaviour among Street Children: The Case of Four Urban Centres', Forum for Street Children, Ethiopia.

FSCE (1999), 'Differential Patterns of Drug Use among Street Children', Forum for Street Children, Ethiopia.

Gardner, B. (1992), 'Changing Economic Perspectives on the Farm Problem', *Journal of Economic Literature* 30 (March), pp. 62–101.

Gebissa, E. (1997), 'Consumption, Contraband and Commodification: a History of Khat in Harerge, Ethiopia, *c*.1930–1991, PhD Thesis, Michigan State University.

Gebissa, E. (2004), *Leaf of Allah: Khat and Agricultural Transformation in Harerge Ethiopia 1875–1991*, London: James Currey.

Getahun, A. and Kirkorian, A. D. (1973), 'Chat: Coffee's Rival from Harar, Ethiopia. I. Botany, Cultivation and Use', *Economic Botany* 27(4), pp. 353–77.

Giannini, A. J., Burge, H., Shaheen, J. M. and Price, W. A. (1986) 'Khat: Another Drug of Abuse', *Journal of Psychoactive Drugs* 18(2), pp. 155–8.

Giffen, P. J. (1991), 'Panic and Indifference: The Politics of Canada's Drug Laws', Ottawa: Canadian Centre on Substance Abuse.

Glennon, R. A. and Liebowitz, S. M. (1982), 'Serotonin Receptor Affinity of Cathinone and Related Analogues', *Journal of Medicinal Chemistry* 25(4), pp. 393–7.

Goldsmith, P. (1988), 'The Production and Marketing of Miraa in Kenya', in R. Cohen (ed.), *Satisfying Africa's Food Needs*, London: Lynne Rienner.

Goldsmith, P. (1994), 'Symbiosis and Transformation in Kenya's Meru District', Unpublished PhD thesis, University of Florida.

Goldsmith, P. (1997), 'The Somali Impact on Kenya, 1990–1993: the View from the Camps', in H. M. Adam and R. Ford, *Mending Rips in the Sky: Options for Somali Communities in the 21st Century*, Lawrenceville and Asmara: Red Sea Press, pp. 461–83.

Goldsmith, P. (1999), 'The Political Economy of Miraa', *East Africa Alternatives*, March/April, 15–19.

Goldstein, P. (1985), 'The Drugs' Violence Nexus: A Tripartite Conceptual Framework', *Journal of Drug Issues* 14(4), pp. 493–506.

Goodhand, J. (2005), 'Frontiers and Wars: the Opium Economy in Afghanistan', *Journal of Agrarian Change* 5(2), pp. 191–216.

Gough, S. P. and Cookson, I. B. (1984), 'Khat-induced Schizophreniform Psychosis in UK', *Lancet* 1(8374), pp. 455–455.

Gough, S.P. and Cookson, I.B. (1987), 'Khat-induced Paranoid Psychosis', *British Journal of Psychiatry* 150, pp. 875–6.

Gough, S.P. and Cookson, I.B. (1988), 'Khat-induced Paranoid Psychosis', *British Journal of Psychiatry* 152, p. 294.

Granek, M., Shalev, A. and Weingarten, A. M. (1988), 'Khat-induced Hypnagogic Hallucinations', *Acta Psychiatrica Scandinavica* 78(4), pp. 458–61.

Green, M. (2001), 'Profiling Refugees in Tower Hamlets to Deduce Their Particular Health Needs and How Best Meet Them', Tower Hamlets Primary Care Trust.

Green, P. (2001), *Drugs, Trafficking and Criminal Policy. The Scapegoat Strategy*, Winchester: Waterside Press.

Green, R. H. (1999), 'Khat and the Realities of the Somalis: Historic, Social, Household, Political and Economic', *Review of African Political Economy* 79, pp. 33–49.

Griffiths, D. (2000), 'Fragmentation and Consolidation: the Contrasting Case of Somali and Kurdish Refugees in London', *Journal of Refugee Studies* 13, pp. 281–302.

Griffiths, P. (1998), 'Qat Use in London: a Study of Qat Use Among a Sample of Somalis Living in London', London: Home Office, Drugs Prevention Initiative.

Griffiths, P., Gossop, M., Wickenden, S., Dunworth, J., Harris, K. and Lloyd, C. (1997), 'A Transcultural Pattern of Drug Use: Qat (Khat) in the UK', *British Journal of Psychiatry* 170, pp. 281–4.

GZAD (1998) 'Gurage Zone Agricultural Development Baseline Information', Gurage Zone Agricultural Department, Wolkite.

Hailu, D. (2005), Review Article, *Journal of Agrarian Change* 5(2) (April).

Halbach, H. (1972), 'Medical Aspects of the Chewing of Khat Leaves', *Bulletin of the World Health Organization* 47(1), pp. 21–9.

Hansen, B. and Twaddle, M. (eds) (1988), *Uganda Now*, London: James Currey.

Hansson, G. (2001), 'Ethiopian Reforms: Government Legitimacy, Economic Growth and Development', in M. Lundahl (ed.), *From Crisis to Growth in Africa*, London and New York: Routledge.

Harris, H. (2004), 'The Somali Community in the UK. What we Know and How we Know it', London: Information Centre about Asylum and Refugees in the UK (ICAAR).

Hassan, C. (2003), 'Le Khat: un mal nécessaire', *La Nation*, 5 juin, p. 5.

Hassan, C. (2004), *Khat the Necessary Evil* (in French), unpublished.

Hassan, N. A., Gunaid, A. A., El Khally, F. M.Y. and Murray-Lyon, I. M. (2002a), 'The Subjective Effects of Chewing Qat Leaves in Human Volunteers', *Annals of Saudi Medicine* 22(1–2), pp. 34–7.

Hassan, N., Gunaid, A. A., Abdo-Rabbo, A. A., Abdel-Kader, Z. Y., Al-Mansoob, M. A. K., Awad, A. Y. and Murray-Lyon, I. M. (2000), 'The Effect of Qat Chewing on Blood Pressure and Heart Rate in Healthy Volunteers', *Tropical Doctor* 30(2), pp. 107–8.

Hassan, N.A., Gunaid, A. A., El-Khally, F. M. Y. and Murray-Lyon, I. M. (2002b), 'The Effect of Chewing Khat Leaves on Human Mood', *Saudi Medical Journal* 23(7), pp. 850–3.

Hebdige, D. (1979), *Subculture: the Meaning of Style*, London: Methuen.

Hill, B. (1965), 'Cat (Catha Edulis Forsk)', *Journal of Ethiopian Studies* 3.

Himmelstein, J. L. (1978), 'Drug Politics Theory: Analysis and Critique', *Journal of Drug Issues* 8, pp. 37–52.

HREFB (2004), 'Statistical Abstract, Harari Regional Economic and Finance Bureau' (in Amharic).

Ihunwo, A. O., Kayanja, F. I. B. and Amadi-Ihunwo, U. B. (2004), 'Use and Perception of the Psychostimulant, Khat (*Catha edulis*) among Three Occupational Groups in South Western Uganda', *East African Medical Journal* 81(9), pp. 468–73.

Isse, H. (2005), 'Working with Somali Khat Users', *Drugs and Alcohol Today* 5(3).

Kalix, P. (1984), 'The Pharmacology of Khat)', *General Pharmacology* 15, pp. 179–87.

Kalix, P. (1991), 'The Pharmacology of Psychoactive Alkaloids from Ephedra and Catha', *Journal of Ethnopharmacology* 32(1–3), pp. 201–8.

Kalix, P. (1996), 'Catha Edulis, a Plant that has Amphetamine Effects', *Pharmacy World and Science* 18(2), pp. 69–73.

Keitetsi, C. (2004), *Child Soldier*, London: Souvenir Press.

Kennedy, J. G. (1987), *The Flower of Paradise: the Institutionalized Use of the Drug Qat in North Yemen*, D. Reidel Publishing Company.

Kennedy, J. G., Teague, J., Rokaw, W. and Cooney, E. (1983), 'A Medical Evaluation of the Use of Qat in North Yemen', *Social Science and Medicine* 17(12), pp. 783–93.

Khalis, S. S. (1993), 'I am a Long [sic] Ranger, *Yemen Times* (San'a) 3(47), (8 November–4 December), p. 18.

Kirsten, J. F., Perret, S. R. and Tefera, T. L. (2003), 'Market Incentives, Farmers' Response and a Policy Dilemma: a Case Study of Chat Production in the Eastern Ethiopian Highlands', *Agrekon* 42(3) (September), pp. 213–27.

Klein, A. (2004a), 'An Evaluation of the Hibiscus Organization', Jamaica Report for the Drugs and International Crime Department, Foreign and Commonwealth Office, London: DrugScope.

Klein, A. (2004b), *Khat in Streatham: Formulating a Community Response*, London; DrugScope.

Knighton, B. (2003), 'The State as Raider among the Karamojong: Where there are No Guns, They Use the Threat of Guns', *Africa* 73(ii), pp. 427–55.

Kujog, S. O. A. (2001), 'From Policeman to Drug User: a Personal Perspective on the Use of Khat', *Journal of Substance Use* 5, pp. 320–2.

Lee, K. (1994), 'Race, Culture and Psychosis: Some Reflections and Warnings, Khat and Health', in Ahmed, S., Proceedings of a Seminar on Khat and Health, Tower Hamlets Health Strategy Group.

Lemessa, D. (2001), 'Khat (Catha edulis): Botany, Distribution, Cultivation, Usage and Economics in Ethiopia, Emergencies Unit for Ethiopia', United Nations Development Programme (UNDP).

Lewis, I. (1962), *A Pastoral Democracy*, Oxford: Oxford University Press.

Lindley, A. (2005), 'Eating with Your Brother when he has Money: Migrants' Remittances in Somali Society', African Studies Seminar paper, St Antony's College, Oxford, 16 February.

Lindley, A. (2006), 'The Dynamics and Effects of Migrants' Remittances in Insecure Settings: The Somali Case', DPhil thesis, University of Oxford.

Litman, A., Levav, I., Saltzrennert, H. and Maoz, B. (1986), 'The Use of Khat – An Epidemiologic-Study in 2 Yemenite Villages in Israel', *Culture Medicine and Psychiatry* 10(4), pp. 389–96.

Mains, Daniel (2004), 'Working, Dreaming, and Chewing: Chat Use Among Young Men in Jimma Ethiopia'. Paper for a workshop organized by the Institute of Ethiopian Studies on Khat and the Ethiopian Reality: Production, Marketing, and Consumption, Addis Ababa, 16 April 2004.

Manifase, T. E. (2004), 'Inside out' www.bbc.co.uk/print/insideout (accessed 3 March 2004).

Mayberry, J., Morgan, G. and Perkin, E. (1984), 'Khat-Induced Schizophreniform Psychosis in UK', *Lancet*, 1(8374), p. 455.

McCrone, P., Bhui, K., and Craig, T. (2005), 'Mental Health Needs, Service Use and Costs among Somali Refugees in the UK', *Acta Psychiatrica Scandinavica* 111(5), pp. 351–7.

McGowan, R. M. (1999), *Muslims in the Diaspora: The Somali Communities of London and Toronto*, Toronto: University of Toronto Press.

Meneley, A. (1996), *Tournaments of Value: Sociability and Hierarchy in a Yemeni Town*, London and Toronto: University of Toronto Press.

Milich, L. and Al-Sabbry, M. (1995), 'The "Rational Peasant" vs. Sustainable Livelihoods: The Case of Qat in Yemen', http://ag.arizona.edu/~lmilich/yemen.html

Miller, N. (1981), 'The Other Somalia', Hanover NH: American University Field Staff Reports.

MOFED (2002), 'Ethiopia: Sustainable Development and Poverty Reduction Program', Ministry of Finance and Economic Development (MOFED). Addis Ababa, Ethiopia.

Mohammed, A. E. (2003), 'The Prevalence of "Chat-Chewing Habit" and Its Incidental Interdependence with Alcohol Drinking Among Addis Ababa University, Main Campus Male Undergraduate Students', *Ethiopian Journal of Development Research* 25(1), pp. 1–51.

MPED (1993), 'An Economic Development Strategy for Ethiopia: A Comprehensive Guidance and a Development Strategy for the Future', Ministry of Planning and Economic Development, Addis Ababa, Ethiopia.

National Drugs Intelligence Unit [NDIU] (1990), 'Khat Misuse in the United Kingdom', *Drugs Arena* 10, London: New Scotland Yard.

Nega, B. (2003), 'Introduction: Development Options for Ethiopia: Rural, Urban, or Balanced', in B. Degefe and B. Nega (eds), *The Role of Urbanisation in the Socio-Economic Development Process*, The Ethiopian Economic Association.

Nielen, R., van der Heijden, F., Tuinier, S. and Verhoeven, W. (2004), 'Khat and Mushrooms Associated with Psychosis', *World Journal of Biological Psychiatry* 5(1), pp. 49–53.

Nielsen, J. A. (1985), 'Cathinone Affects Dopamine and 5-hydroxytryptamine Neurons in Vivo as Measured by Changes in Metabolites and Synthesis in Four Forebrain Regions in the Rat', *Neuropharmacology* 24(9), pp. 845–52.

Numan, N. (2004), 'Exploration of Adverse Psychological Symptoms in Yemeni Khat Users by the Symptoms Checklist-90 (SCL-90)', *Addiction* 99, pp. 61–5.

Odenwald, M. et al. (2005), 'Khat Use as Risk Factor for Psychotic Disorders: A Cross-sectional and Case-control Study in Somalia', *BMC Medicine* 3(1), p. 5.

Opiyo, G. (2004), 'Miraa Farmers', *East African Standard*, 24 November.

Oxfam (2002), 'Coffee Companies under Fire', Press Release, 18 September.

Oxfam (2003), 'Coffee Collapse is Leading to Global Drug Boom', Press Release, 9 December.

Pantelis, C., Hindler, C. G. and Taylor, J. C. (1989), 'Use and Abuse of Khat (Catha-Edulis) - a Review of the Distribution, Pharmacology, Side-effects and a Description of Psychosis Attributed to Khat Chewing', *Psychological Medicine* 19(3), pp. 657–68.

Patel, N. B. (2000), 'Mechanism of Action of Cathinone: The Active Ingredient of Khat (Catha Edulis)', *East African Medical Journal* 77(6), pp. 329–32.

Patel, S., Wright, s. AND Gammampila, A (2005), *Khat Use among Somalis in four English Cities*, London: Home Office.

Peake, R. (1989), 'Swahili Stratification and Tourism in Malindi Old Town, Kenya', *Africa* 59(2), pp. 209–20.

PEDD (1998), 'Gurage Zone Socio-Economic Base-Line Survey', Planning and Economic Development Department, Wolkite.

Randall, T. (1993), 'Khat Abuse Fuels Somali Conflict, Drains Economy', *Journal of American Medical Association* 269(1), pp. 12–15.

Rothman, R. B.et al. (2003), 'In Vitro Characterization of Ephedrine-related Stereoisomersat Biogenic Amine Transporters and the Receptorome Reveals Selective Actions as Norepinephrine Transporter Substrates', *Journal of Pharmacology and Experimental Therapeutics* 307(1), pp. 138–45.

Rudgley, R. (1993), *The Alchemy of Culture: Intoxicants in Society'*, London: British Museum Press.

Ruggiero, V. and South, N. (1995), *Eurodrugs: Drug Use, Markets and Trafficking in Europe*, London: Routledge.

Rushby, K. (1999), *Eating the Flowers of Paradise: A Journey Through the Drug Fields of Ethiopia and Yemen*, London: Constable.

Schechter, M. D. (1990a), 'Dopaminergic Nature of Acute Cathine Tolerance', *Pharmacology, Biochemistry and Behaviour* 36(4), pp. 817–20.

Schechter, M. D. (1990b), 'Rats Become Acutely Tolerant to Cathine after Amphetamine or Cathinone Administration', *Psychopharmacology (Berl)* 101(1), pp. 126–31.

SOVOREDO (2002), 'Qaadka Ma Quud Baa Mise waa Khasaare' (in Somali), Somaliland Volunteers for Relief and Development Organization.

Spanagel, R. and Weiss, F. (1999), 'The Dopamine Hypothesis of Reward: Past and Current Status', *Trends in Neuro Sciences* 22(11), pp. 521–7.

Stacey, Tom (2003), *Tribe*, London: Stacey International.

Summerfield, H. (1993), 'Patterns of Adaptation: Somali and Bangladeshi Women in Britain', in G. Buijs, *Migrant Women: Crossing Boundaries and Changing Identities*, Oxford: Berg.

Taylor, C. (1999), *Sacrifice as Terror: the Rwandan Genocide of 1994*, Oxford: Berg.

Toennes, S. W. et al. (2003), 'Pharmacokinetics of Cathinone, Cathine and Norephedrine after the Chewing of Khat Leaves', *British Journal of Clinical Pharmacology* 56(1), pp. 125–30.

United Nations International Drug Control Programme (1997), *World Drug Report*, Oxford: Oxford University Press and UNDCP.

United Nations International Drug Control Programme (1999), 'The Drugs Nexus in Africa', Accessed online at www.undoc.org/pdf/report_1999-03-01_1.pdf

Varisco, D. M. (1986), 'On the Meaning of Chewing: the Significance of Qat (Catha edulis) in the Yemen Arab Republic', *International Journal of Middle East Studies* 18, pp. 1–13.

Varisco, D. M. (2004), 'The Elixir of Life or the Devil's Cud? The Debate over Qat (*Catha edulis*) in Yemeni culture', in R. Coomber and N. South (eds), *Drug Use and Cultural Contexts: 'Beyond the West'*, London: Free Association Books.

Warfa, N. et al. (2006), 'Legislation to Prohibit Khat Must Balance Case Report and Epidemiological Evidence of Risks for Mental Disorder', *Social Science and Medicine*, forthcoming.

Warsama, A. (1973), 'Khat, Poison of the Territory of the Afar's and Issas', Bordeaux II, Faculté de Médecine et de Pharmacie.

Weir, S. (1985), *Qat in Yemen: Consumption and Social Change*, London: British Museum.

WHO (1984), 'Proceedings of the Conference on the Use and Control of Khat', World Health Organization.

Widler, P. et al. (1994), 'Pharmacodynamics and Pharmacokinetics of Khat: A Controlled Study', *International Journal of Clinical Pharmacology and Therapeutics* 55(5), pp. 556–62.

Willis, J. (2002), *Potent Brews: A Social History of Alcohol in East Africa*, Oxford: James Currey.

Woods, D (2005), 'Khat Chewing and the Mental Health of Adult Somalis in Sheffield', Somali Mental Health Project report.

Woolverton, W. L. and Johanson, C. E. (1984), 'Preference in Rhesus Monkeys Given a Choice Between Cocaine and [dee,#one]d, l-cathinone', *Journal of Experimental Analysis of Behaviour* 41(1), pp. 35–43.

www.borderpatrol.com/borderframe901.html accessed online 26 March 2005.

Yousef, G., Huq, Z. and Lamber, T. (1995), 'Khat Chewing as a Cause of Psychosis', *British Journal of Hospital Medicine* 54(7), pp. 322–6.

Zaghloul, A., Abdalla, A., El Gammal, H. and Moselhy, H. (2003), 'The Consequences of Khat Use: A Review of Literature', *European Journal of Psychiatry* 17(2), pp. 77–86.

Zelger, J. L., Schorno, H. X. and Carlini, E. A. (1980), 'Behavioural Effects of Cathinone, An Amine Obtained from Catha Edulis Forsk.: Comparisons with Amphetamine, Norpseudoephedrine, Apomorphine and Nomifensine', *Bulletin of Narcotics* 32 (3), pp. 67–81.

Zinberg, N. (1984), *Drug, Set and Setting: The Basis for Controlled Intoxicant Use*, New Haven, CT: Yale University Press.

Index

Note: Entries refer to khat cultivation and industry unless otherwise specified. *Italicized* page numbers indicate tables.